LIBERTY AND EMPIRE

LIBERTY AND EMPIRE

*British Radical Solutions
to the American Problem*

1774-1776

ROBERT E. TOOHEY

THE UNIVERSITY PRESS OF KENTUCKY

ISBN: 0-8131-1375-X

Library of Congress Catalog Card Number: 77-84068

Copyright © 1978 by The University Press of Kentucky

A statewide cooperative scholarly publishing agency
serving Berea College, Centre College of Kentucky,
Eastern Kentucky University, The Filson Club,
Georgetown College, Kentucky Historical Society,
Kentucky State University, Morehead State University,
Murray State University, Northern Kentucky University,
Transylvania University, University of Kentucky,
University of Louisville, and Western Kentucky University.

Editorial and Sales Offices: Lexington, Kentucky 40506

To my mother

CONTENTS

PREFACE

DURING the critical two years between Parliament's passage of the Coercion Acts and the American Declaration of Independence the British government's American policy was bitterly opposed in Parliament by the Rockingham Whigs and William Pitt, earl of Chatham. Their arguments against the policy of the king and the North ministry formed the bases of a Whig Opposition which is well known to students of the American revolutionary period. During this time voices of dissent also were being heard from the ranks of a British Radicalism which had emerged in English affairs during the 1760s and early 1770s. This development, deemed "Radicalism" much later by nineteenth-century historians, was the offspring of a London-centered disenchantment with the old Whig ascendancy and fears that the court had ambitions to revive the power of the monarchy at Parliament's expense. Such apprehensions were fomented by the Wilkes affair and what seemed to be the government's calculated attempt to subvert the liberties of the American colonists. There was little unity among the various shades of this Radicalism, and it was unable to create an effective program of reform to prevent disaster in America. Yet among these groups were several individuals who had some extraordinary ideas about British affairs, including the American question, and whose thinking represented a wide range of British Radical opinion in and around London. These persons were able, informed, and innovative thinkers who, among other things, conceived some carefully planned alternatives to the government's American policy and to then current notions of liberty and empire. They presented their ideas to both English and American audiences in books and pamphlets published during the critical, decisive two years prior to the Declaration of Independence.

The five individuals whose ideas are described in this volume made some notable contributions to the great debate over America in 1774–76, and several historians of our own time have shown that these persons were prominent figures in the history of late eighteenth-century English Radicalism. My objective in these pages is to present a synthesis of these British Radicals' ideas about the American crisis and to show that America did not possess a monopoly on men with innovative, enlightened concepts of liberty and empire.

Major John Cartwright urged a scheme of imperial reformation which foresaw the later British Commonwealth of Nations. Granville Sharp's case for the legislative rights of both Ireland and America anticipated Victorian principles like responsible government or home rule. James Burgh wrote a classic argument for parliamentary reform in which the American question was deeply involved. Catharine Macauley made a grand appeal to the peoples of Great Britain and Ireland to stand with the Americans against a corrupt British government in a style that anticipated the republican fervor of the French Revolution's famous citizenesses. Dr. Richard Price wrote one of the period's most eloquent statements on human liberty and what the American Revolution was essentially about. Though their ideas were little understood or supported in the England of their time, they made important contributions to the emergence of late eighteenth-century Radicalism in England and their influence on the Founding Fathers of the American Republic was by no means insignificant. The later history of the British Empire demonstrated that their ideas about liberty and empire on the eve of the American Revolution anticipated some important developments in the British world during the two hundred years after their own generation. Their ideas about America in the tense years of 1774–76 must be considered a notable and interesting part of the American revolutionary drama.

As the United States enters the third century of its existence I think that these extraordinary Englishmen whose enthusiasm for the American cause matched that of legendary American patriots ought to receive well-deserved attention from modern Anglo-American readers who recognize that the American Revolution was and continues to be a unique influence on the histories of peoples and institutions throughout the English-speaking world. Our own generation has good reason to be indebted to them and the principles they stood for.

Numerous historians, both British and American, during the past few decades have written books which show important connections between the emerging radicalisms in England and America early in the reign of King George III. These writers include Dora Mae Clark, Dame Lucy Sutherland, Caroline Robbins, Ian Christie, Bernard Bailyn, H. Trevor Colbourne, and Gordon S. Wood. They furnish evidence that the two radical movements shared notions about liberty, empire, and a "corrupt" English political system which seemed to be undermining the rights of the crown's subjects on both sides of the Atlantic. Anglo-American radical opinions combined to shape the ideological origins of the American Revolution and to sanction both colonial defiance of the British government and the cause of parliamentary reform in the mother country. It will be one of my purposes in this book to describe the climate of opinion about America in England during the 1770s and to show why a few British Radicals were drawn to publicize their ideas on the American crisis—something which contributed to both the American revolutionary experience and the origins of the parliamentary reform movement in late eighteenth-century England. This study describes the Radicals' arguments so that it might be understood that they thought of the American question within the context of the eighteenth-century world in which they lived.

An important consideration in British and American radical displeasure with British politics in the 1770s was the complaint that the existing order had, in effect, betrayed the ideological principles of the Glorious Revolution of 1688. British Radicals called this betrayal "corruption," while their American brethren called it "tyranny." The established order accepted eighteenth-century ideas of a balanced government of the king, the Lords, and the Commons as integral parts of the sovereign Parliament acting for the best interests of Great Britain and its empire, the belief that such an order could and should be sustained by the oligarchy of the realm's great landed families, and the patronage system which made the existing constitution work. It was an order of politics which clung to old mercantilist ideas about the empire and the authority of Parliament to uphold them.

Whereas measures like the Stamp Act aroused suspicions of "tyranny" in American minds, it was the Wilkes affair which seemed to dramatize the apprehension among British Radicals that the structure of English politics was far astray from the principles of

1688. John Wilkes and his associates who had published the *North Briton No. 45* to denounce the king's approval of the Paris negotiations in 1762 provoked angry authorities to issue a general warrant for search and seizure that made Wilkes and the tactics used against him the talk of London in 1763. Wilkes's irresponsible publication of the pornographic *Essay on Woman* served to escalate the scandals wrought by him and by imprudent officials, until the affair toned down with his flight to France. His return to England in 1768 and his celebrated fight to be seated for Middlesex in the House of Commons stirred many British Radicals to join his cause as a crusade for British liberty and to produce the famous Middlesex Petition of 1769 in his behalf. While American radicals fought the "despotic" Townshend Acts, their English brethren in London and Middlesex fought "corruption" in behalf of Wilkes and liberty. But the great men of Parliament and His Majesty's government had no doubts that they were faithful heirs to the principles of 1688 and regarded charges of despotism, whether from London Radicals or American radicals, as absurd.

The old political distinctions between Tory and Whig which may have been obvious in early eighteenth-century England were eroded by Augustan England's prosperity and stability. Old questions over the Church, royal prerogative, and the Hanoverian succession no longer stirred controversy as they had in an earlier generation. The Whig oligarchy, the family of Hanover, and the Revolution Settlement of the post-1688 years were all, more or less, entrenched features of the complacent England inherited by George III in 1760. In a large sense virtually all Augustan Englishmen, including the monarch, were "Whigs." Both old party labels survived merely out of habit, sentiment, or expediency. Such terms took on new meanings during the American Revolution, when progovernment subjects of George III in England and America were called Tories and antigovernment critics were addressed as Whigs. Men like Charles James Fox or Edmund Burke in the House of Commons were among the Whig Opposition in the heat of the American crisis. British Radicals, also antigovernment, included people like Dr. Price and Major Cartwright whom Professor Caroline Robbins describes as "Honest Whigs." It was this group of Whigs who were the true ideological kinsmen of America's revolutionaries.

This was an English political structure without parties as we think of them in the United States or the United Kingdom today. Englishmen of the eighteenth century often thought of party as being analogous to contentious faction, disloyalty, lack of patriotism, or whatever might seem injurious to effective, well-ordered government. The politics of "ins" and "outs," however, was a way of life in the Whig oligarchy. Factions, cliques, connections, or families generated political rivalries which greatly influenced the life of Parliament and court. Motives were rooted in family loyalties, personal ambition, clashes of personality, friendships, or prevailing interest. The patronage system nurtured by the likes of Sir Robert Walpole and the duke of Newcastle was often the glue which gave some coherence to the complicated political alignments of the time. Connections like the King's Friends, the Rockingham Whigs, the Grenvilles, the Bedfords, and the Chathamites were the most prominent such groups which tried to manipulate English affairs early in George III's reign. They often catered to the considerable number of "independents" in Parliament in efforts to achieve their various objectives. Edmund Burke was the only gifted politician of the period who fully grasped the place and value of party organization in accomplishing well-defined objectives. Few British Radicals recognized the value of party organization, but some of them were moving in that direction during the late years of the American war. Men like John Cartwright and Granville Sharp who urged alternative solutions to the imperial crisis in 1774 addressed their ideas to men in Parliament or to public opinion. Such was the political world to which the persons described in the following pages addressed themselves. If such a world paid them little heed, there is nevertheless due cause why the ideas of figures like Cartwright, Sharp, Burgh, Macaulay, and Price warrant the recognition of their Anglo-American heirs of liberty.

I wish to express my acknowledgement and gratitude to those who have influenced and assisted my labors on this volume. I thank Professor Carl B. Cone of the Department of History at the University of Kentucky who initially suggested that I inquire into this problem. My association with Professor Cone has been one of the most pleasant and rewarding experiences of my academic life and I appreciate his influence on my own interest in the world that was eighteenth-century England. I give my thanks to the staffs of the

Department of Special Collections and the Department of News-papers and Microtexts of the Margaret I. King Library at the University of Kentucky whose assistance was so helpful to me in my research. And I am grateful to those members of my family whose encouragement was so important to me in my completion of this work.

ONE

The Crisis of Empire

AS the Seven Years' War came to an end in 1763 Great Britain's position in the world reached unprecedented heights. Under the magnificent leadership of William Pitt, she was victorious in North America, India, and at sea. Her position among the imperial powers of Western Europe was dramatically strengthened at the expense of her traditional French and Spanish rivals. British pride and confidence were echoed in the imperial nationalism of the great Pitt. Under their new king, George III, Englishmen looked forward to a grand era of peace, prosperity, and imperial greatness. Despite burdensome taxes at home and displeasure toward the lenient terms of peace given the enemy powers in Paris, many Britons were satisfied that their country's hard-won primacy in the Atlantic world would soon compensate for the sacrifices of war.

Few men in victorious England gave thought to the potential problems postwar conditions might pose for the eighteenth-century constitution as it had developed by that time. Unlike Englishmen of the preceding century who had been plagued by serious constitutional problems, the generation of Newcastle and Pitt the Elder was little concerned with issues that had been settled a generation before. "In this Augustan age of wealth, success, self-confidence, and enlightenment, the problems of organizing society and government which had vexed previous ages seemed under the direction of a capable and energetic aristocracy to have been triumphantly solved." [1] Old distinctions between Whig and Tory were eroded by Augustan acquiescence to the Glorious Revolution Settlement and Walpolean peace and prosperity. The structure of British politics at the accession of George III was an oligarchic establishment sustained by the king and the great families of the realm. The balanced constitution in which eighteenth-century Englishmen took pride protracted a balance of authority and liberty conducive to the existing order of English life. Traditional notions of empire, much rooted in the old mercantilism, continued to be regarded as a pillar of the prosperity and power of old England. It was thought both logical and necessary that the British Parliament—the king, the Lords, and the Commons—should represent and assert the interests and sovereign authority of the British world at home and in the colonies.

Though they saw nothing in the postwar British Empire which required basic constitutional changes, the king's ministers soon recognized that the grandeur of empire certainly presented the mother country with some enormous problems. The empire was vastly larger. The Indian nations of North America had to be reckoned with. The problems of administration and defense required much attention. The mother country was burdened with a huge national debt and Englishmen were weary of wartime taxation.[2]

Such problems were largely matters of administration and finance. In the decade after 1763 such questions were engaged by practical, worldly men like George Grenville, Charles Townshend, Frederick North, and numerous others whose experience in finance and administration seemed to be commensurate with the pressing needs of the hour. Their programs represented the authority and will of crown and Parliament in accordance with postwar notions of imperial responsibility. Such practitioners of mid-eighteenth-century English politics had no doubts about Parliament's imperial jurisdiction and its competence to legislate for the empire. Modern scholarship by the Namier school has shown that the young George III was firmly committed to Parliament's supremacy at home and in the empire. Despite charges of despotism raised against him by political critics and later Whig historians, the king was sincere in his insistence that he was fighting Parliament's battles in his quarrels with the American colonists. Limitations on the authority of Parliament in the empire of the post-1763 world simply were not envisaged by crown, Parliament, or the great mass of Englishmen.

The efforts of British leaders to make imperial policy on the bases of parliamentary sovereignty and old mercantile laws led to repercussions felt throughout the Atlantic world in the generation following 1763. Though the situations in Ireland and India needed serious attention, events in several American provinces moved swiftly and it was in that quarter of the empire that the British government quickly found itself caught up in a constitutional quandary which severely challenged traditional English notions of empire. Angry, bewildered ministers of the king eventually saw no choice but to use coercion against defiant Americans.

British imperial policy clashed with an American situation changed substantially by the recent war. Of course, colonial displeasure with old mercantile laws restricting American trade and manufacturing had a history dating to the previous century. "Salutary neglect" and smuggling in colonial ports usually had taken the sting out of the letter of the law. London's program of imperial responsibility after 1763 was intended to end such laxities and abuses. British resolve and efficiency in this direction aroused provincials in Massachusetts Bay and nearby colonies to angry opposition against official policy. Such quarrels were compounded by points of view distinctly British and distinctly American, a crystallization of some critical differences which existed between English and American life by the late eighteenth century. The expulsion of the French from the continent left the Americans with greater security and confidence to question British policies affecting trade, taxation, and the future of the West. The heated polemics of men like Daniel Dulany, James Otis, and Patrick Henry elevated the quarrel into the constitutional question of Parliament's jurisdiction in the empire. By 1774 such figures had fomented an American radicalism finding expression in the writings of such men as James Wilson (*Considerations on the Authority of Parliament*), Thomas Jefferson (*A Summary View of the Rights of British America*), and John Adams (*Novanglus*).

By the middle of the 1770s such colonial radicals were arguing that each colony was a distinct political entity under the crown, that each colonial assembly was a duly constituted parliament with legislative jurisdictions which could not be infringed by the mother Parliament, and that, therefore, the British government in London should administer colonial affairs through the machinery of the respective provincial assemblies. Such principles suggested that the American colonies had a constitutional status resembling that of future members of the British Commonwealth of Nations. This argument left the Parliament in Great Britain in a constitutional position entirely out of joint with contemporary notions of parliamentary authority. The crisis of empire which developed by 1774 boiled down to the central question of parliamentary authority in the British Empire. In the words of G. H. Guttridge, "The authority of Parliament was the central issue of the American Revolution, and American claims were directed to justify resistance by limiting or denying that authority."[3] Numerous American radicals raised the difficult issue of how Parliament's authority was to be reconciled with the liberties of the colonists. In brief, the imperial crisis was precipitated by the bewildering problem of authority versus liberty in the British world.

Seldom since the Hanoverian succession were English politics as stormy as during the years following the Peace of Paris. The king, intent on cleansing the body politic, battled the old Whig oligarchy with his own influence and patronage. Newcastle and Rockingham Whigs saw this as a concerted scheme to undo the hard-won ascendancy of the eighteenth-century Parliament. The Wilkes affair served to magnify suspicions about the growing influence of the crown at the expense of Parliament's independence. Despite the king's claims that his American policy was defending Parliament's supremacy in imperial affairs, followers of Rockingham and Chatham were convinced that the imperial question was being used by the King's Friends to strengthen the court's position. Members of the so-called Whig Opposition by 1774 suffered a great disadvantage in their feud with the crown's supporters not because of an actual court conspiracy but largely because the king's views were supported by a broad majority of Englishmen—their opinions still viewed colonies in a mercantilist tradition. Large majorities in both houses of Parliament, because they measured the value of empire by the prosperity and power it gave to the mother country, were ill disposed to accept unorthodox ideas about colonies. Prevailing concepts of empire required effective central authority for order and unity. The British government and Parliament under the existing constitution should maintain the delicate balance of authority and liberty in the crown's domains. An imperial order which had so blessed England in the past should not be changed in ways that could threaten tried and proven modes of economic activity. Guttridge makes an accurate description of English policies of the time: "Mercantilism had changed from the control of trade in the interest of national policy to the control of national policy in the interest of trade."[4]

Regardless of traditional notions of empire and British leaders' mistakes in American policy, the colonial crisis of the 1770s could not have been resolved easily by even the most capable statesmanship. The blunders and stubbornness of the men who actually made policy have strengthened history's vindication of the American rebellion. But responsibility for the debacle was not one-sided. Professor Keir argues, "Responsibility for the failure of the eighteenth century constitution to find any means of harmonizing imperial unity and colonial self-government may not be unequally divided between British and American politicians, the former for their lack of realism in dealing with the problems involved, and the latter for their irresponsible repudiation of imperial obligation."[5]

Aside from the small groups of colonial hotheads and punitive politicians in England, most men on both sides of the American question thought they were moved by principles compatible with their senses of right and reason. To British leaders the concern for imperial authority and unity seemed no less reasonable than the colonial arguments about liberty. But history can be acrimonious toward men who fail, like the men who lost America. None of them has been so maligned as the king. John Brooke, his recent biographer, has written, "In the mythology of American history King George III is the would-be tyrant whose wicked plans were foiled by the courage and resistance of the American people. He is the scapegoat for the act of rebellion. . . . In the mythology of British history King George III is the scapegoat for the failure of imperialism. The Americans have charged him with tyranny, the British with corruption. In the literal sense, he has had the worst of both worlds."[6] As for the men who loyally followed the king through the American crisis, most of them had abilities and experience which might have enabled them to do rather well in less extraordinary times. Lewis B. Namier, John Brooke, and other modern historians have shown that these men were not the scheming villains they long were ascribed to be. Yet history has rightly judged them as men in power at the wrong time. Shortsighted and tactless, they failed to foresee the results of their policies. They lacked the insight, the magnanimity, and the sense of history to govern a great empire successfully.

The parliamentary opposition to the government's American

policies was concentrated in the men of the Rockingham connection and the few who attached themselves to Chatham. By the standards of great statesmanship, their understanding of the imperial dilemma also left much to be desired. Prevailing notions of the constitution, the politics of faction, and economic interest were as likely to be at the root of their cause opposing the government as any interest in America or sympathy for colonial complaints. The Rockinghams saw the American question as part of their confrontation with the court's supporters over the more central issue of Parliament's independence from the monarchy. In theory, they had no quarrel with the king on the principle of parliamentary sovereignty either at home or in the colonies. They opposed his tactics in defense of that principle by his collaboration with those who shaped court policy. As Dora Mae Clark put it, "The government advised coercion to uphold a theory; the opposition, conciliation for the sake of expediency."[7] Edmund Burke's eloquent speeches on America represented the Rockinghams' case for expediency and conciliation while still upholding the concept of an imperial Parliament as sovereign in the British Empire. It was left to Chatham and Shelburne to challenge the theory of Parliament's unlimited sovereignty in favor of rationales that could guarantee the indefinite unity of Great Britain and America. Political factionalism and clashes of personality among the opposition, along with the unpopularity of their views on America, seriously disabled their efforts to influence basic changes in imperial policy in the mid-1770s when war might have been prevented. Though the speeches of antigovernment parliamentarians like Burke and Fox were widely read by colonists who applauded them as the friends of America, they were voices in the wilderness of progovernment English opinion at the outset of the American war. Not until the frustrations and blunders of trying to prosecute an exhaustive war became burdensome was the climate of British opinion disposed to change. By then it was too late for reconciliation with America. The British and American peoples were left to confront the future in their own separate ways.

It is not the views on the American dilemma among men in the king's government nor in the parliamentary opposition, however, with which this volume is essentially concerned. For outside the halls of Westminster there was emerging in English affairs during the 1770s a small but forceful undercurrent of opinion which later historians such as Élie Halévy were to describe as "Radicalism." From this rudiment of opinion appeared a number of ideas and individualists which crystallized into an interesting English counterpart to the colonial radicalism surging to the foreground of American affairs by the middle of the 1770s. The following story suggests that this occurrence was no unimportant chapter in the history of the American revolutionary experience—nor, for that matter, the modern history of the Anglo-American peoples.

TWO

~~~~~~~~

On the Eve of the American Revolution

WHAT is described as Radicalism in the England of the American revolutionary period formed only a secondary and divergent expression of British opinion at the time. The possibilities of organized parties were as remote to Radicals as they were to the men who sat in Parliament. Radicalism was concentrated mainly in London and Middlesex and represented the views of very few people out in the country. Lack of unity and common objectives among Radicals made it difficult to develop broad, firm agreement on the great issues of the period, including the American question. It will be the purpose of this chapter to describe the broad spectrum of English Radical opinion at the outset of the American Revolution and to account for the variety of Radical reaction to unorthodox ideas about the nature and future of the British Empire.[1]

Lucy Sutherland traces City and Middlesex Radicalism during the years of the American Revolution back to William Pitt's war ministry in the 1750s. It was nurtured by the Wilkes affair and unrest among the "middling citizens" of the livery companies due to inflation, some bad harvests, and the effects of some industrial changes around London. Therein were the seeds which grew into their cries for parliamentary reform during the early 1770s. They talked of annual parliaments, an expansion of male suffrage, and single-member constituencies. Most of them were not interested in sophisticated arguments over the American problem. But the Wilkes affair made them sensitive about the principle of British liberty and they often gave lip service support to liberty-minded Americans. Most of them were men of trade with much at stake in what was happening in America, and it was only human that commercial interest was an important, even dominant, factor in their reaction to the crisis. If they might lack enthusiasm for splendid arguments and schemes on imperial reformation, they could certainly like the antigovernment tone in the writings of empire reformers such as John Cartwright and Richard Price. The variety of opinion about the empire and proposals to reform its structure which existed among British Radicals may be shown by briefly describing the Radicals' reaction to the American question before Lexington and Concord. For, as we shall see, it was the only substantial audience in which new ideas about the structure and future of the empire might be given favorable receptions.

First of all, what about John Wilkes? Was he a man who, for all his pro-American professions about liberty, was sincerely disposed to support radical changes in the imperial system as proposed by well-intentioned Radicals? The Wilkes controversy had received wide attention in America and many colonists saw him as a symbol of liberty crusading against a government which they despised. For several years Americans entertained hopes that Wilkes might win enough support to pressure the British government into changing its American policies. His apparent failure to do so led them to conclude that the government was incapable of making changes in basic policy either in England or America.[2]

After Wilkes finally took his seat in the House of Commons in 1774 and thus resumed his career in that body, he was something of an "indoor champion" of America and the pro-American ideas of British Radicals. His famous proposal for parliamentary reform on the floor of the Commons in 1776 was influenced by the *Political Disquisitions* of James Burgh and other Radical reformers whose ideas will be discussed in these pages.[3] But he offered nothing comparable to the proposals of Radicals like John Cartwright on the subject of imperial reformation.[4] Some historians, such as Leslie Stephen, Lucy Sutherland, and Ian Christie, have taken a dim view of Wilkes's sincerity about any contemporary issues other than those which conveniently served his own personal and political objectives.[5] O. A. Sherrard and Pauline Maier are more apologetic.[6] Even contemporary Americans in London were divided over Wilkes.[7] Some British Radicals idolized him, while others disliked the man but supported his cause. I seriously doubt that Wilkes's attitude toward America or Radical ideas on imperial reform had an integrity comparable to that of men whom I shall be discussing in the succeeding chapters. A man of his character was capable of many things and his pro-American professions have to be considered in the perspective of a career filled with demagoguery. Nevertheless, it is clear that his professions, whatever their motive, had a significant impact on American attitudes and the City Radicals' reaction to ideas of empire in the pamphlets of John Cartwright and others.

As for the broad range of opinion among the politicians and liverymen of London and Middlesex, it should be understood that there were those among them, some quite influential, who held conservative political and even anti-American attitudes. Many of them, despite complaints against the government, considered it their patriotic duty to support Britain's case against America and loathed those Englishmen who made scathing attacks on the government's American policies during the 1770s. At the same time, City politics and livery companies were the largest seedbeds of Radical disenchantment with the establishment and were the most potent audience for Radical imperial reformists, if for no other reason than to embarrass a government all Radicals disliked. Their enthusiasms tended to ebb and flow with the tide of economic trends precipitated by the imperial crisis. Political activity, whether in behalf of American liberties or reform at home, was often fomented by considerations of business stability due to the memory of the Stamp Act crisis. Some of the most influential and outspoken personalities among the City Radicals were diehards like James Townsend and John Sawbridge, Catharine Macaulay's brother, who were devoted to reforming the English political structure and to combating forces inimical to their ideas of liberty. Such people as these in London and surrounding Middlesex were among the most ardent admirers of ideas expressed in the writings of Mrs. Macaulay and other Radicals who wrote pro-American propaganda.

When 1,565 City freeholders presented their famous Middlesex Petition to Parliament in Wilkes's behalf in 1769, it included proposals—put in the petition at Arthur Lee's request—for a more conciliatory attitude toward Americans angered by the Townshend duties. Many of these petitioners did not relish an official policy which brought diminishing returns to London merchants. But they also questioned the legality of Parliament's authority to legislate such duties. Some of these people were Wilkesites whose arguments were based on principle and on idealistic notions of liberty. Many of them feared that such arbitrary measures could lead to similar devices in England, especially against City politicians with reputations of opposition to the government.

In March 1770, five Radical City aldermen—John Sawbridge, James Townsend, Barlow Trecothick, William Beckford, and Sir William Stephenson—drafted a remonstrance in behalf of the livery companies against the government's American policy. It also was around this time that several City Radicals connected with the Society of the Bill of Rights created American-type committees of correspondence to coordinate their opposition to the government with political allies in Northumberland, Cumberland, and Durham. Such activity came to little. But evidence of pro-American attitudes was obvious when, in 1773, two Americans—William Lee, Arthur's brother, and Stephen Sayre—were elected as sheriffs in the City.[8] In late 1774 when City Radicals learned of hardships in Boston caused by the Coercion Acts, the Lord Mayor and several aldermen donated money to a local fund for distressed Bostonians.

The general election in October 1774 was the occasion for much pro-American sentiment being shown among liverymen who met at the Guildhall to elect City members to the House of Commons. The chairman of the assembly started the proceedings by admonishing all voters to remember what was taking place in Massachusetts Bay at the time and to consider the ominous implications of the Coercion Acts for all Englishmen. He urged the candidates for London's four seats to pledge themselves to parliamentary legislation more conciliatory toward the Americans, including recognition of the colonial assemblies' rights to legislate their own tax laws. Four of the five candidates did so.[9]

On the eve of Lexington and Concord, the livery council publicly expressed its gratitude to Pitt, then the earl of Chatham, for his dramatic speech earlier in the year appealing for conciliation with America. In March, 1775 the same council voted in favor of a petition against Parliament's passage of the Restraining Act directed against New England. In April pro-American liverymen sent an address to the king arguing the justice of colonial resistance to the Coercion Acts. This was very irritating to George III, and he ordered that no petitions from the livery companies be presented at court unless they represented the views of the whole livery. Angered by the royal rebuke, twenty-five hundred livery members assembled once more and adopted a new resolution against the North ministry's American policy. They also gave public praise to Lord Effingham's highly publicized resignation from the army to avoid military service in the colonies.[10]

Demonstrations of pro-American sentiment in the livery companies reached their crest during the summer of 1775 after news of hostilities outside Boston reached London. Fiery criticisms of the government were heard in their meetings, and the conduct of City aldermen made them vulnerable to accusations of sedition. Rumors spread about London that the livery was donating £2,000 to the rebels. Progovernment citizens were angered in August when the Lord Mayor entertained members of the Bill of Rights Society at the Guildhall. When royal heralds proceeded to Temple Bar and the Royal Exchange on August 23 to proclaim the Americans as rebels and publicly to forbid His Majesty's subjects to correspond with them, the Lord Mayor refused to allow them to ride in state through the streets of the City and to carry the mace.[11] Shortly afterward, the City aldermen sent seven livery representatives to present another petition to the king. Signed by 1,029 liverymen this time, it implored His Majesty to an act of clemency toward the rebels and warned him against misguided policies urged upon him by his advisors.[12] Such overtures provoked progovernment citizens to reaffirm their loyalty to the Crown and its American policy. The king himself chose to dismiss his livery critics as "irresponsible" and took no action against them lest he give them new cause for complaint: "I have no doubt but the Nation at large sees the conduct of America in its true light and I am certain any other conduct but compelling obedience would be ruinous and culpable. . . ."[13]

English Radicalism also manifested itself in several societies which appeared in London around this time. Radical opinion on domestic reform in general and the American question in particular caused much discussion in debating societies like the Robinhood of Butcher's Row in Temple Bar. Such organizations were convenient forums for Radicals who wished to air their views to audiences which were not always amenable to their polemics. In most cases traditional concepts of empire prevailed after heated exchanges. In the Robinhood, for example, there existed a strong pro-American group, but when the war started in 1775 most of the membership supported the government for patriotic or expedient reasons.[14]

Two Radical reform societies appeared in London during this time which consistently gave support to Radical spokesmen on imperial reformation. Both the Society of the Supporters of the Bill of Rights and the Constitutional Society originated in support of specific Radical causes under the more general banner of liberty. They were Radical in membership and intent. To the members of such organizations, the principles of British Radicalism and American rights shared common causes against the British government. They had long-range objectives for remedying wrongs in English life and were, therefore, essentially more concerned with the affairs of their own country. But many of them had strong convictions about the existence of dangers to their liberties and they substantiated their fears by raising a fuss over British tactics in the colonies. A large number of these society men had pro-American sentiments which went further than lip service. Their reform programs included demands for redressing colonial grievances. They welcomed the ideas of English Radicals who argued that the imperial system should be changed. During the early years of the American war some of the most outspoken opposition to the conflict came from these organizations, a position which disposed them to urge schemes of imperial reform outlined by the figures described in the succeeding chapters.

The Society of the Supporters of the Bill of Rights was an offspring of the frenzy provoked by the Wilkes matter. It was founded in February 1769 when about fifty City Radicals organized the society to provide assistance to Englishmen whose rights had been "violated." Its defense of Wilkes was its primary occupation between February 1769 and early 1771. In addition, efforts were made to defend City printers who published parliamentary debates and to use the organization as a base from which to promote the members' influence in City politics. Their activities were in the tradition of City aversion to a constitutional establishment dominated by the Whig oligarchy. Many of the members were liverymen or figures on the ascendancy in City politics—Sawbridge; his father-in-law William Stephenson; Townsend; the West Indians Thomas Oliver and his cousin Richard Oliver; the Dissenter Frederick Bull; Sir Joseph Mawbey, the Vauxhall distiller; Sir Robert Bernard of the Huntingtonshire gentry; Sergeant John Glynn; and above all, Parson John Horne, who is known to later generations as John Horne Tooke.[15] Many of these were men of wealth or aspirants to it. Though they often championed controversial figures, they were not obsessed with any consuming sense of injustice. They were reformers, but they usually were thinking of the City's best interests. Parliamentary reform was an issue mainly thought of as something to promote the influence of London in English political life. G. S. Veitch suggests that the society's chief importance lay in the experience it acquired in organizing public opinion for agitation on the issues of the day—something not fully understood even by many of the society's members at the time.[16]

The society was largely the creation of John Horne Tooke, who founded and dominated it until April 1771. Christened John Horne, he took the surname of his friend and political patron William Tooke in the midst of his reform career. In February 1769 he was the leader among the followers of Wilkes who assembled for the purpose of raising a sum of £3,340 to pay Wilkes's court expenses and creditors.[17] This led to their organization of the Bill of Rights Society to help Wilkes and other causes in defense of British liberty. In early March Horne Tooke raised another £300 for Wilkes. It was under Horne Tooke's leadership that the society announced its support of parliamentary reform, "the redress of the grievances of Ireland, and the restoration of the sole right of self-taxation to America."[18] Shrewd, alert, and tenacious, Horne Tooke was Wilkes's ablest defender and himself reveled in political notoriety. He was one of the great society organizers of his time.

> ... Like Pericles, he rarely laughed, like Alcibiades he could suit himself to the humours of other men: That he could enjoy his wine with Homer and Ennius, could draw a character with Tacitus, and was as ready to accept money from his friends as Pliny and Cicero.
> ... He was the earliest, and for practical business the ablest, of a class of men to whom Englishmen owe a debt of gratitude which they are, not inexcusably, somewhat unwilling to acknowledge.[19]

The life of the society through early 1771, however, came to be plagued by a bitter rivalry which developed between Horne Tooke and Wilkes. The former concluded that Wilkes was using the soci-

ety for its money and to serve his political ambitions. The breach
between the two men was widened in the winter of 1770–71 when
Wilkes contested Horne Tooke's effort to raise money for the defense of a printer being prosecuted for publishing some of Wilkes's
own writings. Matters came to a head when they had a violent
argument before a society audience at the London Tavern on 9
April 1771. Rather than allow the organization to serve Wilkes's
private and political designs, Horne Tooke made the motion that
the society dissolve itself. It lost by two votes. Thereupon Horne
Tooke and his followers left the room and organized their own
Constitutional Society. Those who remained in the room were die-
hard Wilkesites who formed the nucleus of the Bill of Rights Society
during the next few years. The departure of Horne Tooke resulted
in less effective propagation of the society's program despite its
continued support of reform and America. Its funds subsidized
three City newspapers during the early 1770s. Even Horne Tooke
joined hands with the society's members in opposition to the war in
1775.

Because John Horne Tooke was the dominant figure in the or-
ganizational work of the Bill of Rights Society in its early years—
and because his views were supported by many Radicals—it is
useful to examine his ideas on the American question and their
relation to the ideas of other Radicals. There was a strong tint of
ideology in his personal principles, and this influenced many of his
colleagues. He considered the society to be a voice in defense of the
principles of the Revolution of 1688. At the same time, there can be
little doubt that such enthusiasm was amenable to the desires of
City politicians for promoting their own causes. Most society
members regarded the American question as closely related to their
own concerns—reforming Parliament and pursuing their own
careers in business and politics. Yet men like Horne Tooke and
Sawbridge saw common ground upon which their own cause and
that of America could meet—both had a mutual foe, the government, and Horne Tooke tried to use the society for swaying British
opinion toward a more conciliatory position with the colonists. He
believed that both Englishmen and Americans shared a common
interest in the cause of parliamentary reform. While under his
leadership, the society drafted a "test" for members standing for
Parliament in which they were expected to pledge their support

of the American arguments on taxation and representation.[20]

Horne Tooke shared part of the responsibility for a serious quarrel between the crown and the South Carolina Assembly in 1769 when he encouraged the Carolinians to donate £10,500 to the Bill of Rights Society out of the public treasury. When the assembly did so the king was furious, and the royal governor had a bitter argument with the legislature. Calmer tempers in Parliament led to permission of the donation with orders to the governor that such measures not be allowed again. The society, in a letter of thanks to the Carolinians, wrote, "Our cause is one—our enemies are the same."[21] In a speech before Middlesex freeholders in 1770, Horne Tooke declared, "The security of their freedom and their rights is essential to the enjoyment of our own. We should never for a moment forget the important truth, that when the people of America are enslaved, we cannot be free; and they can never be enslaved whilst we continue free. We are stones of one arch, and must stand or fall together."[22] During his campaign for a seat in the House of Commons at that time, Richard Oliver made the American cause the leading principle in his platform and enjoyed the support of the City livery for doing so.

With Horne Tooke gone from the society after April 1771, the membership continued their support of the Americans. In June they adopted a resolution urging parliamentary reform and soon afterward formed a committee which drafted a program of eleven points supported by all members. Among them was support for restoring to America "the essential right of taxation, by representatives of their own free election; and the universal excise so notoriously incompatible with every principle of British liberty, which has been lately substituted in the colonies for the laws of custom."[23]

The society steadfastly stood with the citizens of Boston during the crisis following the Tea Party in 1773–74. John Adams was elected to its membership.[24] When Parliament passed the Quebec Act in 1774, the society published and circulated the names of M.P.'s supporting the bill to all the counties and boroughs of England.[25] In early 1775 the membership voted £500 for the relief of Bostonians besieged by the consequences of the Coercion Acts. When Wilkes entered Parliament in late 1774 the Bill of Rights men saw it as a triumph for the same principle of liberty which they associated with the American predicament. Colonists had been encouraged by Wilkes's successes and support given by the society. Though members of the society promoted the notion that they had common cause with America, it is not clear whether the membership fully understood or supported the American position taken on the issue of Parliament's authority in the British Empire by 1775. It has been argued that the Bill of Rights Society was disenchanted with Parliament because it did not represent adequately the British nation, whereas American dissatisfaction with it was due simply to its not being American. Even some members of the society seem to have believed in the supremacy of Parliament.[26]

Whether all members of the society agreed with the American ideology which evolved by 1775 or the imperial ideas of people like John Cartwright and Richard Price is difficult to say. It is evident that many of them did. All of them welcomed the government's failure to suppress the American rebellion, as it encouraged them to continue their cause for parliamentary reform. Catharine Macaulay found some of her most enthusiastic supporters in this group. They applauded Dr. Price's *Observations on the Nature of Civil Liberty* for both its ideological and propaganda values. When John Sawbridge and Richard Oliver castigated the British government's military actions against the colonials, they were representing the Bill of Rights Society's vigorous support of City politicians' opposition to current American policy.

As previously shown, the Constitutional Society was the offspring of the feud between Horne Tooke and Wilkes in early 1771, a rift which had been greatly fomented by the pro-Wilkes rantings of the notorious "Junius." Friends including John Sawbridge, William Tooke, Sergeant Glynn, and Richard Oliver followed Horne Tooke into the new reform society. Its activities and propaganda during the early 1770s paralleled those of the Bill of Rights Society while its organization and program were dominated by Horne Tooke. It joined with the Bill of Rights people in sympathizing with the Americans and promoting the cause of parliamentary reform in behalf of London Radicalism. It was as the leader of the Constitutional Society that Horne Tooke gained most notoriety in the eyes of the English public for denouncing the government after hostilities began in America. And, as with the Bill of Rights Society, this reform group endorsed the ideas of Radical imperial reformers at the outset of the American Revolution.

There was another shade of British Radicalism which appeared in English life at this time and among which the imperial reformers described below might have been most welcome. Professor Caroline Robbins identifies them as "Honest Whigs" and discusses them at length in her masterly *The Eighteenth Century Commonwealthman*. They were not necessarily active in the organized Radicalism of City politics or reform societies, but they most certainly endorsed organized criticism of the government and Radical reform principles. Most of the Honest Whigs were respectable men of property and learning. They were patriotic and well-intentioned and came from the ranks of English Dissent. By the time of the American war they represented some thinking about the British Empire which suggested significant departures from traditional concepts of empire. Their notions of empire were significantly influenced by their strong moral estimations of the American question, as well as by political and practical considerations. Their pro-American sentiments were probably the most sincere to be found among British Radicalism. Dr. Franklin and other colonists often were in their company before the war. As a result, many of the Honest Whigs had an extraordinary understanding of the American point of view. None of them desired a separation of England and America nor, pending the conduct of the British government, did they think it necessary—a view Franklin shared with them up to 1774. But when the Americans declared independence in 1776, they supported the decision while thinking such an event tragically to have been forced on the colonists by British mistakes.

The Honest Whigs included figures who formed a kind of intelligentsia of British Radicalism. Dr. Joseph Priestley, one of the most eminent Englishmen of his time, was among their number. He wrote an important treatise on liberty and reform in his *The Present State of Liberty* (1769).[27] Dr. Andrew Kippis, Presbyterian clergyman, biographer of Dissenters in his *Biographia Britannica*, and apologist for America, often represented Radical opinion in articles published periodically in the *Gentleman's Magazine* and the *Monthly Review*.[28] William Hazlitt,[29] father of the famous essayist, and Dr. John Fothergill,[30] the affable, well-known Quaker physician and merchant, also were among this group. The eccentric author of the children's book *Sandford and Merton*, Thomas Day, came to be connected with the Honest Whigs during the war and published antislavery views like those of Granville Sharp.[31] He admonished his American friends to exemplify the ideals of the Declaration of Independence by freeing their slaves. Though not a Dissenter himself, Sir William Jones, the great jurist, classical scholar, and Oriental linguist whom Dr. Samuel Johnson called "the most enlightened of the sons of men,"[32] was another reputable advocate of Honest Whig principles during the American war.

Several Anglican churchmen of liberal views also were connected with the Honest Whigs, including Jonathan Shipley, bishop of Saint Asaph; Richard Watson, bishop of Llandaff; and John Hinchcliffe, bishop of Peterborough. Bishop Shipley was one of Dr. Franklin's closest friends and made several pro-American speeches in the House of Lords.[33] William Paley was one of the finest minds in the church during this time and wrote an analysis of the British constitution which Caroline Robbins describes as "perhaps the most subtle and thoughtful of the period."[34] It has been ranked with the political writings of Richard Price and Joseph Priestley.[35] Dr. John Jebb, the kindly physician whom a friend described as "the most perfect human being he had ever known," also came from the Anglican fold. He became John Cartwright's co-worker for parliamentary reform.

Honest Whig emphasis on the moral ramifications of the imperial crisis, as well as the issue of liberty, was obviously shared by many Dissenting Englishmen throughout the country.[36] There is no reason to think they had objections to radical changes in the imperial system proposed in the name of human liberty. This was certainly the case among the Unitarian congregation of Theophilus Lindsey's chapel in London's Essex Street. Lindsey, another Honest Whig, founded his chapel in 1774 after his disappointment over the failure of the Feathers Petition in 1772.[37] His congregation was visited by Price, Priestley, and Franklin on numerous occasions. This little group was respected, but its pro-American sentiments sorely irritated many Londoners during the revolutionary war years.

Caroline Robbins's *The Eighteenth Century Commonwealthman* shows that the Honest Whigs of the American revolutionary era were the heirs of a rich liberal Whig tradition that went back to the time of Oliver Cromwell and the Puritan Revolution. This legacy enlivened Honest Whigs' disdain toward Augustan complacency during the early years of George III's reign, a resurgence fanned by the Wilkes affair and fears over the alleged growing influence of the court. This branch of British Radicalism was familiar with classical thought, the history of the English constitution, and the reform theories of seventeenth- and early eighteenth-century "commonwealthmen" like James Harrington, Algernon Sidney, Robert Molesworth, and others. They accepted the political theories of John Locke as gospel truth and were inspired by the ideological principles of the Glorious Revolution. Unlike many City Radicals, these Honest Whigs—including those to be studied in the following chapters—did not enter public life or politics in the strict sense. Consequently, they were less reluctant to raise questions about the constitution and the British Empire. They spoke with greater independence and variety of opinion than men in office. Like eighteenth-century politicians, however, they did not understand party organization in the modern sense. They admired the British constitution and believed in its great possibilities to enhance their concepts of liberty. Unlike most Englishmen, they were willing to change the constitution for the betterment of their country. They were men of the Enlightenment who had much faith in human nature, believed in progress, and recognized the value of education for the improvement of society. Robbins considers their chief significance to have been their preservation of an impressive liberal tradition and their elevation of ideas about liberty which had an enormous impact on successive generations. J. H. Plumb describes them as a gifted lot of Englishmen known among contemporaries for their intellectual abilities and sincere intentions. They viewed the great questions of their day with historical perspective, philosophical insight, and moral sensitivity.[38]

Because many of the Honest Whigs were Dissenters, they valued ideas about liberty which are understandable in the light of earlier Dissenter history in England. They often viewed the society and politics of Augustan England moralistically. They used the word *corruption* to describe the evils of their time. Though most of them disliked Wilkes, they supported his cause in behalf of liberty. They saw the rise of a court clique early in George III's reign as the consequence of a corrupted body politic. They concluded that radical parliamentary reform was imperative if British liberty and public integrity were to be restored. Gordon S. Wood's *The Creation of the American Republic* describes the notion of liberty which both Honest Whigs and American radicals were propagating on the eve of the Revolution:

> The liberty that was now emphasized was personal or private, the protection of individual rights against all governmental encroachments, particularly by the legislature, the body which the Whigs had traditionally cherished as the people's exclusive repository of their public liberty and the surest weapon to defend their private liberties. ... Men now began to consider "the interests of society and the rights of individuals as distinct" and to regard public and private liberty as antagonistic rather than complementary. ... Government was no longer designed merely to promote the collective happiness of the people but also ... "to protect citizens in their personal liberty and their property" even against the public will. ... Unless individuals and minorities were protected against the powers of majorities no government could be truly free.[39]

Such a concept of liberty caused Honest Whigs to regard the parliamentary ascendancy of the Whig oligarchy, not to speak of old Tory ideas on the royal prerogative, as inconsistent with the principles of 1688. Since the early eighteenth century Whig theorists like Robert Molesworth and John Trenchard had lamented the rise of the Whig oligarchy as a betrayal of the Glorious Revolution. The Honest Whigs of the American revolutionary period continued that tradition of complaint and urged parliamentary reform which would facilitate the enjoyment of true liberty.

It was the specter of a court conspiracy threatening British liberty, however, which especially aroused Radical (and Whig) fears by the time of the American crisis. The court's reaction to Wilkes and the growing complaints of American colonists contributed to British Radicals' sense of urgency about parliamentary reform. Bernard Bailyn's *The Ideological Origins of the American Revolution* emphasizes the intensity of this alarm: "They saw about them, with increasing clarity, not merely mistaken, or even evil, policies violating the principles upon which freedom rested, but what appeared to be evidence of nothing less than a deliberate assault launched surreptitiously by plotters against liberty both in England and in America."[40]

Honest Whigs like Joseph Priestley and Thomas Hollis of Lincoln's Inn connected this threat to liberty with the British government's policies in America several years before the Boston Tea Party. But it was not until the incident in Boston Harbor had precipitated great tensions in both America and England in early 1774 that several Honest Whigs began to comment publicly about the imperial crisis and to offer clearly defined principles and alternatives to present policies. In the light of history, their ideas proved to be enlightened and somewhat prophetic. They showed that America did not possess a monopoly on men with advanced ideas about liberty and empire. Lewis Namier writes that the only way in which the American colonies could have been kept under the British crown was through a policy which reflected the ideas of these remarkable Englishmen.[41] They were a group who felt an especial kinship with their fellow subjects across the sea. "To them alone, who knew no hierarchy either in religion or politics, the colonists were so many congregations of brethren beyond the seas. In their own depressed condition, they followed the growth of those communities with a sincere and active love, and with a hope that the new England would some day right the wrongs of the old."[42] Throughout the years of the American war they saw the conflict as a civil war, in the tradition of 1688, over the critical issues of liberty, authority and the unity of the king's subjects.[43] When American independence came, they wished their old friends well and set about the task of reform in their own country. They were at heart British patriots, and their ideas on the imperial crisis were proposed in the good interests of their own country as well as the colonists'.

The panorama of Radical reaction to the ideas of Radical imperial reformers reveals that there was general approval of anti-government arguments, pro-American sentiments, the nature of British liberty, and the justice of parliamentary reform. Such approval, however, was accompanied by a variety of motives. There was no "united front" either in motive or objective. Principle, personality, demagoguery, alarm, interest, and expediency all were ingredients which help to explain why Radical opinion reacted as it did to such ideas. To some Radicals the issue of righting wrongs done to America was an end in itself—as in the opinions of moralists like Dr. Kippis and Dr. Fothergill. The personality of a man like John Horne Tooke showed that a passionate sense of justice for America could be integrated with strong disenchantment with the contemporary political establishment of one's own country. The demagoguery of Wilkes showed that the American issue could be a convenient stepping stone to serve ulterior motives. Many Radicals easily found reason to fear that official oppression in the British colonies abroad could lead to tyranny at home, a prevalent view among the men of the Radical reform societies. Radicals in the livery companies expressed displeasure with colonial policies that were injurious to business. Most English Radicals' interest in the American quandary was qualified by primary concern about their own situations at home. And there was no unanimous agreement on the extent of parliamentary reform or the expansion of civil liberties in England.

THREE

~~~~~~~

Radical Spokesmen on Imperial Crisis, 1774-1776

THE materials which shed light on extraordinary figures like John Cartwright, Granville Sharp, James Burgh, Catharine Macaulay, and Richard Price are not nearly as extensive as those which tell historians about the great men of the Whig Opposition in Parliament who opposed the government's American policy. Yet there are sufficient sources of information available to us upon which we can form some concrete judgments about their roles in the imperial drama. Some of them were quite prominent in their day and their opinions were known on both sides of the Atlantic. Much information about them can be found in contemporary correspondence, memoirs, periodicals, and other recorded recollections of men who knew them. Of especial value to the historian are the books and pamphlets written by these individuals. In an age when pamphleteering was a common means of addressing large audiences, their pamphlets provided forums for expressing their opinions. Numerous biographies and other secondary sources published in the recent past in both Great Britain and America contribute to our knowledge of the British Radicalism of which these persons were a part.

In the following pages I will present a synthesis of the ideas of these five figures who publicly addressed the American question during the critical two years between the Boston Tea Party and the Declaration of Independence. Recent research by the American historian Thomas R. Adams on British pamphlets of the American revolutionary era indicates that the pamphlets of Cartwright, Sharp, Macaulay, and Price—Burgh's *Political Disquisitions* was a political treatise in three volumes—were the only ones published during this juncture that urged solutions to the American problem from the British Radical vantage point.[1] These five were among the leading Radical political thinkers of the day and they made some singular contributions to the history of English Radicalism. Their interest in the constitutional ramifications of liberty and empire furnished part of the later legacy of Whiggish interpretations of the American Revolution.[2] It should be understood that this work, essentially a history of ideas, does not argue that their ideas were causal factors of later developments in some parts of the British Empire, such as responsible government and free trade. At the same time, their proposals certainly had some influence on contemporary American leaders and therein lies their immediate significance. As for the long-range connection of such ideas with important trends in the nineteenth-century British Empire, British Radical ideas preceding the Declaration of Independence anticipated such tendencies in the tradition of liberal Whig reformism, rather than becoming powerful forces which directly influenced developments like the Durham Report or the British North America Act of 1867. It is to the credit of British Radical thinkers of the American revolutionary era that many of their ideas envisaged imperial innovation in the nineteenth and twentieth centuries.

James Burgh and Richard Price were among a company of Honest Whigs who regularly attended informal social gatherings in London coffeehouses over a period of several years in the 1760s and 1770s. This company seems to have started out as a weekly supper club which met at the homes of Burgh, Price, and Thomas Rogers, father of the later author Samuel Rogers, outside the City in Newington Green. Its growth caused the group to move their gatherings into several London coffeehouses, such as Saint Paul's Coffeehouse, the London Coffeehouse at Ludgate Hill, and the Crown and Anchor Tavern in the Strand. Their numbers included notable Dissenters, some liberal Anglicans, a few M.P.'s, and the best-known American in England, Benjamin Franklin.[3] These meetings were held fortnightly on Thursday evenings and were occasions for pleasant conversation and supper. The company discussed various subjects, including politics, empire, and reform. There is no doubt that these men carried on some of the most stimulating discussions of the day on philosophy, religion, science, history, and human liberty. They were interested in reform and human improvement. They sought the moral regeneration of their country as well as pragmatic changes to improve British institutions. "Their faith was science, education, and the application of the principles of good reason to the problems of the day. Earnestly dedicated to doing right, they believed in the power of common sense and knowledge to improve the lot of their fellowmen." [4]

James Burgh was the erudite headmaster of a Dissenting Academy in Newington Green during the generation before the American Revolution. His *Political Disquisitions* (1774–75) was a classic statement of British Radical opinion and a masterly argument for parliamentary reform. The volumes included some forceful ideas about the American problem. Burgh may have had a greater influence on John Adams and Thomas Jefferson than did Thomas Paine. Caroline Robbins suggests that the *Political Disquisitions* possibly was the most important political work of its kind to appear in England during the first half of George III's reign. [5] Bernard Bailyn calls it the "key book of this generation." [6]

A Scotsman, Burgh originally came from Perthshire, where he was born in 1714. His father was a Presbyterian clergyman and his mother was the aunt of the historian William Robertson. He attended Saint Andrews University for a short time with aspirations for the clergy. Bad health and perhaps need of money caused him to abandon his studies, and he turned to the linen trade. He failed in business and was in London by 1740. There he found work as a proofreader and indexer. Burgh came to have pedagogical ambitions and taught at schools outside London for about three years. He won a national audience in 1746 when he published a treatise called *Britain's Remembrancer*, a moralistic commentary on the "Forty-Five" that warned against the profligacies of Augustan England. The reputation and earnings resulting from the pamphlet's success brought better times. Burgh started his own academy in Stoke Newington in 1747, and its success permitted him to move the school to a larger building in adjacent Newington Green in 1750. He married during the following year. For the next quarter of a century Burgh was a distinguished headmaster and a notable writer on moral, political, and academic subjects. A bad case of gallstones forced him to retire from the academy in 1771. He spent his last years finishing his most important political work, the *Politi-*

cal Disquisitions. Burgh completed the third volume shortly before his death in the summer of 1775.[7]

Burgh's students and neighbors in Newington Green knew him as a benevolent, industrious gentleman with an acute mind and great enthusiasm in his academic career.[8] He was a devout man. All his endeavors, in teaching, in writing, and in his politics, were callings to high and worthy goals. He was loved and respected by the Prices and the Rogers, who lived near him. Both his character and abilities were respected by the Honest Whigs and numerous celebrated associates of his in London, including Arthur Onslow, Speaker of the House of Commons, and Stephen Hales, clerk of the closet to the Princess Dowager Augusta. Burgh became a friend of the princess herself.[9] The Newington Green schoolmaster got to know various men connected with City Radical politics during the 1760s, and he probably influenced some of the members of the Bill of Rights Society in its early years.[10]

Richard Price and his wife Sarah lived across the green from the Burghs for many years. The two men had much in common in their views on life and the great issues of their time. Price was one of the most respected men in England by the time of the American Revolution and one of the most prominent figures in the history of eighteenth-century English Dissent. His contemporaries knew him as an accomplished clergyman, theologian, moral philosopher, and actuarial statistician. His *Observations on the Nature of Civil Liberty*, first published on the eve of the Declaration of Independence, was one of the most important publications of the period. Price's ideas about liberty eloquently viewed the American crisis in a perspective which transcended the constitutional issues over which Englishmen and Americans had been quarreling for a decade. Dr. Price's pamphlet won broad attention on both sides of the Atlantic and, had he accepted an American invitation to come to Philadelphia during the war, this gifted and kindly man might have played an important role in the creation of the Republic.

Price was born in Glamorganshire, Wales in 1723. Like Burgh, he was the son of a clergyman. He was sent to Dissenting academies in Wales before the premature deaths of both his parents when he was around eighteen years old. In 1740 his uncle, Samuel Price, sent for him from London and placed him in the Fund Academy of the Dissenter William Coward. Young Price studied for the Presbyterian ministry and was ordained after graduation from the academy in 1744. He became chaplain to the wealthy Dissenting family of George Streatfield in Stoke Newington and, shortly afterward, assistant to Samuel Chandler at the London Presbyterian chapel in the Old Jewry. Stoke Newington and Newington Green were pleasant rural retreats from the nearby City during those years, and many respectable families of English Dissent resided in the area. Many of the residents were baptized, married, and buried by the Reverend Price over a period of nearly half a century. The Rogers family also provide testimony about Price, who was one of the best-known, most-loved residents in the vicinity.[11] His writings and actuarial studies in life insurance and national debt brought him into association with people in many stations of life. He even found his way into the company of Lady Elizabeth Montagu and her Bluestocking companions. It was through Lady Montagu that he began his long friendship with Lord Shelburne. Price's visits to Shelburne House and Bowood enabled him to meet some of the most celebrated people of the age.[12]

The Reverend Price was financially well-off after he received substantial inheritances upon the deaths of his uncle and Mr. Streatfield in 1756. He married the gentle Sarah Blundell in 1758 and, after a brief residence in Hackney, they lived in Newington Green until Sarah's death in 1786. Price served several congregations through these years and became one of the most prominent Dissenting clergymen in England. His *Four Dissertations* (1767) on theology earned him an honorary doctorate of divinity from Aberdeen University. His work in actuarial statistics caused the Equitable Assurance Company in Coleman Street in London to seek his advice. Shelburne consulted with him about the national debt, and this made it possible for Price to obtain valuable information about public expenditures by the government during the American war. The long work on national debt estimates and his interest in the principle of the sinking fund led to two important publications in the early 1770s, *Observations on Reversionary Payments* (1771) and *An Appeal to the Public on the Subject of the National Debt* (1772).[13]

Dr. Price was one of the first and best-known figures of the Honest Whig gatherings in London coffeehouses. Burgh once spoke of his neighbor and friend as "the incomparable Dr. Price." Price also was one of Benjamin Franklin's closest friends during the American's long residence in England. Perhaps Dr. Price's association with Americans is the most notable example of the extraordinary understanding which existed between English Dissent and American revolutionaries.

Dr. Price was a man of peace and did not like controversy, private or public. Though his writings came to have great influence on Radical activists in London, he himself kept a respectable distance between the placid routine of a Newington Green clergyman and the stormy politics of City Radicalism. The American question obviously came up for discussion among the Honest Whigs during their frequent gatherings, but Price apparently did not think it necessary to publicize his opinions outside the company of his companions. Like other Englishmen who questioned the wisdom of the government's American policy, he was very alarmed by the passage of the Coercion Acts in 1774, the grave possibility of their actual enforcement, and the even more grave possibility of a war. In 1775 he was deeply affected by the departure of Dr. Franklin from England and, a few months later, by the accounts of the actions outside Boston sent to him by American friends.[14] Late in that year, when it became clear to him that the government was resolved on a policy of coercion, Dr. Price had no doubts about the justice of the American cause and the distressing effects which an American war would have on England. He decided to present his views on the American issue publicly and, when his *Observations on the Nature of Civil Liberty* appeared in early 1776, he was surprised that his ideas became "the talk of London" and an inspiration to American patriots in Philadelphia.

Though not a Dissenter like Burgh and Price, Granville Sharp's life and career resembled the endeavors of many reformers among English Dissenters who were interested in social improvement. He is mainly remembered as "the father of the anti-slavery movement" in eighteenth-century England. His friends knew him as a humane, good man whose enthusiasm and willpower made him a lifelong crusader for good causes in behalf of the Negro slave, the victim of the press-gang, and the poor of London. George Otto Trevelyan once described Sharp as "a man who was the forerunner of a class which . . . has played an unostentatious and unrecompensed, but a most commanding, part in the history of moral and social progress."[15] Granville Sharp's *A Declaration of the People's Natural Right to a Share in the Legislature* (1774) was another contribution to the American debate and sheds some important light on how some English Radicals looked at the problem of legislative jurisdiction within the larger perspectives of English history and the cause of social justice.

Sharp was born in Durham in 1735 and was one of the fourteen children of Thomas Sharp. Granville's grandfather was an archbishop of York and his father was archdeacon of Northumberland. Young Sharp was taken to London when he was fourteen and apprenticed to a linen draper of Tower Hill. In 1757 he completed his apprenticeship and became a freeman of the City as a member of the Fishmongers' Company. Life as a tradesman soon lost its flavor for him and he gave it up in 1758. He secured a place in the government's ordnance department and worked there as a salaried clerk for the next eighteen years. Sharp never married. During his early years at the ordnance department he lived in rooms at Garden Court Temple and spent much of his time with two brothers who also lived in the City. He devoted many of his leisure hours to private biblical studies and arrived at some conclusions about biblical prophecy which his acquaintances probably found somewhat eccentric.

Sharp apparently got to know London quite well, especially its poor sections. He was distressed by the vice and depravity he saw and was outraged by the work of the press-gang. His philanthropic career began in 1767 when he befriended a desperate Negro slave named Jonathan Strong who was in danger of being carried away to the West Indies. Sharp took the case into a widely publicized court battle and succeeded in assuring Strong's freedom. During and after this ordeal he studied English law and raised the question of why English law should respect the legality of some 14,000 slaves being kept in servitude while residing on English soil. His studies led to his publication of an antislavery treatise called *A Representation of the Injustice . . . of Tolerating Slavery in England* (1769). All this helped to bring on his famous role in the *Somersett* case in 1771–72 when he challenged prevailing legal opinions, including William Blackstone's, before William Murray, earl of Mansfield, who was lord chief justice of the Court of King's Bench. Sharp's contention that "as soon as any slave sets his foot upon English territory, he becomes free" prevailed when Judge Mansfield made his famous decision in Somersett's favor in June 1772. The case was a sensation. Sharp was a celebrity. Still working at the ordnance office, he continued to be active in numerous causes—the most important being his crusade for the abolition of slavery in the British Empire. He won the recognition and friendship of the Quaker Anthony Benezet, who was beginning a similar cause in Philadelphia. Sharp eventually was made chairman of the Anti-Slavery Society in London, but he came to be overshadowed by the great William Wilberforce. He was one of those Englishmen whose longtime efforts anticipated abolition of the slave trade in the British Empire in 1807. Defense of America in 1774 was one of his many causes.

John Cartwright's reputation as a Radical reformer traditionally has been connected with his longtime advocacy of parliamentary reform based on principles he first espoused publicly in his *Take Your Choice!* (1776). He is usually known in the history of English reformism as Major Cartwright. Some of his contemporaries considered him the "father of parliamentary reform." His work for parliamentary reform extended over a period of half a century, from the years of the American Revolution to the eve of the Great Reform Bill.[16] Unlike Burgh, Price, and Sharp, Cartwright was unknown to the English public in 1774 when he publicized some imaginative proposals for settling the American crisis in his *American Independence the Interest and Glory of Great Britain* (1774). Though not taken seriously by most of those who read the pamphlet, his ideas, as R. G. Adams once wrote, "do not seem so impractical in the light of later experience."[17]

Cartwright was born to a family of the Nottinghamshire gentry in 1740. His younger brother, Edmund Cartwright, was the inventor of the power loom. His formal education went no further than grammar school. During the Seven Years' War he entered the Royal Navy in time to serve in the actions in Quiberon Bay off the French coast. Before the war ended he was a first lieutenant on the flagship staff of Admiral Richard Howe. He served at the Newfoundland Station from 1766 to 1770, suffered from the climate, and almost lost his life in a shipwreck. Poor health forced his return to England in 1770 for convalescence. He divided the next few years' time between home in Nottinghamshire and business in London. Cartwright, by then, was a self-educated man who read widely and had

seen much of the world. He evidently read extensively about English history, the constitution, and contemporary politics. By the
time of the Boston Tea Party he was interested in parliamentary
reform and the American problem. The colonial crisis during the
winter of 1773–74, the impending actions of Parliament, and a
pamphlet published by the anti-American dean of Gloucester
Cathedral, Josiah Tucker, prompted him to publish ideas which
might have been running through his mind for some time.

This was the young John Cartwright rather than the kindly,
eccentric, old gentleman known to the English public many years
later. One of his friends complimented the reformer's character as
being "purely English." [18] His friends respected him enough to over-
look his eccentricities. Later nineteenth-century reformers could not
help admiring an Englishman whose faith in English institutions
was so great that he waged a fifty-year campaign for parliamentary
reform until he died at the age of eighty-four in 1824. He had many
qualities which present him as a worthy eighteenth-century Englishman. Even his severest critics thought of him in his late years as
a well-meaning old nuisance. He liked to tinker in ideas, like his
more famous brother, and among them were some notable, if
idealistic, ideas about the future of the British Empire.

The life and career of the lady historian Catharine Macaulay
should be very attractive to twentieth-century feminists. She irritated, even shocked, both her friends and critics by behaving
unconventionally in a London society which expected adherence to
convention. Her ideas about womanhood and her Radical political
sentiments made her one of the most talked about women in the
British world. The eight volumes of her Whiggish *History of
England from the Accession of James I to That of the Brunswick
Line* sorely annoyed conservative Englishmen like Dr. Johnson and
delighted Radicals on both sides of the Atlantic. [19] She thought of
herself as a crusader against all forces which she believed inimical to
her principles of liberty. And she welcomed the American Revolution as history's greatest triumph for the cause of freedom. Along
with men like Shelburne, Burke, and Wilkes, she was toasted by the
Sons of Liberty in the taverns of Boston as one of those worthy citizens of the "Republic of Letters" who shared their enthusiasm for
liberty. [20] Her grandiose *Address to the People of England, Scot-*

land and Ireland on the Present Crisis of Affairs (1775) appealed to
the inhabitants of the British Isles to unleash the fury of public
opinion in America's behalf around the time when Britons received
news of Lexington and Concord. Her outspoken views on the imperial crisis marked "the eruption of woman into public life, a
meteor flashing across the sky foretelling the dawn of romantic
freedom"—something which added to the aura of the American
Revolution in the minds of Englishmen.[21]

The celebrated Mrs. Macaulay was born in 1731 to a well-off
family of Kentish gentry. She was the sister of John Sawbridge, a
prominent London Radical. The young Catharine Sawbridge was
given all the advantages a wealthy, indulgent father could provide
for his two sons and two daughters. As a young, bright, and impres-
sionable girl she studied classical literature and history. She grew up
to become an attractive, independent woman with an acute, erudite
mind and political ideas rooted in her admiration for the classical
republics of Greece and Rome. Her unconventional feminism and
republican idealism fashioned her notions of English politics in her
time as corrupt and disloyal to the lofty principles of the Glorious
Revolution.

Catharine Sawbridge was twenty-nine in 1760 when she married Dr. George Macaulay, a physician at the Lying-In Hospital in
London's Brownlow Street. She became a familiar figure in London
society but was not the sort of woman to be bound by the quaint
femininities of her friends' drawing rooms. When David Hume's
very popular *History of England* received the plaudits of the reading public, she was ruffled by Hume's Tory-like treatment of the
Stuart reigns. In 1761 she set out to write her own version of Stuart
history and managed to finish the first of her eight volumes in 1762.
This was the threshold of her growing prominence. She enjoyed a
wide social circle in London, ranging from the fashionable salon of
Lady Montagu's Bluestockings to the Radical friends of her
brother. She probably knew numerous Honest Whigs and certainly
James Burgh. The Macaulays especially knew and liked Thomas
Hollis of Lincoln's Inn, who was a frequent visitor in their home.[22]

The Macaulays had a daughter before Dr. Macaulay died suddenly in 1766. His death was a severe blow to his widow but the
pain was eased by her active life and the *History*. She finished the

fifth volume by the end of 1771, but the final three had to wait completion until ten years later. Her independence and Radical politics led to her interest in the American issue. Her pro-American sympathies did not sit well with the refined ladies of London society. Critics dismissed her as a female gadabout. John Wilkes, of all people, accused her of neglecting her daughter. Bad health caused her to leave London in 1774 and take up residence in Bath. Even her friends never forgave her when in 1778, at the age of forty-seven, she married the twenty-one-year-old William Graham, a surgeon's mate. They eventually moved to Binfield in Berkshire where they lived until Catharine's death in 1791.

Catharine Macaulay was an extraordinary woman and one of the most celebrated females of her time, both in England and America. It is strange that she has not received more attention from students of the period. She figured more prominently in the minds of British Radicals and American revolutionaries as a gifted propagandist rather than as a serious historian like her contemporaries Gibbon, Robertson, and Hume. Her strengths as a writer, however, were admirable. Caroline Robbins argues that her research was better than Hume's and that she had a "certain detachment and independence in her commentary that entitles [her] to more serious study than she normally provokes." [23] Lecky described her as "the ablest writer of the new Radical school." [24]

The course of human events seldom can be foreseen with any large degree of certitude, and few of the king's subjects on either side of the Atlantic could have known where the events of 1774–75 were going to lead them. Not until the Americans declared independence in 1776 did the Radicals described above think it was too late to settle the imperial crisis in some way that might preserve a union of the two peoples and fashion their notions of a proper balance of liberty and authority throughout the British world. During the two years between March 1774 and March 1776, these five loyal but disconcerted subjects of King George III published their views on the American issue in hopes that an unnecessary, unjust, and tragic war would not be unleashed upon the colonists by the British government. These spokesmen represented some important features of British Radical thinking on both domestic and imperial questions. Their ideas, which will be described in the order of their initial appearances in London publications, were well received among the Radicals of the City and Middlesex, while being regarded by the mass of informed Englishmen with resentment or indifference.

Three months after the East India Company's tea cargo was dumped into Boston Harbor, John Cartwright publicly urged upon Parliament his extraordinary proposals for building a grand Anglo-American commonwealth which might have been inspiration for a Rudyard Kipling. The social reformer Granville Sharp appealed to his interpretations of the history of English law and argued that the crown's subjects both in America and Ireland should have a more equitable legislative representation—notions which envisaged the "home rule" principle of a later age. James Burgh presented a classic argument for parliamentary reform as the central consideration toward solving many problems, the American crisis being only one of them. Catharine Macaulay spoke as a republican citizeness who wanted to animate among the British public the passion for liberty which beat in her own breast. Dr. Richard Price, at a time when American leaders were preparing to argue their case for independence before the world, wrote one of the period's most eloquent and definitive statements on what the American Revolution was about. How did these people conceive of liberty and empire? What concrete proposals did they submit as alternatives to the policy of their government? Were they practical? How did the ranks of British Radicalism react to their principles? What were the reactions of great men like Chatham, Burke, and others in the Whig Opposition? And how were they connected with the men who made the American Revolution? We shall see that these Radical spokesmen nurtured ideas which were ahead of their time. Their own generation could not or would not understand them. But these individuals' place in the history of the American Revolution was noteworthy and their ideas show us that the mother country, along with America, had persons with enlightened concepts of liberty and empire which merit the recognition of their posterity on both sides of the Atlantic.

FOUR

~~~~~~~~~

A Commonwealth of Nations: John Cartwright

JOHN CARTWRIGHT, at the time a first lieutenant in the Royal Navy, was residing in London during the winter of 1773–74 when news about the Boston Tea Party was raising a furor among Englishmen. He probably thought intently about the American problem long before his recognition that Parliament, once it was reconvened at Westminster, was likely to vote for reprisals against the city of Boston. His decision to address himself to Parliament was probably prompted by that body's initiation of the historic Coercion Acts and the appearance of a remarkable pamphlet written by the anti-American Josiah Tucker, dean of Gloucester Cathedral, and entitled *The True Interest of Britain* (1774). Because of his extraordinary ideas and their unintentional connection with Radical principles, it is important to give some attention to Dean Tucker. Cartwright's proposals, as will be seen, apparently were influenced by the cantankerous dean.

Dean Tucker had long been a prolific writer on controversial issues. A theologian and polemicist, he was also one of the most original economic theorists of the eighteenth century. His unpublished *The Elements of Commerce and Theory of Taxes*, completed in 1755, anticipated some of the antimercantile arguments in Adam Smith's *The Wealth of Nations* published two decades later.[1] He accepted the old mercantilist notion that a country's economic activity should be regulated by government in a manner consistent with national interest. But he complained that some of Britain's old mercantile laws no longer served that central, critical purpose. By the eve of the American Revolution Tucker was convinced, after a decade of quarreling between the mother country and some of its American colonies, that it was not in Great Britain's best interests to hold onto troublemaking provinces like Massachusetts Bay. Whereas John Cartwright was to make some distinction between what he described as a British nation and a rising American nation, Dean Tucker saw a growing distinction between two differing "interests." The Boston Tea Party convinced Tucker that he was right and that British and American interests would move further apart in the years to come.

Dean Tucker published *The True Interest of Britain* in January 1774 and addressed himself to both Parliament and the public. What course of action is it in "the true interest of Britain" to take at this critical time when Parliament is about to meet? As Tucker sees it, Britain has five possible courses of action:

> To suffer things to go on for awhile, as they lately have done, in hopes that some favourable opportunity may offer for recovering the jurisdiction of the British legislature over the colonies, and for maintaining this authority of the mother country.
>
> To attempt to persuade the colonies to send over a certain number of deputies or representatives, to sit and vote in the British Parliament; in order to incorporate America and Great Britain into one common empire.
>
> To declare open war against them as rebels and revolters; and after having made a perfect conquest of the country, then to govern it by military force and despotic sway.
>
> To propose to consent that America should become the general seat of empire; and that Great Britain and Ireland should be governed by viceroys sent over from the Court residencies, either at Philadelphia or New York, or at some other American imperial city.
>
> To propose to be separate entirely from the colonies, by declaring them to be a free and independent people, over whom we lay no claim; and then by offering to guarantee this freedom and independence against all foreign invaders whomsoever.[2]

Tucker curtly dismisses the first four alternatives. Procrastination, a position taken by the Rockingham Whigs at the time, would achieve nothing in the light of past experience. It would be naïve to believe that the headstrong Americans could be brought around to accepting principles of imperial responsibility that would not coincide with American interests. Admitting Americans into Parliament would be impractical and solve nothing. It would only bring more faction and quarreling to the floor of the House of Commons. An American faction would surely develop and be more obliged to colonial interests than to imperial responsibility. The dean of Gloucester hated war and the prospect of armed force against the colonists was repugnant to him. The costs in British blood and treasure would be immoral, impractical, and self-defeating. The bitterness of war would sour relations between the two peoples for years to come. If British arms prevailed, the expense of ruling a conquered people would be prohibitive. And no serious thinker could suggest the removal of the imperial capital to distant America. And so Dean Tucker argues that Great Britain, for the sake of her best interests, grant American independence. This is the measure with which Parliament should be concerned when it convenes at Westminster. "And, in fact, what is all this but the natural and even the necessary corollary to be deduced from each of the former reasons and observations? For if we can neither govern the Americans, nor be governed by them, nor ought to subdue them;—what remains, but to part with them on as friendly terms as we can?"[3]

His countrymen's fears over such a radical measure, argues the dean, will prove to be groundless. There will be no disastrous decline in Anglo-American trade. An independent, prosperous America would remain Britain's chief customer and market because of British ability to buy from abroad and the growing American demand for British goods. The Royal Navy, bolstered by the British taxpayer, can leave the defense of American waters to the Americans, while His Majesty's fleet can be concentrated in Channel and Mediterranean waters. British departure from the colonies will not be followed by the appearance of the French. The Americans would make French masters more miserable than English ones. American independence could slow down emigration from the British Isles of those industrious people whose skills and productivity are needed at home. And it is no longer rational that the British government expend between £300,000 and £400,000 a year for American administration and defense. With the perspective of two centuries' hindsight, it is evident that Tucker's case had much substance. Professor Vincent Harlow praises him as a theorist and prophet whose ideas anticipated the founding of the second British Empire.

"Tucker's economic principles were too revolutionary to win a large following; but as the nation began to feel the drain and disappointment of an unsuccessful war, bellicosity began to fade into war-weariness and a longing for peace, and Tucker's arguments that the American connection was a source of weakness for Britain became increasingly representative of a public opinion which was deciding that the colonial grapes were sour."[4]

John Cartwright's arguments on the crisis were presented in a much different perspective, but he seems to have been impressed by the dean's economic arguments. It is likely that *American Independence the Interest and Glory of Great Britain* was a counter-proposal to that of Tucker. Cartwright devised his own concept of American independence and, unlike Tucker's, it was inspired by principles readily acceptable to British Radicals. He put the American problem within the more general framework of a grand scheme of imperial reformation. His vision of a mercantilist empire translated into a commonwealth of self-governing states was the groundwork for some ideas which, like Dean Tucker's, proved to be prophetic about the course of Anglo-American history.

Cartwright publicized his views in a series of ten open letters addressed to Parliament, then sitting at Westminster. They originally were published over a period of several weeks in March and April 1774. Under the pen name of Constitutio, they appeared in the London *Public Advertiser*. They came out in the London *Chronicle* during the following autumn and also were distributed, in pamphlet form, to members of Parliament. A second pamphlet edition with a long postscript was published in the spring of 1775. The first American edition was printed in Philadelphia by Robert Bell in early 1776.

Cartwright shows no extraordinary qualities as a writer in *American Independence*. He does not have James Burgh's erudition or Dr. Price's eloquence. His narrative rambles and his arguments lack coherence. But this is owing to their initial appearance in a series of letters written over two months' time. If his work has little literary merit, that is offset by the author's grasp of the subject and great enthusiasm for his own ideas. He was one of those young English Radicals of the American revolutionary period whose veneration of the ancient constitution was integrated with a zealous, benevolent reformism rooted in the tradition of the anticourt, anti-ministerial Whig reformers of Sir Robert Walpole's generation.[5] He saw the American question essentially as a constitutional problem that could be resolved in the British empirical tradition. Though the Boston crisis at the time might be seen as a local matter, he fears that serious trouble will soon spread through much of British America. Like other British Radicals in early 1774, he does not think it either necessary or desirable that the mother country completely break away from America. Desiring the preservation of Anglo-American unity and harmony, he is convinced that this is still possible through a clever reformation of the old imperial system.

Cartwright begins his case with the assertion that the basic rights of all Englishmen are rooted in England's great constitutional traditions, including those which build a proper balance of liberty and authority. His philosophy of liberty is Lockean and is tempered by the spirit of the eighteenth-century Enlightenment. Englishmen's rights, he insists, go back further than Magna Charta and are consistent with the laws of nature. The constitution's evolution is the world's finest manifestation of man's basic aspirations to life, liberty, and property. Those free and enterprising Englishmen who had gone out to create colonies in the New World carried the constitutional traditions of old England with them. Free Englishmen on English soil abroad are as free as Englishmen in the native isles. English colonization, in a large sense, was an expansion of English liberty abroad. The American peoples of his own day, writes the author, are his fellow Englishmen across the sea.

The history of the American provinces is analogous to the growth of a strong, healthy young man. They were once infants in need of the mother's care and protection, weaned through a necessary dependency on the mother country. In time these transplanted Englishmen built the fabrics of their own social and economic progress. The historic result has been the growth of a self-reliant American nation which has come of age. The recent war against France both tested and confirmed American manhood. The subsequent quarrels with the mother country are no more than a family squabble roused by a young nation's will to make its own way in the world. Britons at home can no longer expect Englishmen in America to accept old and irritable parental restrictions on American liberty and progress. If the family of Anglo-American peoples is to live in peace and unity, it is necessary to change the old colonial system. Failure to do so can only lead to preventable clashes which may endanger and possibly destroy the unity of these peoples who have so much to gain by preserving union. If the present British government is serious about the use of the Coercion Acts, it is employing Prussian methods against free Englishmen. Americans will be subjected to outrages that would not be tolerated by Englishmen at home.

Cartwright expresses distaste for Dean Tucker's anti-American feelings and failure to appreciate the grand possibilities of keeping England and America linked together. Yet he is impressed by the dean's criticism of outdated mercantile restrictions. His generation of Englishmen defend the supremacy of the mother parliament in the British Empire as necessary to maintain a harmonious commercial system. But the old Trade and Navigation Acts, in his opinion, no longer give sustenance to American growth, but rather impede it. They have become a kind of economic bondage inconsistent with the liberties of free, promising Englishmen. The old laws no longer make good economic sense either. American economic potential is so vast that it demands a freedom for growth that is possible only through revision of the old mercantilism. Such a step is in the vital interest of both Great Britain and America. England would surely gain from a blossoming of American economic growth. And, as matters presently stand in Boston, the mother country does not have much of a choice. Indefinite prolongation of the old colonial system will require the use of force. Peaceful enforcement will become impossible. The sooner His Majesty's government and Parliament abandon their view of America as a means to protect solely English interests, the greater will be the prospects for an imperial reformation that will serve the best interests of both peoples.

Through his constitutional and economic arguments Cartwright shows his notion of American independence. He does not propose complete separation as argued by Dean Tucker. Cartwright urges a scheme for American autonomy from Parliament while maintaining an Anglo-American allegiance to the titular sovereignty of the British crown. Such a measure, he contends, is entirely workable under the constitution. It would be a kind of imperial reform with vast potential for the futures of Great Britain and America. The idea for such a plan leads Cartwright to an elaborate explanation of the constitutional machinery through which it might be carried out. He raises a curious challenge to Parliament's right to exert legislative authority in the British Empire.

Essentially, Cartwright challenges eighteenth-century notions of Parliament's right to legislate for the American colonies. He argues that the Revolution of 1688 had been a victory for English liberty throughout the British Empire. But the subsequent Revolution Settlement did not establish a parliamentary supremacy in the colonies. The Glorious Revolution and its aftermath left undisturbed the royal prerogative's responsibility to administer colonial affairs. It is unfortunate, he argues, that Parliament's ascendancy in the eighteenth century had led to its increasing influence in colonial matters on behalf of powerful commercial interests. An inept monarchy had contributed to this state of affairs. The passage of the Declaratory Act in 1766 was a recent manifestation of this irresponsible infringement of the royal prerogative. Unfortunately, the present monarch has been a party to it. Cartwright is suggesting that many problems of the time were rooted in widespread ignorance, including the king's, of the constitution's true principles. The rightful responsibility for the government of the colonies lies with the crown as first magistrate of the British Empire.

It is curious that a man like Cartwright seems to be upholding the prerogative in such a way almost a century after the Revolution of 1688. Not even George III himself would have concurred with the concept in 1774.[6] But Cartwright explains himself with the argument that the colonial assemblies, not Parliament, are the rightful bodies to legislate for the Americans and that the crown's administration of the colonies should have been sanctioned not by Parliament's interests but by those of the respective colonial assemblies. The British Parliament's business is to legislate on British affairs in the home isles in collaboration with the king.

> The House of Commons can claim no power of imposing laws on the colonists, for they derive no such power by election. The power of the Commons of Great Britain is a legislative power, and that power bears no relation to the purposes for which it was given; which was to impose laws on the people of Great Britain, but by no means the people of America because the power of the electors extended only to themselves. The three orders united, i.e., the parliament have a most extensive power over the people of Great Britain because every power in the state meets in that body; but considered with respect to

the colonies, their pretension to such a power there clashes with the legislatures of those colonies, they can never submit together in the same place.[7]

Therefore, insists the author, it is the colonial assemblies which are duly authorized to represent and to legislate for Englishmen in the colonies. Whereas the king in Parliament act for the British nation itself, the king in colonial parliaments should act for the imperial provinces. Within the spirit of the constitution the mother Parliament has no authority to speak for colonists who have no role—nor should they—in the electoral procedures which send men to the House of Commons. Cartwright's reasoning is similar to that of numerous American spokesmen of the time. His idea of true legislative representation is the same as that of the colonists who were contesting the principle of virtual representation. Under the circumstances, he does not even think the British people are fairly represented under such a system.

Like Dean Tucker, Cartwright rejects recent suggestions that the Americans be conciliated by being given several seats in the Commons. It simply is not practical. The Commons would still be dominated by English interests. A vast ocean would still impair necessary and frequent communication between American legislators and their constituents. American M.P.'s would have little interest in strictly British matters. Speaking in behalf of the colonial assemblies, Cartwright reminds the mother Parliament that colonial Englishmen are subjects of the crown, not Parliament, and that the colonial legislatures hold the same relation to the king on colonial affairs as Parliament does on British affairs in the home islands. "Is not the end of government to the Americans the same as to all peoples, that is to say, the welfare and happiness of the society? Can these [sic] be welfare and happiness without freedom. . . . Is it agreeable to common sense to imagine that an American representation in the British Parliament could answer the true ends of representation to the people of that country?"[8]

Cartwright next takes up the heated issue of colonial taxation. If Parliament is not constitutionally authorized to legislate for Englishmen in the colonies, it stands to reason that it has no right to impose taxes—internal or external—on them. Again, he appeals to the natural rights of property belonging to all Englishmen in the

British world. Only that legislature which is representative of and accountable to its constituency may regulate their right of property by taxation. Parliament may exert such authority in the British Isles, but the colonial assembly is the rightful authority to tax in the colony. "It would require no learning, but only common sense and common honesty, to have known that a man hath no property in that which another can take from him without his consent." [9] The current situation in America requires a British resort to force to maintain the government's policy on taxation. Given the colonies' size, growth, and determination to resist such taxation, coercion would be self-defeating. It is obvious that American attitudes toward the British government in the near future are going to be determined by the way London decides to resolve this critical issue.

All of Cartwright's arguments seem to locate the responsibility for imperial reformation in the crown—that is, the king in collaboration with the colonial assemblies. Historically, it had been the prerogative through which the original colonial charters had been granted. The machinery for the administration of the colonies had been created by and was responsible to the crown. This essentially remained true in 1774 through the roles of the secretary of state for the American Department and the Board of Trade. Cartwright insists such machinery has some serious responsibilities to the colonial assemblies and this should offset arguments about the rights of an imperial Parliament. Parliament's claims in the Declaratory Act clashed with the principles of the constitution. Constructive changes in the imperial structure should be worked out through a collaboration of the king's officials on colonial affairs with colonial assemblies independent of the mother Parliament's claims.

Was Cartwright naïve or ill informed to think that the court could be brought around to such a position? George III and his ministers certainly were not well disposed to think of the British Empire in any light but that of the old mercantile system. The crown was allied with powerful interests which were hostile to any major alteration of the imperial structure. Cartwright recognizes all this. He seems to have made his case for imperial reform through action by the prerogative in order to demonstrate how far removed such a possibility was from the political realities of the time. The crown was also corrupted by the present structure of English politics. Neither king nor Parliament possessed a proper sense of responsibility to the colonists. Such a situation gave little reason for hoping that Cartwright's scheme could be adopted as a way of conciliation with the Americans. Aware of the political facts of life in his country, he places his reform hopes in the parliamentary Opposition. In the preface of his first letter to Parliament, he addressed his case to the liberal-minded Sir George Savile of Yorkshire and other M.P.'s with the potential for timely statesmanship. The cause of imperial reformation would have to begin with bold and selfless agitation among a small group in Parliament. Perhaps the turn of events in America would make their case more convincing in due time. Cartwright was to become a very frustrated man when such a development failed to materialize.

Hopes that his proposals might win converts from English merchants and other middling groups were to be just as frustrated. Having attacked the restrictive nature of mercantile policy, Cartwright holds out prospects of even more profitable trade with America under a much less regulated commercial exchange. Such notions succeeded no more than those of Dean Tucker. As for the mass of British opinion, Cartwright's ideas found no fertile ground. Public sentiment was too prejudiced against such a radical scheme. Most Englishmen, like their government, still viewed colonies as inferior, static repositories of the mother country's surplus population and products. Notions of colonial subservience to British interests were reenforced by a long tradition of such thinking. Nor could national pride allow such an accommodation with colonials. There was much sentiment that the Americans had a moral obligation to England for the latter's sacrifices in their behalf during the recent war.

Cartwright's failure to win support for his reform plan outside the circles of British Radicalism, however, does not warrant an historian's neglect of his extraordinary proposals. He unfolded his case on liberty, the constitution, and the means of reform in order that he might show how his scheme could transcend the present crisis through a new imperial order which would produce enormous benefits for both Britain and America. Basically, his aim is to see the old imperial structure transformed into a confederation of sovereign Anglo-American states under the common British constitution and with a common allegiance to the British crown. Such a union would consist of Great Britain and the newly "independent" states of British America—that is, American states with legislative jurisdictions autonomous from the mother Parliament. American independence is to be succeeded by the formation of eighteen sovereign entities from Canada southward to the Floridas and the West Indies. He evidently discards the idea of forming a federal "United States of America" because of his belief that a confederated union would be more commensurate with promoting Great Britain's vital interests in a system under the general British constitution. American governments and laws will correspond to those of the mother country under the British constitution. Each country will be governed by a national parliament with a status equal to that of the mother Parliament. The crown's essential role is to be titular sovereign of the confederation and symbol of its common constitution and Anglo-American unity. "The King was to be separately the King of each of the constituent nations of the League and to be the 'protector of the whole against foreign powers.' This would make the constituent nations separate units in international law, despite the declaration that they were 'free and independent states,' a fact which once more emphasizes the inadequacy of our political terminology, which finds it so difficult to admit the existence of an entity thus composed." [10]

Cartwright does not offer suggestions on how parliamentary leaders or cabinets in America might execute administrative responsibility. If his arguments are carried to their logical conclusions, it would seem that such cabinets would be more responsible to their own parliaments than to the crown in distant England. Each state in the confederacy is to be complete master of its domestic affairs. Cartwright is optimistic enough to believe their common heritage, constitution, and interests to be sufficient bases for general harmony, especially on matters of trade and defense. The problem of making foreign policy is not completely clear. He does propose that Britain assume the major responsibility for the defense of the league by way of British naval power. The Royal Navy's presence in the Atlantic Ocean and American waterways will be a defense from foreign dangers and a guarantee of the great American rivers as international trade routes accessible to all friendly nations. Each state in the confederacy, however, is to have its own armed militia with the authority to determine its use. Evidently, the American states are not to be bound to support British foreign policies or to be wartime allies of Britain against their will. It is also suggested that the mother country act as an international arbitrator among disputing members of the league. Cartwright does not elaborate on possible conflicts between the decisions of such arbitration and the sovereignty of league nations.

It would seem that Britain's extraordinary responsibilities in defense and arbitration would leave its position in foreign policy somewhat superior to the other states. Be that as it may, Cartwright apparently believes that the Americans could accept such a scheme. He is dealing with a problem that was successfully resolved in the twentieth-century British Commonwealth. It is also interesting that Cartwright's appreciation of British naval capacity anticipated the connection of such sea power to the interests of both the United States and Great Britain in the nineteenth century. The Royal Navy did not come to be the grand protector of an Anglo-American union such as that conceived by Cartwright in 1774. But British naval power most certainly had an important influence on the growth of the American Republic in the nineteenth century. It stood between an America concerned with internal development and European powers capable of interfering in American affairs.

Cartwright's "Grand British League and Confederacy" was a remarkable anticipation of the British Commonwealth of Nations which came into existence a century and a half after the American Revolution. With common loyalty to the British constitution, nominal allegiance to the British crown, parliamentary government, and national identities similar to those of the future dominions, the states of Cartwright's confederacy show striking likenesses to the members of the twentieth-century Commonwealth. Ideas enunciated in the *American Independence* foresaw the essence of the Statute of Westminster in 1931. The scheme of imperial reformation in 1774 envisioned the translation of Britain's national constitution into a commonwealth constitution. According to Cartwright, it is in the interest of the mother country to become a part of America's economic destiny. It will be to her glory that the British constitution and liberties be extended throughout the confederation and possibly to the far reaches of the globe. Great Britain in 1774 stands on the threshold of a magnificent opportunity to

resolve the American question and make way for a splendid union
with advantages to be shared by the British and Americans alike.

It evidently was Parliament's passage of the Quebec Act in 1774
that prompted Cartwright to express his views on the western territories in British America. These are discussed in his postscript to
the second edition of his pamphlet in 1775. His scheme for an organization of the western lands possibly was influenced by a veteran
of the recent war named Captain John Knox, who had published a
volume entitled *Historical Journal of the Campaigns for the Years
1757, 1758, and 1760.* The work included a map with territorial
divisions drawn by a cartographer named Thomas Kitchen. Cartwright may have copied it. In any event, his own scheme is an imaginative solution to the western problem.

Cartwright argues that the population growth of America
makes western expansion imminent and logical. The Quebec Act,
like other British restrictions of the time, does not consider the obvious trends of American growth, including western expansion.
Acts of Parliament cannot stop the inevitable. As a result, the
British government must face the realities of the situation and deal
with the western problem in ways commensurate with the ambitions of would-be settlers and the rights of Indians.

Cartwright proposes that the British government permit western expansion with guarantees of orderly settlement. Negotiations
with the Indian nations will be of cardinal importance as a prelude
to white settlement. Treaties must guarantee respect for mutual
agreements and the territorial rights of both Indians and settlers.
Cartwright does not elaborate on what Indian reaction to such proposals might be. And he is not clear in explaining the future connection between Indian nations and the settled territories. He indicates
that new American states might exist alongside formally recognized
Indian states. If necessary, states with mixed populations may be
created under British law. One point is made clear. Cartwright pre-
supposes the integrity of the Indian territories and the treatment of
Indian peoples as equals of whites under the law. How far he is
extending the abstract notion of natural rights to the Indians is a
matter for speculation.

Execution of the western scheme is to be under British administration. Territorial divisions of the West are to be based on natural

river boundaries. Such frontiers can minimize territorial disputes and offer an international network of river routes. Such waterways as the Ohio and Mississippi rivers could facilitate both Anglo-American trade and defense.

Cartwright recommends that the British-American West be organized into nineteen territories from the Great Lakes to the Gulf of Mexico and from the Appalachians to the Mississippi River. Political development will be in accordance with the principles of the British constitution. The four conditions for ultimate independence and nationhood must include a population of 50,000, establishment of the Protestant religion, allegiance to the British Crown as titular sovereign, and agreement to join the Grand British League and Confederacy. Ultimately, Cartwright's confederation would include Great Britain and at least thirty-seven American states.

This remarkable program for the future organization of western territories in America, conceived sometime in 1774, bears a striking resemblance to the plan of Thomas Jefferson as set forth in the Land Ordinance of 1784.[11] It also anticipates the intent of the Northwest Ordinance of 1787. The manner of separating the western lands from the coastal states, orderly administration and settlement under a central authority, along with preliminary conditions for statehood, are principles consistent with Cartwright's ideas. An American historian has speculated on the possible connection of the two men's ideas: "These ideas occur as fundamental bases of the Ordinance of 1784. It seems, therefore, that the policy adopted by the United States of enlarging the federal union by the admission of new members created by territory hitherto independent—that epochal policy which so successfully solved the political problem caused by the rigid settlement of the western wilderness—might conceivably have had Cartwright's plan as one of its sources."[12] The possibility that Jefferson may have been influenced by Cartwright's proposal has never been substantiated by tangible evidence. But the second edition of Cartwright's pamphlet was available in Philadelphia in 1776, and people such as Jefferson and Franklin were familiar with it. Whether Cartwright may be linked with the Land Ordinance of 1784 or not, it is obvious that his scheme was a feasible one. It is interesting that his western proposals were his only ideas on the American problem in his time which, to a great degree, were put into practical application. The results were phenomenal.

It would be presumptuous and simplistic to argue that Cartwright's schemes were obvious and logical solutions to the American question in 1774. He did not sufficiently appreciate some strong differences between the society of his own country and the wilderness society of America. Possibly he underestimated geographic difficulties in making such a system work and he most likely overestimated American colonial desires to maintain such bonds as those he was proposing with the crown and a league dependent on British protection. Nevertheless, his ideas suggest a comprehensive and remarkably prophetic concept of a new form of imperialism which would emerge in the British world in later generations.

Despite some important differences between the British and American societies of his time, Cartwright's conception of an Anglo-American commonwealth of nations did indeed illustrate a strong future interdependence of British and American interests in the world. Their common cultural, economic, and strategic interests were destined to build a mutual dependence that profoundly affected their respective histories in the nineteenth and twentieth centuries. These ranged from the importance of British sea power to both countries during the nineteenth century to the stature of American economic and military power in the twentieth century.

There is also something of the Victorian imperialist in Cartwright. His hopes for an Anglo-American union of nations were inspired by his conviction of a British mission to carry the supreme benefits of Anglo-Saxon culture to the rest of the world.

This has, under a most singular Providence, been our own peculiar blessing. I trust that it will be the blessing of our posterity to the latest generation, and that when we shall have given birth . . . to as many independent states as can find habitation on the vast American continent, that Britain will still be great and free: the respected mother, the model, the glory of them all: and I will, I must indulge the fond hope, that the pure religion, and the constitution of Britain, will gradually spread themselves over all America; and in every other part of the globe, as to become the chief instruments in the hands of almighty God of bringing about, in his due time, that universality of Christianity, that harmony and happiness among the nations of the earth which are entimated [sic] in the prophetic writings.[13]

These words have the ring of Carlyle and Kipling. Cartwright is confident of the benevolent potential of British constitutionalism and Protestantism to expand throughout the world of the late eighteenth century, when Captain James Cook's expeditions were preparing for Britannia's appearance in the Pacific.

His ideas on the progressive character of Anglo-American history also made Cartwright, along with Dean Tucker and Adam Smith, an early spokesman for abandonment of the old mercantilism. Such an economic argument was crucial to his case for the constitutional reformation of the British Empire. His estimation of the economic potential of an Anglo-American union through less regulation and greater free trade showed a keen anticipation of the liberal economic thought of the following century.

Finally, Cartwright's ideas were closely interwoven with the Radicalism that revived the liberal Whig advocacy of parliamentary reform in the 1770s. His pamphlet of early 1774 was inspired by his distress with the existing structure of English politics as well as his enthusiasm for changing the constitutional relationship between Britain and America.[14] His career in behalf of parliamentary reform in the half century after 1774 took root in the crisis of empire. In his view, the failure to achieve imperial reform made parliamentary reform imperative. The old parliamentary system was not conducive to responsible solution of the problems which Cartwright and his fellow reformers were beginning to recognize in British life. The old structure had to be changed through such radical steps as annual parliaments and universal male suffrage.[15] The obstinacy and ignorance of men in the current Parliament on the American issue were committing British colonial policy to an intransigence that made conciliation impossible.[16] Given the strength of traditional notions about empire in England at the time, however, it seems improbable that even the parliament sought by John Cartwright would have accepted the imperial reformation described in his pamphlet. Nevertheless, Cartwright's public appearance on the stage of Radical reformism in 1774 led to his associations with people such as Granville Sharp, Richard Price, John Horne Tooke, Dr. John Jebb, and numerous others among the Radical reform circles of the time. It was these men, not the Whig Opposition in Parliament, who corresponded to those known as Whigs in America.[17]

To Cartwright and others who thought like him, the American Revolution was a civil war among common heirs of the same constitution in which the colonists were struggling for liberties other Englishmen had won in 1688.[18] The Americans' eventual success inspired Cartwright's crusade for parliamentary reform down to the eve of the Great Reform Bill.

FIVE

~~~~~~

"Home Rule" for Ireland and America: Granville Sharp

GRANVILLE SHARP completely agreed with Cartwright's ideas. His *A Declaration of the People's Natural Right to a Share in the Legislature* first appeared during the spring of 1774, only a short time after the initial appearances of the Tucker and Cartwright publications. His principles of social justice and activities as a reformer, along with his familiarity with *The True Interest of Britain* and *American Independence the Interest and Glory of Great Britain*, stirred him to express his own ideas about the imperial situation. He combined the American problem with the even more ancient one of Ireland. Sharp drew upon his amateur study of English law and history in order to demonstrate his argument that English wrongs done to the Irish and Americans were strongly rooted in the past, when Englishmen refused to allow these two peoples to enjoy their due liberties as subjects of the English crown. His arguments that justice be done in Ireland and America were consistent with his other causes against slavery and impressment. His pamphlet reads more like a hair-splitting legal treatise than an eloquent argument for human justice, but it represents some important features of British Radical opinion on the eve of the American war.

Sharp versed himself in English law during the years before his successful efforts in the Somersett Case in 1772. His studies reenforced his belief in the British constitution as the grandest expression of laws and liberties sanctioned in the Judeo-Christian scriptures and the laws of nature. His ideas about human justice in the British Empire moved him to urge an imperial equity consistent with the spirit and intent of the ancient constitution. In his view, the imperial dilemmas in 1774 were rooted in English failure to recognize the right of colonial subjects to enjoy liberties prescribed in the constitution, most specifically the right of colonial subjects to a representative government which served their immediate, singular interest and welfare. Somewhat like Cartwright's argument on legislative autonomy in America, Sharp's pamphlet is an interesting case for both Irish and American self-government in ways which anticipate the "responsible government" or "home rule" principles of a later generation.

The pamphlet focuses mainly on English misrule in Ireland. Present wrongs done to America in 1774 are representations of English injustices which go far back in Irish history. Current wrongs in Ireland and America have been reenforced by eighteenth-century notions about Parliament's authority in the British Empire. The plight of the Irish in 1774 is no less tragic than that of the Americans. Indeed, the Irish quandary has social and economic ramifications much more distressing than those in America. A major step in the right direction for due justice to both peoples, he contends, is British respect for their right to govern their own internal affairs through Irish and American parliaments under the common British crown but independent of the mother Parliament at Westminster. Failure to do so mocks the constitution of England.

Sharp's interpretation of English law convinced him that the right of crown subjects to representation is as old as the constitution itself. The Irish had possessed such a right under the kings of medieval England, only to have it illegally usurped in modern times. Agreeing with Cartwright, he argues that the British nation which has perpetrated such an inequity across the Irish Sea is now trying to impose it in America.

The pamphlet's central theme is the proposition that "law, to bind all, must be assented to by all."[1] Sharp recalls biblical and Greek traditions that sanctioned the dignity of man and the responsibility of government to uphold the rights of man in accordance with eighteenth-century notions of natural law. Those ancient legacies formed the ethical foundation of the English constitution and common law. As "voluntary popular assent, the only true foundation of all valid contracts," is an intrinsic part of the constitution, the legislature is the means by which the consent of the governed renders the laws of the nation just and valid. That is the role of the British Parliament in its government of the British people. And it is in accordance with the constitution also that unjust laws be resisted when they are legislated without the consent of those to whom the laws apply. Therefore, the Irish and American peoples, who live under the same illustrious constitution as Englishmen in the native isles, have a justifiable complaint against the British government.

Citing ideas in Baron Samuel von Puffendorf's *Law of Nature and Nations*, Sharp holds that if the British Parliament acts as an arbitrary judge of the people's will without giving them due representation to express their own will, Westminster could be claiming an omnipotence for itself that is "a kind of popery in politics." In the debates over the administration of the British Empire in 1774, he writes, Parliament is assuming certain prerogatives not consistent with British law. Even many Englishmen are now inadequately spoken for at Westminster and, obviously, the peoples of Ireland and America have no representation truly consistent with British liberty.

Sharp in order appeals to English history and legal precedent to demonstrate that the imperial debate in 1774 has roots which go far back into the story of English misdeeds in Ireland. Insisting that "advocates for the liberties of Ireland have truth and justice on their side," he sets out to build a case that could justify both Irish and American complaints. In addition, he holds his views to be consistent with plain common sense.

> It plainly appears, that the right of legislation, is not less inseparable, by natural equity, from the people of every part of the British Empire, than the right of granting or with-holding taxes; for otherwise, the free subjects of one part of the empire would be liable to be most materially injured in their greatest and most valuable inheritance, the law, by the hasty decisions of men on the other side of the empire, with whom probably they would be totally unaquainted [*sic*] and whose interest might perhaps be as widely different as their situation upon the face of the globe is distant; that is, as widely different as the east is from the west.[2]

Sharp claims that Irish liberty, under the English constitution, is as old as that of England. When Ireland became part of the domain of King Henry II during the twelfth century, the common crown of England and Ireland had allowed for Irish assent to royal measures affecting Ireland. No less an authority than William Molyneux, in his *The Case of Ireland* (1698), had maintained that the kings of the thirteenth and fourteenth centuries had called Irish "knights" and "burgesses" for consultation with the crown before imposing laws on Ireland. During the reign of Henry VI in the fifteenth century statutes legislated by the English Parliament had not been applicable to Ireland unless that country was mentioned specifically in the laws and then only after the crown's prior consultation with Irish peers. Therefore, Sharp argues, the crown's position as sovereign over medieval Ireland had resided in its acting through an Irish parliament. Though the Irish might assent to a law of the English Parliament, the latter has no authority to impose its will on Ireland by virtue of a "supremacy" over the parliament in Dublin. There is no legal precedent or record from the past in which the Irish conceded a position of legislative supremacy to the Parliament of England. Both legislatures of England and Ireland possess an equal constitutional position under the crown.

> ... The king, together with the people of every different province, subject to the imperial Crown of Great Britain, and detached (as Ireland is) from this island, ought to be and have been esteemed, from the first establishment of our colonies, the only proper and constitutional legislature for each province respectively; because the representation of the people, in every part of the British Empire, is absolutely necessary to constitute an effectual legislature, according to the fundamental principles of the English constitution; for none of them, separately, can be esteemed a competent legislature to judge of the other's rights, without the highest injustice and inequity. . . .[3]

Sharp scrutinizes the implications of Poyning's Laws of 1495. These measures, consented to by the Irish Parliament, "made applicable to Ireland all statutes lately made in England" and provided that future Irish parliaments should meet only after the reasons for convocation and agendas were approved by the king and the Privy Council through the lord lieutenant and his council in Ireland.[4] The Irish tragedy, according to Sharp, began when Sir Edward Poyning summoned the Irish Parliament to Drogheda in 1495 and secured its assent to measures later exploited by Englishmen to destroy Irish liberty. Parliamentary statutes enacted during the Stuart and Cromwellian eras in the seventeenth century assumed the supremacy and authority of the English Parliament to impose its will on

Ireland without the prior consent of Dublin. The assumption had been sustained by eighteenth-century English parliaments through such dubious measures as the Declaratory Act of 1719.

Sharp is arguing that all the bases upon which eighteenth-century parliamentary statutes presumed the authority of the English Parliament to legislate for Ireland are without constitutional foundations. He refuses to accept the premise that the Irish Parliament had accepted a status of inferiority to that of England when approving Poyning's Laws in 1495. To have done so would have been contrary to the common constitution of England and Ireland and the crown's obligation to rule both countries through their respective legislative bodies. His contention is that the Irishmen of 1495 had made Ireland subject to all statutes lately made in England for the expedient purposes of more efficient and practical means of royal administration and justice.[5] This assent merely applied to English laws of a recent date and did not surrender the Irish Parliament to the mercy of its English counterpart. The legislature in Ireland gave its approval of Poyning's Laws in the belief that English laws would never bind them without their consent. Accustomed to the practice of prior consultation by the crown before its imposition of laws on Ireland, they evidently had reason to believe that the laws of 1495 in no way threatened their equal status with the English Parliament. "Thus it appears probable, that the Irish have been represented in England, as well in separate as in joint Parliaments; and upon such equitable terms of representation in England, I presume no Irish patriot will object to the bindings of English statutes whether Ireland will be especially named or not . . . ."[6] In addition, Sharp cannot believe that the Irish could have ever knowingly sacrificed the traditional rights of the Irish Parliament by approving the Poyning measures in 1495. He cites the opinions of several English judges during the reign of King Henry VII who had expressed doubt that such laws meant that England could arbitrarily impose its will on Ireland without the consent of the Irish legislature. Thus, insists Sharp, "it is manifest that the Irish subjects stand most in need of due representation, which cannot therefore be denied them at such a time, without the most flagrant violation of justice and natural equity."[7]

The Declaratory Act of 1719 is given special attention as an example of misguided eighteenth-century English notions about Ireland. With the objective of asserting the British Parliament's supremacy over the Irish House of Lords as the final appellate court of Ireland, the act declared that Ireland was "subordinate unto and dependent upon the Crown of Great Britain," meaning that both crown and Parliament had "full power and authority to make laws and statutes" binding on Ireland, including the right to make "null and void" the rulings of the Irish peers as the High Court of Ireland.[8] That the British Parliament could make such a claim in the eighteenth century was evidence of the sad usurpation of Irish liberties since the sixteenth century. Sharp insists that such claims are illegal. As king in Parliament at Westminster is the lawful government of the English nation, so is king in Parliament in Dublin the rightful government of Ireland. The British legislature has no right to speak for another legislature in the British Empire. This suggests that the growth of the empire's dominions—to sustain the ancient right of legislative representation under the common constitution—means the extension of the number of parliaments through which the crown governs those dominions. Such reasoning has no place for an imperial parliament or even the principle of virtual representation anywhere in the British world. If Ireland has the constitutional right to be governed by the crown through its own autonomous parliament, so also do the provinces of America. (Sharp and Cartwright are in accord here.) Though the position of the British Parliament might be diminished, the prestige of the crown and the glory of British liberty would be enhanced.

Sharp recognizes that British suzerainty in Ireland had been sanctioned by numerous renowned English jurists, including Edward Coke and William Blackstone. In the early seventeenth century Coke contended that many Irishmen had accepted King John's declaration in the thirteenth century that Ireland was to be governed by the laws of England. Though the Irish acceptance had not received unanimous support, Coke had taken the position that the precedent was a sufficient basis for upholding laws enabling the crown to rule Ireland effectively.[9] Sharp interprets Coke's opinions to mean that the crown and English Parliament of the seventeenth century had the authority to rule Ireland, with the Irish Parliament obligated to accept the will of Westminster. If the Parliament in Dublin still has any legislative rights, it is with the permission of London. All statutes enacted at Westminster are binding on Ireland when so specified in the wording of the laws. Sharp cannot understand how Coke could take such a position when even Coke himself, who appealed to precedent, was aware that medieval kings had called Irish peers to England for consultations prior to making decisions on matters related to Ireland—a practice which Coke himself even pronounced to be "an excellent precedent." Sharp challenges Coke by citing the opinion of Daines Barrington in the *Observations on the More Ancient Statutes*. Barrington had maintained that Henry II's conquest in Ireland had not extended beyond the Pale. Hence there is no precedent by which later kings could rule Ireland beyond Dublin without the consent of Irishmen outside the Pale. In addition, English rule in medieval Ireland was through the crown, and there was no valid precedent by which the Parliament of England could arbitrarily legislate for Ireland without the latter's consent.[10] In brief, Sharp rejects Coke's appeal to precedents of dubious validity as bases for asserting the right of the English Parliament to exert authority over its Irish counterpart. This, in effect, challenges the legality of the Trade Acts in Ireland during the seventeenth and eighteenth centuries.

The "right of conquest" principle upheld by Sir William Blackstone is also refuted. In his *Commentaries on the Laws of England*, Blackstone had asserted the British Parliament's right to legislate for Ireland—and, in effect, the American colonies—by stating that Ireland was a distinct but dependent and subordinate kingdom. Conquered, planted, and governed since King Henry II, Ireland was a subordinate of England by the right of conquest. All subsequent laws, such as the Declaratory Act of 1719, were therefore legal. "And as Ireland, thus conquered, planted, and governed, still continues in a state of dependence, it must necessarily conform to, and be obliged by, such laws as the superior state thinks proper to prescribe."[11] Sharp denounces such a position as contrary to the law of nature, the law of nations, and the very spirit of the British constitution. That America could be ruled by the right of conquest is irreconcilable with the historic fact that the colonies were settled by free Englishmen who had full rights to legislative representation consistent with their best interests and the liberties prescribed by the British constitution.

Disagreeing with the positions of Coke and Blackstone, Sharp attempts to strengthen his own case by citing English jurists of the past whose interpretations of legislative representation agree with his own. He quotes the Elizabethan theologian Richard Hooker and the early eighteenth-century Lord Chancellor John Somers. He refers to the following passage from the writings of Hooker:

> ... The lawful power of making laws, to command whole politic societies of men, belong so properly unto the same entire societies, that for any prince or potentate, of what kind soever upon earth, to exercise the same of himself and not either and not by express commission immediately and personally received from God, or else by authority derived at the first from their consent upon whose persons they impose laws; it is no better than mere tyranny! Laws they are not, therefore, which public approbation had not made so. [12]

He also quotes Lord Somers: "... That of having a share in the legislation, and being to be governed by such laws as we ourselves shall choose, is the most fundamental and essential, as well as the most advantageous and beneficial." [13] It is therefore plain, argues Sharp, that Ireland is entitled to all the liberties of the British constitution under the sovereignty of the British crown.

> The respective Parliaments of the two islands are entirely independent of each other; they separately grant, from time to time, the necessary supplies to the state; and no man may presume to deny their right of enquiring respectively into the application of them. But, notwithstanding this distinct economy, and the entire independency of the natives or subjects, with respect to each other, yet they are firmly united, by the bands of allegiance, to one head (or monarchy) of limited power, whereby they enjoy the privileges of the same reasonable common law, and the same excellent constitution of state. . . . [14]

The rights of the American colonies and their respective legislatures are no less than those of Ireland. Having read Tucker's *The True Interest of Britain*, Sharp objects to the dean's curt dismissal of the basic constitutional issues at stake in the American question. Of the dean's five proposals, he remarks that "not one of them (not even the fifth and last which he himself prefers) can possibly be reconciled either to law, equity, or sound politics. . . ." [15] The dean of Gloucester would do well to add a sixth proposal—that of giving the Americans due justice with the recognition of their right to legislative representation and taxation only by their assent. At the same time, Sharp opposes the dean's advice that the Americans be turned loose from the mother country. American independence might diminish the "importance, strength, and security" of both Great Britain and America. He does not share Tucker's opinion that a free America would be safe from French and Spanish designs.

Sharp's case for Ireland leads him to conclusions on the nature of the British Empire and legislative representation which, in turn, make him an ally of John Cartwright on the American issue. The argument that the British parliament has the authority to legislate for Ireland and America without their consent, upheld by such men as Coke and Blackstone, is based on "mere assertions" inconsistent with the constitutional right of all the crown's subjects to be duly represented in legislatures truly reflecting their will.[16] The British, Irish, and American subjects of the crown are "equally free" and their respective legislatures have equal positions under the constitution. The basic facts of geography make it logical that the king govern through a diversity of equal legislatures rather than through an imperial parliament that would not be adequately informed on the problems of subjects in distant parts of the British Empire. The concept of virtual representation is unrealistic in an empire that is spread across the globe.

"America," in Sharp's view, "was no conquered country; feudal tyranny had no historic right in America; Americans possessed title to all the fundamental rights embodied in English common law. Any other verdict . . . would be 'treason against the constitution.' "[17] Sharp's notion of justice causes him to regard his fellow subjects in Ireland and America as "congregations of brethren across the seas" who are entitled to the same rights as Englishmen at home.[18] He insists that mercantile considerations be made subservient to the principles of British liberty extended on an equal basis throughout the British Empire.

Some of Cartwright's ideas show up in the reasoning of Sharp. Nevertheless, it appears that Sharp's attitude toward imperial questions was that of an independent thinker and that he would have come to the same conclusions without Cartwright. He does not spell out a grand imperial scheme of union like Cartwright's but does seem to conceive some sort of "empire of the world" in which all the crown's subjects are equal under the common British constitution. Each domain in the British Empire can govern its own internal affairs through its own legislature in collaboration with the crown, a principle which became the essence of later notions of home rule in the British Empire.

Sharp never mentions India in his arguments. However, he was to express his views on the subject in later years when the East India Company came under heavy fire. He saw the necessity to reduce the company's political power in India—as well as undue political influence at Westminster—and subsequently to develop the machinery for native participation in the government of those Indian states under British domination.[19]

The common denominator in Sharp's various causes was his deep sense of the human justice to which all inhabitants of the British world were entitled. Eighteenth-century notions of empire in the minds of most Englishmen were irreconcilable with Sharp's arguments that the peoples of Ireland and America shared constitutional rights and liberties which were no more, no less than those of Englishmen living in the home isles. For this position he was applauded by other English Radicals. His study of Irish history and English law convinced him that the people's right to be represented in a legislature responsible to the electorate was deeply rooted in the ancient laws of England and that there were sufficient precedents whereby both the Irish and Americans of his time could press strong cases against contemporary concepts of parliamentary authority and jurisdiction. He refused to believe that an imperial parliament could be consistent with the spirit and intent of the constitution; nor could he accept current mercantilist concepts of empire as commensurate with human justice. Such notions were similar to those of numerous American leaders at the time. Like arguments on both sides of the constitutional issue of Parliament's jurisdiction, it is difficult to isolate fine theories from the historical circumstances in which men conduct human affairs. Sharp was, in effect, attacking English attitudes toward Ireland which traced from the distant past. At the same time, his impressive use of legal knowledge equipped him to raise moral and constitutional questions about British rule in Ireland and America. The few Englishmen who read his pamphlet and took it seriously must have been very impressed by its moral earnestness.

Like Cartwright, Sharp did not want to see a separation of Britain and America but rather a union of the two peoples under the crown in full constitutional equity. Nor did he argue in behalf of a separation from Ireland. He believed that past British injuries in both America and Ireland could be partly redeemed by forms of self-government not far removed from nineteenth-century principles of home rule. Along with Cartwright, Sharp anticipated the concept of a British commonwealth of nations. Like numerous British Radicals, he viewed the American question as only part of a greater imperial problem in which the Irish people were deeply involved—something which American radicals neglected.

Perhaps the finest attribute of Granville Sharp was the fact that he represented some of the best qualities of the humanitarianism that was maturing in English life during the eighteenth century. In an age that had its crassness and brutalities, his faith in God and the better part of human nature moved him to believe in man's capacity for social improvement. He appealed to the consciences of men in all classes and stations of life. His sense of humanity and will to combat injustice were the inspiration for lifelong causes which earned him the respect of many in his own generation and afterward.

SIX

*Parliamentary Reform:
James Burgh*

JAMES BURGH's ideas were permeated by a lofty moral tone which derived largely from his Presbyterian upbringing in Scotland. It was a quality often found among eighteenth-century Dissenters who were critical of English society and politics. He shared Catharine Macaulay's scorn for aristocracy. He considered the Whig oligarchy of his day to be as morally iniquitous as it was politically corrupt. Radicals like Burgh often used the word *corruption* within the context of contemporary Radical notions of personal morality, civic virtue, and political reform—an approach toward the existing political establishment which was far removed from Walpolian concern for its workability and the Namierites' view that the issue of corruption is a matter of opinion. Burgh's notions of civic virtue led him to think that British America could be fertile ground for nurturing the probities of Rome's early republic, which might put Augustan England to shame. Much of his writing sermonized on the evils of the England he knew. It had wide appeal to Englishmen, Irishmen, and Americans who, by the time of the American Revolution, had great interest in the shortcomings of English political life.

It appears that the upright schoolmaster of Newington Green tried to measure up to his own standards of integrity. His writings reveal Burgh to have been a deeply religious man who felt strongly about the necessity of honor in public life. His notions about the "corruption" of his age were, like Granville Sharp's, greatly influenced by the conditions he saw in London. Whereas Sharp lamented the plight of London's poor and oppressed, Burgh deplored the luxury and opulence of its high society and the structure of politics which sustained it. The squalor, scandal, and greed which he saw among London's high and mighty convinced him that the great city of empire was a latter-day Babylon.

> O London, London, how hast thou degenerated! Where are now those happy days, when thy greatness and superiority to the other cities of England, consisted more in thy superior virtue and piety than in thy enormous wealth, trade and commerce. . . . Thy riches have exalted thee to heaven; beware lest thy pride humble thee to the dust. For, when thy sins have brought upon thee the hour of thy destruction, it will not be in the power of thy riches, thy commerce, or thy mighty fleets, to protect thee. . . .[1]

Such moral indignation appealed to many English Dissenters, including some of Burgh's neighbors in placid Newington Green. His conversations with Benjamin Franklin, who provided much of his information about conditions in the colonies, may have given him occasion to suggest that America would be better off without the corruption and greed with which old England ruled the empire. Ringing denunciations of "our degenerate times and corrupt nation," when people wallowed in "luxury and irreligion . . . venality, perjury, faction, opposition to legal authority, idleness, gluttony, drunkenness, lewdness, excessive gaming, robberies, clandestine marriages, breach of matrimonial vows, self-murders" must have appealed to American colonists caught up in the fervor of the Great Awakening.[2] A portrait of the mother country's descent to perdition encouraged colonial readers' belief in the superior moral tone of American life over that of England.

Burgh was not merely a man who judged his generation by the rigorous standards of his moral idealism. He was a man of reason and common sense. His work at Saint Andrews University gave him a good dose of the Scottish Enlightenment. He placed great value on the study of history, with its lessons about noble men and ideas associated with the great states of the past. The history of ancient Rome provided many warnings against the consequences of eroding virtues and political corruption in high places. Men of public affairs should study history and biography to learn the past's lessons about virtuous and responsible government. They could sustain good government if they recognized the importance of exemplifying the private and public virtues necessary for good leadership. But if Englishmen were willing to be governed by men who have their price, they should be reminded of the circumstances which doomed the Roman Republic and other great states of the past.

Burgh's ideas obviously were influenced by the writings of political theorists who lived during the Stuart and early Hanoverian periods. The ideas of Harrington, Locke, Bolingbroke, and numerous "commonwealthmen" are readily recognized in his writings. Like Dr. Price and other Radicals of his own day, he admired the British constitution but thought it to have been betrayed by an ignoble Whig ascendancy.

There also can be no doubt that many of the ideas contained in the *Political Disquisitions* owed something to Burgh's association with the Honest Whigs. Men such as Price and Franklin easily stimulated an academician who delighted in discussing weighty issues with such persons. As a group, these men were distressed by the cynicism and corruption abroad in the land. They were impressed by the notion that Great Britain was confronted with a moral and constitutional crisis that could ruin the country and dismantle its great empire. They regarded the Wilkes matter as a manifestation of the wrongs Englishmen had suffered or tolerated for too long.

Since he was an academic man, it is not surprising that Burgh's ideals were affected by an exacting pedantry. His *Thoughts on Education* stressed the importance of learning, especially in the classical disciplines and religious instruction, as the foundation for self-improvement and public service. Teaching young boys to become virtuous subjects of the king was of paramount importance at his academy. Such goals were "well worthy the attention of the nation, and likely to contribute greatly to its advantage."[3] In his own academic world in Newington Green, Burgh devoted his academy to the production of honorable and public-minded young men who he hoped might bring about the moral and political regeneration of his country. He sought the kind of England whose public affairs would reflect great values like prudence, knowledge, virtue, and revealed religion described in his most notable moral treatise, *The Dignity of Human Nature*. They represented "what is truly great, ornamental, or useful in life; to call the attention of mankind to objects worthy of their regard, as rational and immortal beings

. . . to show the certain and established means for attaining the true end of our existence, happiness in the present and future states." [4] Such ideas had wide appeal to Englishmen, including Princess Augusta and her son Prince George. Burgh's ideas impressed American readers long before the Revolution. By 1776 colonial readers welcomed an Englishman's views which might help confirm their prejudices. Burgh's early writings were well known in learned American circles, and they probably gave him a ready and enthusiastic audience for his *Political Disquisitions* on the eve of the American Revolution.

The *Political Disquisitions* brought to light conclusions which Burgh had reached after many years of reflection about the state of English society, the constitution, politics, and the British Empire. The work was published in three lengthy volumes between January 1774 and the summer of 1775. The first volume evidently was timed to appear prior to the general election of 1774. The latter two seem not to have come out until after the elections. [5] Burgh wanted to impress upon Englishmen, as they turned to the elections, his argument that the kingdom had reached a critical point in its history. He saw it confronted with a quasi-revolutionary crisis both at home and in the empire. The country's social degeneracy and political corruption were bringing England to an impasse in which it would face tragic consequences if major reforms were not forthcoming. At the heart of the kingdom's dilemma, argues Burgh, is a corrupt and irresponsible Parliament at Westminster. Using Richard Price's figures on the approximate size of Britain's population, Burgh estimates that the country is ruled by about eight hundred men from an overall population of around five million. Parliament, he argues, is as unrepresentative of the British nation as it is morally corrupt. He intends to present his case by treating various facets of contemporary British affairs, including the imperial questions in America and Ireland. But his basic theme in the *Political Disquisitions* is an educated, comprehensive argument for parliamentary reform as the first necessary step toward setting things aright in the British world. He makes liberal use of long passages from classical writers, modern historians, political theorists and publicists such as Charles Davenant and Bolingbroke, and speeches of the parliamentary opposition under George I and George II to substantiate his arguments. Announcing his intention to demonstrate the inefficacies of Parliament, Burgh remarks in his preface that he seeks "to teach the people a set of solid political principles, the knowledge of which may make them proof against such gross abuse [as] one great object of this publication." [6]

The first volume and parts of the second describe political corruption in English life originating from such abuses as inadequate parliamentary representation, long parliaments, undue influence of the court in Parliament, the evils of placemen and pensioners, dishonest elections, and irresponsible treatment of the Irish and Americans. Having a strong moralistic intonation, Burgh refers to the examples of biblical, classical, and English history in an effort to illustrate the consequences of corrupt government. One of the greatest tragedies of such a state of affairs, he argues, is the destruction of liberty. When governments become estranged from the citizenry they are prone to employ coercion in maintaining their authority. This observation gives Burgh occasion for a lengthy polemic against standing armies in times of peace. The heavy expenditures for the maintenance of British armies since the late war against France are ample testimony to the government's potential resort to military force against discontented subjects in the home isles and the British Empire. "The King is guarded by the love of his subjects." [7] If British leaders are not willing to make long due readjustments in the country's political structure, public allegiance to abusive government will dissolve. Official resorts to coercion for maintaining law and order can bring the despotism and demagoguery that will mock the constitution and British liberty.

Burgh insists that liberty and political integrity in British life can be restored by reforms which accept the principle of popular sovereignty. The people are the "fountain of power." "All lawful authority, legislative and executive, originates from the people." [8] Representative government is the most logical and natural form of government and it must maintain civic integrity and responsibility to the commonweal. The current condition of the British Parliament is an insult to such principles. The effects on Britain's domestic and imperial life are disastrous. Burgh advocates the expansion of suffrage to democratic proportions, annual parliaments, the rotation of parliamentary membership, public sessions of Parliament, integrity of Parliament's members and procedures, adoption of the ballot system in elections, respect for the legislative rights of Ireland and America, and the end of placemen, pensioners, pluralism, and the court's influence in Parliament.

Burgh's third volume is an indictment of an English society that tolerates abuses described in his previous volumes. He deplores the decline of decency in English life. "Where the manners of a people are gone, laws are of no avail. . . . Liberty cannot be preserved, if the manners of a people are corrupted. . . . God forbid that ever any future political writer should have occasion to describe and account for the decline and fall of the British Empire, as . . . that of the Roman."[9] Burgh casts his hopes upon men of high station whose high moral principles and civic virtue would make them leaders of the country's moral and political regeneration. The great men of the kingdom should exemplify and encourage both private and public virtues reminiscent of early Rome. The schools of Britain should place great importance on religious instruction and the development of good character. "The true love of liberty is founded in virtue."[10]

Burgh implores his countrymen to look across the sea to America, where they might see a young, vigorous nation emerging from a mass of hardy, virtuous yeomen and industrious merchants. The agrarian setting of America nurtures private lives of independence, fruitfulness, contentment, and happiness. Public virtue among American leaders possesses a noble simplicity and civic responsibility that shame the corrupt political life of the mother country. American towns and villages are cradles of virtue and liberty, while London is a great lair of squalor and greed. Burgh's disdain for abusive government, mercantile rapacity, and large cities is reminiscent of the Jeffersonian ideal of agrarian democracy. His romantic notions of the American character are a powerful, if flattering, attraction to American prejudices which relish notions of colonial righteousness that shame the evils of the Old World.

Burgh's imposing case for parliamentary reform includes his appraisal of the current crisis of empire then being dramatized by the American situation. Book 2 of his second volume is entitled "Of Taxing the Colonies," and it contests the moral justice and constitutionality of the government's American policy since the end of the Seven Years' War. He is convinced that the court not only had sought illegally to impose burdensome taxes on the colonies but also had planned to build a large imperial bureaucracy as a haven for the many placemen and pensioners who hounded British officials for favors. The Americans, argues Burgh, have as much reason to complain against British political corruption as Englishmen do. The crisis in America is an offshoot of the sordid conditions in Parliament and the electoral system which breeds them. Any fair solution to the American question is contingent on reform at home.

Burgh argues that even Robert Walpole had the prudence to warn both court and Parliament against nuisance taxes on America and filling colonial administrative posts with placemen. The colonies, Walpole used to tell Parliament, more than repay the mother country's sacrifices for them with their trade. Nevertheless, charges Burgh, the government's conduct since 1764 seems intent on squeezing revenue monies out of American pockets illegally and doing so by building a tax bureaucracy filled with court favorites and jobbers. Court cronies were among the most enthusiastic supporters of the Grenville and Townshend tax measures. The men who legislated the Declaratory Act in 1766 had shown an imagination no greater than that of "a tradesmen's clerk." They had not only failed to recognize the constitutional ramifications of such devices but were so morally bankrupt that they were inadvertent tools of court extravagance and patronage. The Americans who had established civil and religious liberties in the vast wilderness of North America, Burgh writes, deserve much more respect from England. America should not be a dumping ground for the mother country's rogues and court jobbers. Colonial trade with Great Britain has been a major cause of the latter's wealth and power, and it is deplorable that English politicians should risk the loss of America merely to satisfy their corrupt political and economic ambitions. The government and Parliament "were risking the loss of four millions of customers for the manufactures of this country—all for the sake—of making a few places for collectors, and commissioners of duties and taxes, that [they] might have somewhat to stop the Cerberian barking of a pack of hungry court-curs." [11] The government has arrogantly blundered its way into a predicament in Massachusetts Bay causing the most self-defeating restrictions on that province's trade. The clumsy punishment of all Boston for the acts of a few "persons unknown" has aroused American indignation from New England to Charleston. A favor rendered by Parliament to the East India Company might well cost England an empire. The politicians in London have only themselves to blame.

Burgh was not the sort of person who could readily condone some of the violent tactics of the Sons of Liberty in Boston or even the Tea Party. But he sympathizes with all the complaints that had been raised by colonial agitators on such issues as trade restrictions, billeting of soldiers, putting Americans on trial in distant courts, and appointment of bad colonial governors. He cites Dr. Franklin's comment that there had been a serious decline of American respect for British leadership. British subjects in the colonies have more than ample cause to raise the cry of tyranny. British government in America has reached a point of estrangement from the people where the use of threats and coercion are found necessary to maintain compliance with unjust decisions made under dubious circumstances in London. "Every act of authority of one man (or body of men) over another for which there is absolute necessity is tyrannical." [12]

The attacks on the corruption and high-handed tactlessness of British policy are followed by Burgh's arraignment of "taxation without representation." Even the provinces of the despotic Roman Empire, he notes, had a protector in the Roman Senate. During Flanders' wars against Spain its leaders had taxed the people only after obtaining their assent. John IV of Braganza, when leading Portugal's war of independence from the Spanish, had done the same. Yet British officials have betrayed their own constitution in the belief that they can arbitrarily tax the crown's subjects 3,000 miles from Westminster. Englishmen themselves, Burgh reminds his countrymen, rebelled against "oppressive" taxation during the reigns of Edward III, Richard II, Henry VI, Henry VII, and Henry VIII.

> Nothing produces so much ill-blood, as touching people's money. . . . We know that no people ever were more peaceable, or better affected, than the colonists have all along shewn themselves, 'till we bethought ourselves of insulting them with taxes imposed upon them by our Parliament, in which they had no representation, and with the

direct design of raising money upon them for our own advantage. . . .
To provoke three millions of people [the Americans] to their utmost
rage, is no slight affair.[13]

English history, Burgh argues, has many precedents to show flaws
in the "virtual representation" theory. English knights and burgesses used to pay their taxes from their own resources rather than
assume a virtual representation of their neighbors in order to obtain
money not belonging to them. Most certainly "they did not grant
the property of people at the distance of 3000 miles, who had not
one representative among them." [14]

Burgh reasons that there are instances in which Parliament
might have pragmatic causes for legislation on the colonies; but
taxation is not one of them. Even the House of Lords cannot alter
the Commons' money bills because they have no constitutional
power over the property of other people. It is because the House of
Commons is supposedly representative of the British nation that it
has the power to tax its constituents. Such principles contradict the
opinions of current politicians that they can tax Americans who
have no representation in Parliament. "What could be more absurd
than the commons [*sic*] giving and granting what was neither their
own property, nor that of their own constituents, what they had no
more right to give and grant than they have to give and grant the
property of the people of Holland and France." [15] Burgh cites the
maxim of King Edward I "that what concerns all, may be approved
by all." In protesting the Stamp Act and the Townshend duties, the
Americans were only doing what John Hampden had done against
ship money. Common sense shows that parliamentarians might tax
unrepresented boroughs in England; for they are familiar with conditions in all parts of their own country. But common sense also
makes it clear that this is not true in taxing the distant Americans.
"If the people of Britain are not to be taxed, but by Parliament;
does it now directly follow, that the colonists cannot, according to
Magna Charta, and the bill of rights, be taxed by Parliament, so
long as they continue unrepresented, because otherwise they may
be taxed without their own consent?" [16]

There are also practical considerations that should influence the
government's taxing policies. Burgh believes that most colonists are
comparatively poor farmers whose incomes are vulnerable to nui-

sance taxes like the stamp duty. Too many Americans are likely to be inconvenienced and disgruntled by the impositions of British politicians. With the propensity of the Court to "overgovern," Americans would not long tolerate an arbitrary taxation that originates from across the Atlantic. In a more conciliatory tone, Burgh asks why Grenville could not have called American delegates to London in 1765 and negotiated some kind of arrangement in which colonial assemblies could have, with the assent of their constituencies, voted sums of money for colonial defense and administration. Even then, he rejoins, it would have been expecting a great deal of the Americans to assist the financial problems of a corrupt Parliament. In brief, both Americans and Englishmen have cause for complaint against the character and wisdom of the Parliament. The favoritism shown to the East India Company by the passage of the Regulating Act in 1773 is an insult to both peoples.

> In short: The new method of taxing our colonists in parliament, where they have no representation, adequate or inadequate, is subversive of liberty, annihilates property, is repugnant to the genius of the people, oppressive to their indigence; it strikes at the root of their charters, as colonists, and of their privileges as British subjects ever loyal and unoffending; it is derogatory from the faith of government, omnius [*sic*] to the liberty of the British empire, unjust in its principles, rigorous in its execution, and pernicious in its operation alike to the mother-country and the colonists.[17]

Warning Englishmen of the danger signals in America, Burgh urges them to heed the arguments of Parliament's Whig Opposition and men in the Stamp Act Congress against the Stamp Act in 1765–66. If officials in the government and Parliament do not reverse the course of their policies in America, they will lead Great Britain into unnecessary disaster.

The lengthy but imposing conclusion of the *Political Disquisitions* makes an appeal to crown subjects in all parts of the British Empire to join in a common cause for the restoration of the constitution and preservation of their liberties. Englishmen have the right to government that is truly representative, led by men of integrity who are responsible for the welfare of the whole nation. The American colonists have the right to tax themselves, to trade without undue hindrance, and to enjoy liberties equivalent to those of their brethren in the mother country. Burgh believes that a major crisis is at hand in the life of the British nation and that events in America are a manifestation of serious ills at home. A revolt in the colonies might be the signal for insurrection in Ireland and England. The inertia of Englishmen is a distressing reason why British leaders have been allowed to blunder their way into the explosive situation that currently exists in America. The men in the government and Parliament can either come to their senses and take steps toward overdue reforms at home and in the British Empire or resort to despotic actions that could be disastrous. What is needed, argues Burgh, is a means of putting effective pressure on the politicians to move in the direction of reform.

Burgh submits some concrete proposals for creating public pressure in behalf of reform. It is a scheme for the realization of meaningful parliamentary reform with far-reaching ramifications for the whole British Empire and an extraordinary resort to ultra-parliamentary procedures for achieving a program of reform. It may have been anticipated by his remarks in *Crito*, his political prologue to the *Political Disquisitions* initially published in 1766. "We read newspapers. We dispute in coffeehouses and taverns. We drink party-toasts. But we have not yet come to a resolution for associating, petitioning, or instructing." [18] In order to engage the quasi-revolutionary situations which currently exist in England, Ireland, and America, Burgh urges the formation of a "Grand National Association for Restoring the Constitution." Though the name might suggest an organization of purely British composition, he is addressing his proposal to "the independent part of the people of Great Britain, Ireland and the colonies" and submits that the association's membership include advocates of reform in Ireland and America as well as all lovers of liberty in the British world to participate in the movement:

> There must be established a GRAND NATIONAL ASSOCIATION FOR RESTORING THE CONSTITUTION. Into this must be invited all men of property, all friends to liberty, all able commanders, etc. There must be a copy of the Association for every parish, and a parochial committee to procure subscriptions from all persons whose names are in any tax-book, and who are willing to join the Association. And there must be a grand committee for every county in the three Kingdoms, and in the colonies of America. . . .

By the readiness of people to enter into the associations, it may be effectually determined, whether the majority are desirous of the proposed reformations. This, as has been observed before, is a matter of supreme consequence, for resistance to government, unless it be a clear majority of the people, is rebellion.[19]

Burgh, whom Herbert Butterfield describes as a "fanatic on the subject of associations," is proposing a truly revolutionary idea here.[20] The schoolmaster of Newington Green suggests that such an association be a pyramidal organization built upwards from local parish committees in Britain and county committees in Ireland and America to a grand national—or, more accurately, imperial—representative assembly that takes on the character of an ultra-parliamentary body. He entertains the hopes that the king himself might assume the headship of such an organization as the champion of British liberty and justice. If not, the leadership might be provided by men of the "independent nobility," that is, the Rockingham Whigs. If these fail, then "let the great, the rich, the independent City of London take the lead."[21] He sometimes refers to the organization as the "London Association." He is suggesting, evidently, that a London organization would have the talent and numbers which could furnish experience and initiative for the creation of chapters in other parts of the British world.

The Grand National Association, with massive support from subjects all over the British Empire, should devote its initial endeavors to four basic objectives—a more representative and virtuous Parliament, securing the faltering public credit, presenting Parliament with petitions on other specific reforms, and maintenance of a perpetual pressure on British leaders for achieving other future reforms recommended by the association. Burgh submits that some form of action should be available to the organization to guarantee official responses to its petitions, "to raise the strength of the nation against the government."[22] The association might also be presented as a reflection of public opinion, a ready and willing petitioner when circumstances demand it, and an organizer of popular resistance to official apathy when warranted. But Burgh stops short of encouragement to violence. If Parliament refuses to act, however, the association, because it would be more truly representative of the nation and the British Empire than the House of Commons, should assert itself as a legislature. He does not describe clearly the course of action to be taken if the association is confronted by official repression. He is no revolutionary and recognizes the pitfalls of upheavals which can bring even worse forms of despotism. Possibly he thinks that British politicians have sufficient common sense to·accept reforms if sufficient pressure is put on them in peaceful, constitutional ways. That proved to be the case in 1832 and was the theme of reform agitation from 1780 onwards.

Burgh urges Americans to take their own initiative in the organization of association chapters which can complement those in England. Their grievances can be linked with those of Englishmen in a common cause against British politicians. It is curious that he says so little about what the Americans themselves already had been doing in organizing complaint groups against the British government. Over eighty committees of correspondence had been distributing antigovernment propaganda in Massachusetts Bay since 1772. Colony committees, actually standing committees of colonial legislatures, originated in Virginia in 1773. So-called county committees chosen by local units acted as agents of central colonial committees of correspondence about the same time. Nor is Burgh moved to comment on the potential of an intercolonial or "continental" assembly reminiscent of the Stamp Act Congress as a powerful voice of American opinion. The history of the period shows how important these American organizations were in dealing with unpopular British policies. As long as figures such as Samuel Adams played powerful roles in their activities they would not have been very likely contributors to the kind of enterprise Burgh had in mind. Adams and his kind were no more interested in an imperial responsibility for the cause of reform than they were in the imperial responsibility of administrative finance and defense. Be that as it may, Burgh advises the Americans to do whatever may be necessary if London turns deaf ears on their complaints. If British politicians refuse to give them due recognition of their liberties and rights, he admonishes the colonists to assume responsibility for redressing their grievances in their own way!

The *Political Disquisitions* draws to a close with a quasi-revolutionary admonition to the leaders of Great Britain to rise to the occasion in one of the nation's most crucial moments. Burgh declares to the peoples of the British world that he had described for them "the condition of public affairs in this great empire." Knowing that his painful illness will soon take its fatal toll, Burgh ends the *Political Disquisitions* with a dying man's prayer for his country:

> In thy hands, O Father and Preserver of all, doth thy servant desire to leave this King and country, in the hope that they shall be safe under thy heavenly protection; and to Thee doth he consecrate this and all his but well-intentioned labours for the good of his fellow creatures, humbly hoping, that his infirmities shall be overlooked, and his offenses blotted out; not on account of any merit in himself, but through the magnanimity of him who is hereafter to judge the world in righteousness and mercy. Amen.[23]

Each volume of the *Political Disquisitions* was reviewed by the *Monthly Review*. Burgh's work was acknowledged as well intended, ably presented, and worthy of serious attention. As a writer, he was considered "judicious, and sensible, though not elegant." The integrity of his motives was respected and, though his opinions were shared by few Englishmen, the *Political Disquisitions* was recognized as an important contribution to the rational analysis of important issues in British affairs:

> It is to be wished that people of all ranks should pay a sober regard to these subjects. . . . Those readers who may not agree with him [on America] in the whole, will yet allow that he possesses no small strength of argument. . . . Considered merely as a matter of curiousity [*sic*] and entertainment, the book is really valuable, at the same time it is replete with knowledge, drawn from the best sources. The worthy compiler merits the respect and esteem of the public for the great zeal and labour which he has employed; and we heartily wish that his earnest endeavors may be followed by some answerable success, for the advantage and honour of these kingdoms.[24]

Though the editors of the *Monthly Review* usually avoided controversy, they had been sympathetic with Americans' complaints for several years before Burgh's volumes appeared. They evidently concluded that Burgh's appraisals of British affairs were not without substance.

Ian Christie comments that Burgh wrote not as a political philosopher, but rather as a propagandist of ideas circulating in London's Radical circles at the time and reflecting the City's prejudices

against the old oligarchy.[25] Like Catharine Macaulay, he was contemptuous of aristocracy and something of an idealist republican.
He believed that the difficult problems at home and in the British
Empire had been fermented by corrupt oligarchical elements whose
chief interests were their own self-serving designs, mercantile and
political, at the expense of everyone else. In regard to the American
situation, Burgh concluded that Great Britain, governed by such
people, was forfeiting its moral and constitutional right to govern
America. Officials who violated colonial charters could easily do
the same with English laws. Such convictions had great attraction
for Englishmen who were disenchanted with the current failures of
English institutions and politics. This explains the evident influence
which Burgh had on the Wilkesites and the Bill of Rights men.

Yet Burgh was no revolutionary who desired the destruction of
existing institutions. He sought a purification of English political
life in order to promote the essential goodness of the British constitution and the extension of liberty. The government's reaction to
the American question gave no indication that it was prepared to
adopt needed reforms. As a result, he urged a massive, peaceful
pressure on the politicians in order to bring the full force of British
opinion at home and in the British Empire to bear against officials
in London. He placed faith in the effectiveness of such widespread
pressure to influence men in high places. "His writings aimed to
strengthen rather than to overturn the existing order; and so they
were interpreted by his English contemporaries who hoped that a
reading of the *Political Disquisitions* would persuade the 'men at
the helm' to 'remove all those evils' which the book exposed." [26]
Though Burgh's scathing invective against English politicians delighted men like John Wilkes and Patrick Henry, his ideas were still
within the bounds of peaceful, pragmatic approaches to the great
problems of the day. His proposals fell on deaf ears in the government as well as among the great majority of his countrymen who, in
the tense months of 1774–75, were animated by the desire to have
His Majesty's forces teach the ungrateful upstarts in America a hard
lesson. Though members of the Whig Opposition in Parliament
may have winced from Burgh's sermonic lamentations, they found
much to agree with in his talk about corruption.

In the final analysis, Burgh's argument for parliamentary reform
laid the basis upon which he believed the difficult problems of his

time could be resolved. His thesis went further than the proposals of Tucker, Cartwright, and Sharp in 1774. Dilemmas such as the American crisis required the statesmanship and insight which only a reformed Parliament could provide. Ideas about economic objectives, imperial reorganization, and responsible government in British domains abroad were anathema to the existing Parliament. As Burgh saw it, a more virtuous and representative Parliament would be much more disposed to accept major changes in British domestic and imperial life. Among these would be the disposition of a reformed Parliament to settle the American issue. In the short run, Burgh was wrong. Not even a democratic Parliament in 1774–76 could have understood or accepted the ideas he was urging. They were out of joint with prevailing notions about politics, economics, and empire. A more representative Parliament at that time would have meant a more representative pillar of "interest" politics, mercantile imperialism, and popular demand to give the ungrateful Americans a bloody nose. And there was the question of American reluctance to support any cause outside their own range of interest. It is doubtful that they would have been any more accommodating in 1774–76 to Burgh's kind of Parliament than to the Whig oligarchy.

In the long run, however, there is much to say for Burgh. He eventually was shown to be right in his belief that fundamental changes in the British world could come only after parliamentary reform. The important reforms of the early Victorian years came only after the Reform Bill of 1832 became a reality, though Pitt the Younger in the 1780s and William Huskisson in the 1820s did make some progress in that direction. Free trade, the Durham Report, and other things anticipated by British Radicals in the 1770s came only after the appearance of a liberal parliamentary climate which was more receptive to such changes. Also to Burgh's credit is his concept of influencing government through the exertions of extraparliamentary organization. Such a principle came to be an important factor in the history of nineteenth-century reformism. The Anti-Corn Law League and Chartism both owed something to Burgh's concept of the Grand National Association. It also is interesting that, while Burgh was urging such organization in 1774–75, Americans were developing their own forms of organized pressure to serve strictly American aims. The Stamp Act Congress, the committees of correspondence, and the Continental Congresses were all, in a sense, colonial versions of extraparliamentary associations created to contest the British Parliament which Burgh so deplored. The Second Continental Congress even waged war against the might of the British Empire for six years. The republican virtue of the men who sat in it, like Franklin and Jefferson, and the men who served it, like Washington, would have been an inspiration to a man like Burgh. But, most importantly, Burgh was one of the chief architects of the British Radical reform movement that would eventually have a role in deciding the outcome of the American Revolution.

SEVEN

The Force of Public Opinion:
Catharine Macaulay

FEW people in England received Burgh's *Political Disquisitions* as enthusiastically as did Catharine Macaulay. During the spring of 1775 she took up her own pen at her home in Bath and entered the current pamphleteering fray with *An Address to the People of England, Scotland and Ireland on the Present Crisis of Affairs*, a polemical appeal to all freedom-loving men in the British world to rally around the banner of American liberty. Her ideas carried the principles of James Burgh to their logical conclusion. If governments are negligent of their responsibilities to the citizenry, she wrote, then the people have the right to initiate the might of public pressure, even defiance, against their leaders when suffering injustice is the only alternative. Like her friend Burgh, she was not far from sanctioning the right of revolution against the English political establishment. The timely appearance of the pamphlet became evident to its author when the the news of Lexington and Concord reached England late in the spring.

Catharine Macaulay's opinions on the American question obviously were foreseen in the early volumes of her *History of England from the Accession of James I to That of the Brunswick Line*, the first five of her eight volumes having been published bv 1775. The *History* presents an interpretation of the seventeenth-century constitutional struggles from the mind of a talented, doctrinaire Englishwoman of the eighteenth century who deeply believed in the political philosophy of John Locke. Mrs. Macaulay's skillful use of the past furnished welcome propaganda for British Radicals who wanted parliamentary reform and Americans who wanted to justify

a revolution. Her enthusiasm for the ideology of liberty, no doubt
encouraged by her brother John Sawbridge, John Wilkes, Thomas
Hollis, and other Middlesex Radicals, suggests that she was the
most zealous of the several Radicals who publicly urged unorthodox solutions to the imperial crisis in 1774–76. Having a flair
for the dramatic, she nurtured romantic notions about liberty and
revolution drawn from her longtime study of the classical past. At
the beginning of the first volume of her *History* she writes, "From
my early youth I have read with delight those histories that exhibit
liberty in its most exalted state, the annals of the Roman and Greek
republics; studies like these excite the natural love of freedom
which lies latent in the breast of every rational being, till it is nipped
by the frost of prejudice or blasted by the influence of vice." [1] She
sees herself as a successor to the great John Milton in taking up her
pen for "the defense of freedom, morals, and the religion of
England." The principles of liberty which stream through the volumes of the *History* are addressed to all inhabitants of British civilization.

The *History of England* presents the story of Stuart rule as an
illustration of the natural enmities which exist between monarchy
and liberty. The author makes no effort to conceal her contempt for
kings, be they the Stuarts of the seventeenth century or the Hanove-
rians of her own age. Her republican scorn for English aristocracy is
no less sardonic. She regards the Whig ascendancy of the eighteenth
century as having betrayed the Glorious Revolution's great promises for Englishmen. The politics of Robert Walpole and the duke of
Newcastle have corrupted the constitution and perpetrated abuses
as antagonistic to liberty as was Stuart despotism. The England of
her own day is little better off than it had been a century before.
Even men like Rockingham and Burke, because of their accommo-
dations with the present structure of politics, she considers ignoble
heirs and accomplices of an order which has eroded liberty in Great
Britain and its colonies. She wants her volumes to show how contemporary English life is plagued by incongruities between the
country's political realities and true liberty. Consequently, the *History* is, as Bernard Bailyn describes it, "an imaginative work in
praise of republican principles under the title of a *History of
England*." [2] Or, in the words of Lucy Martin Donnelly, it is "a
Whig pamphlet in a large sense." Catharine Macaulay's stature as a

historian is given a candid estimation by Donnelly. "Republican zeal, energy and industry, however useful in controversy, are insufficient qualifications for a historian. ... As a historian Whig prejudice constituted her whole point of view."[3] Rather than regarding Mrs. Macaulay as a serious historian, we must see her as an attractive, talented propagandist.

Notwithstanding her shortcomings as a historian, it is true that Catharine Macaulay's work was competent, acute, forthright, and written in a most engaging prose. It was splendid propaganda. The volumes enjoyed a large audience among the curious and the zealous. They brought the author a large income and fame both in Europe and North America. British and American radicals ranked her with Gibbon, Robertson, and Hume. One of the most celebrated women in the British world by the time of the American Revolution, she must be considered among the most influential British Radicals to take public positions on the American crisis in 1774–76. Standing on the forum of Clio to propagate her notions of British liberty, she became an imposing figure in the ideological debates which grew out of the constitutional confrontation between the British government and the American colonists. Her predisposition to look at the past in black and white terms caused her ideas to have a strong appeal to a revolutionary generation which wanted to crystallize the great issues of its time. Because she reminded her American readers of an English tradition of resistance to tyranny, she gave the disenchanted colonists a historical justification for revolution. She recognized her value to the Americans: "Nothing can console me from being precluded by my engagement to the English public from defending the cause of the Americans but that I think the general principals [*sic*] of the rights of mankind, inculcated in my great work, is of more advantage to them than the more suspected arguments framed for the service of a particular purpose."[4]

The ideological intonation generated by her work on the first volumes predisposed Catharine Macaulay to interpret events in America after the Stamp Act crisis as justifiable colonial resistance to imperial policies rooted in the corruption and greed of English politics. She aired her pro-American sentiments in London drawing rooms and in her frequent conversations with Radicals like Hollis, Wilkes, and others whom she knew through her brother. James

Burgh was one of her many acquaintances and she doubtless was familiar with his reform ideas before the *Political Disquisitions* appeared in public. Whereas Burgh wrote his volumes with initial hopes of influencing the outcome of the parliamentary elections in October 1774, Catharine Macaulay wrote her pamphlet in the spring of the following year because of the elections' disappointing results. She was distressed by the passage of the Coercion and Quebec acts, and this was compounded by her recognition that little or no public resentment against such measures was shown in the 1774 general election.

An Address to the People of England, Scotland and Ireland on the Present Crisis of Affairs originally appeared during the spring of 1775 shortly before Englishmen learned that the king's troops had been fired upon outside Boston. The pamphlet's pro-American sentiments are in character with the grandiose republicanism of the author. She places herself in the role of a Roman citizeness expressing her indignation in the name of British liberty against a misguided and corrupt government. She chastises British leaders for their refusal to heed the enlightened opinions of honest Britons, the Radicals of London and Middlesex, "at a time when a dark cloud hangs over the empire." Because Parliament has failed the nation and is not truly representative of the people, she addresses herself directly to the peoples of England, Scotland, and Ireland as "my friends and fellow citizens."

Catharine Macaulay declares that the government is guilty of having "attempted to wrest from our American colonists every privilege necessary to freemen;—privileges which they hold from the authority of their charters, and the principles of the constitution." [5] Englishmen, Scotsmen, and Irishmen have allowed the Stamp Act affair to pass by without showing any sense of indignation or realization of the serious issues at stake for all inhabitants of the British Empire. "With the same guilty acquiescence" they have tolerated Parliament's outrageous passage of the Coercion and Quebec acts in the past year. The citizens of Massachusetts Bay are being oppressed by martial rule which abolishes trial by jury, dissolves their assemblies, and mocks their rightful liberties. The citizens of Quebec are confronted with the ominous threats of authoritarian government and Roman Catholicism. For many years the

American people have borne such injustices with "almost blameable patience." Their defiance of the Coercion Acts proves that they have had enough of the outrageous policies made by corrupt British politicians. Is it not time for the peoples of England, Scotland, and Ireland to join their fellow citizens in America in popular fury against the adversaries of liberty?

Among the many sins of the British leadership, alleges Mrs. Macaulay, is their skillful deception of the British people about the nature of the American crisis. Officials cloud the most critical constitutional issues with arguments that men in office are the best judges of how to deal with the colonists in the national interest and that popery in Quebec will be of no consequence in other parts of the British world. These men are also responsible for the corrupt, unrepresentative character of Parliament, many unkept promises to the British people, and colonial policies that can destroy liberty in the home isles. While committing outrages in Massachusetts Bay in the name of national interest, they arrogantly make policy on the presumption that they are entitled to the people's unquestioning respect and loyalty. Excuses that British troops in Boston must behave as though they were in "an enemy town" are deplorable.

Mrs. Macaulay admonishes Britons who refuse to recognize the government's duplicity over the American issue to look at what is happening in their own country. The British people are encouraged by their leaders to think that "the times cannot be better." This is far from the truth! Lord North's poppycock! There is a decline in British trade. Serious unemployment problems are obvious in London. One needs only to visit the poor sections of London and the country's ports to see that there is much amiss in the land. Surely Great Britain is living in one of its darkest hours!

The lady historian's indignation is no less aroused by the Quebec Act. Her disregard for many conventions of her day did not include a strong Anglican prejudice against Catholicism. This was a time when many Englishmen could still be animated by the spirit of popery, as shown by the Gordon Riots a few years later. Catharine Macaulay fears that the Quebec Act will menace both the religious and the political liberties of Englishmen in Canada and the provinces to the south. She considers British tolerance of French Canadian Catholicism a hypocritical gesture when English Dissenters are subjected to the Test and Corporation acts in their own country. Only the lovers of liberty in London and Middlesex, she writes, have refused to be blinded by the government's postures in the name of national interest:

> It was the Canada bill, and other transactions of the government, which equally threatened your security and welfare, that enraged the city of London, and the county of Middlesex, to exact from those they elected into the very representative office, an engagement, by which their members were bound to endeavor to the utmost of their abilities, the repeal of the unconstitutional laws respecting America, which passed in the last session of the last Parliament. And as septennial Parliaments are found to be the root from whence all our political grievances spring, they were also bound to endeavor the restoration of our ancient privileges in respect to the duration of Parliaments.[6]

Mrs. Macaulay also refers her readers to Burgh's *Political Disquisitions*. "I have hitherto endeavored to prevent your being misled by the sophistry of those who have an interest in deceiving you. I shall now give you some of the judicious observations of one of your best friends, in regard to the conduct of your government toward America."[7] She reiterates all of Burgh's complaints about extravagance in public spending, placemen, pensioners, bribery, military costs, and other sins of the present ministry and Parliament. Such profligacies mock the venerable constitution and true liberty. If the people of the British Isles do not heed the cry of their American brethren, the consequences will be American independence and civil war at home. The loss of America will do irreparable economic harm to Britain, and Englishmen will be forced to squeeze the national livelihood from the limited resources of "these foggy islands."

Macaulay and Burgh obviously share the opinion that quasi-revolutionary conditions exist in England in 1775. The times demand honorable and responsible government, which is nowhere to be found. Mrs. Macaulay writes that "men of true virtue" must arouse the people of Britain into a determined opposition to an obstinate, irresponsible government. "To oppose government with success, such honest individuals must make use of the assistance of the multitude, and consequently, of good and bad citizens, of the rich and the poor, the learned and the unlearned, of the wise and the foolish, that of every man who will co-operate with them in their designs, whether he be led to such co-operation by the principle of justice, by interest, or by passion."[8] Such men will be doing a greater service for their country than the men now in office. Their endeavors will be acts of duty, not treason. "The subject can only be bound to obedience on the considerations of the public good; but the Sovereign, on these considerations, and a thousand others equally binding, is tied to the exact observance of the laws of that constitution under which he holds his power."[9] The author portrays the England of 1775 in the image of 1688. Just as an "Immortal Seven" did their duty to rid the realm of Stuart despotism, she looks to "men of true virtue" who appreciate the implications of the Coercion and Quebec acts to animate the force of public opinion in ridding the land of corruption. Mrs. Macaulay's idea of popular sovereignty pervades her appeal to the peoples of England, Scotland, and Ireland to bombard the government with petitions, demonstrations, and kinds of pressure which might push the government into a reversal of its American policy and a movement toward domestic reforms:

> Rouse, my countrymen! rouse from that state of guilty dissipation in which you have too long remained, and in which, if you longer continue, you are lost forever—Rouse! and unite in one general effort; till, by your unanimous and repeated addresses to the throne, and to both houses of parliament, you draw the attention of every part of the government to their own interests, and to the dangerous state of the British empire.[10]

And what is to succeed such dramatic manifestations of public pressure if government refuses to yield? For whatever reasons, Mrs. Macaulay does not venture into an overt encouragement of violence. But her rhetoric, preceded by years of glorifying seventeenth-century English revolutions and Lockean ideas on the right of revolution, leaves little room for doubting that she might have welcomed a little bloodspilling if it would awaken the country's leaders out of their slumber of complacency. She certainly never doubted the Americans' right to defy British authority. Few colonials could have been more satisfied with what Massachusetts citizens had just done at Lexington and Concord. She came to venerate General Washington in the same way she had long honored her heroes of the Greek and Roman past. In the final analysis, the logic of Catharine Macaulay's argument led to her sanctioning the right of revolution.

Like Burgh, Catharine Macaulay refused to accept the fact that her alarm was not shared by the mass of Englishmen, who viewed the imperial crisis in an entirely different perspective. Yet her appeal to the force of mass opinion against the government in 1775 was unique in showing her understanding of the potential strength of such pressure. It is also to the credit of the country in which she lived that public opinion certainly counted for something in the councils of government, even during the eighteenth century. But it was the government and its American policy, not figures like Catharine Macaulay, which enjoyed the support of so-called public opinion in 1775. When public support for the North ministry disintegrated after 1778, public opinion was a critical factor in the government's decision to make peace in 1782.

Mrs. Macaulay's eloquent appeals to right the wrongs of her country were an attractive representation of current feeling among many English Radicals, especially John Horne Tooke and numerous others in Middlesex. They held that Englishmen might appeal to higher laws of justice to secure more honorable and representative government. But notions of popular sovereignty and the right of revolution were rejected by cooler heads even among British Radicals who scorned the established political structure. Anyway, the voice of the British people was heard in 1775 and it commanded the king's armies to march against the rebellious Americans. Most Radicals themselves were men of peace and kept their faith in the capacity of the constitution to accommodate change in due time. Organizers of opinion like John Cartwright, John Jebb, and Christopher Wyvill realized that it took much effort and time to bring public opinion around to support of changes which work for the public good.

Catherine Macaulay was an attractive, intelligent, somewhat vain lady with an acute sense of justice and human longing for freedom. Both British Radicals and American revolutionaries had ample reason to admire her. Though she was doctrinaire, outspoken, and simplistic in her opinions, she recognized that men who fight good causes, as well as bad ones, must have their faith refurbished by the propagation of general principles which might seem unsophisticated to the more detached and reflective philosopher. She was inclined to the dramatic and revolutionary and thus she lived in an appropriate time. A revolutionary age requires its Catharine Macaulays.

> She posed confidently in the likeness of the learned goddess [Clio], imagining herself another Brutus, a martyr to republican freedom. But the role that really suit [*sic*] her was the Amazon leading charge after charge on behalf of a Great New Cause. By instinct a fighter of high mettle, she eagerly exchanged the light skirmishes of drawing rooms and literary clubs for heavy warfare in the world of men and politics, and was prepared, even, for the streets and be dubbed "poissard" for her pains. . . . Mrs. Macaulay represented the crusader of eighteenth century life and, it may well be, influenced the public more potently than the Blues and fine ladies whose memoirs make agreeable reading for a gentle posterity.[11]

EIGHT

A Question of Human
Freedom: Richard Price

TO understand Richard Price the man is to understand a great deal
about his ideas. Professor Carl B. Cone says,

> Those who knew him best called Richard Price good. . . . He was a
> good man in ideas, purpose, and conduct. . . . Unlike the eighteenth
> century philosophers whose heavenly city was nothing beyond a fu-
> ture earthly community to be built by enlightened secularist sophisti-
> cates, with deep humility he found the origin of everything and the
> destiny of everything in God, the wise and watchful and immediate
> ruler of the universe. He shared his century's confidence in the steady
> progress of mankind toward perfection.[1]

Dr. Price believed that man's highest destiny would not be realized
until mankind enjoyed a universal freedom in which men might find
and do the will of God both to His glory and the improvement of
humanity. His religious faith and moral philosophy deeply valued
the dignity and freedom of man. A man of peace and good will, he
did not like controversy. But when the American situation took on
the dramatic character of a protracted conflict during the winter of
1775–76, both his conscience and his reason compelled him to
wage a battle of principles in the Americans' behalf. His "gentleness
and humility" were accessories to his "vigor, tremendous courage,
and forthrightness." He was an "apostle of liberty." His *Observations on the Nature of Civil Liberty* might be considered a finer
statement of American revolutionary ideology than anything written in America. Indeed, most of the Americans who took up arms

against the British crown cherished the principles enunciated by Price more than they did the lofty rationalism of the Declaration of Independence.

Price's ideas about liberty were deeply rooted in his heritage of Dissent. Nonconformity in eighteenth-century England still suffered the vestiges of discrimination which restricted the freedom of Dissenters in English life. Dissenters had long possessed strong sentiments about the dignity and freedom of man, his right to rebel against injustice and his accountability to God for his actions. Institutions such as government did the will of God when they preserved freedom rather than suppressed it. In a large sense, "the perfect life was the free life." [2] It is understandable why Price sympathized with the good causes of other Radicals like Sharp and Burgh or the ideology of the American Revolution.

One also might remember that Price influenced, and was influenced by, some of the finest minds in the British world. [3] He was a respected figure in the Royal Society. His friends among the Honest Whigs included Burgh, John Horne Tooke, John Howard, Joseph Jeffries, and many others. He was an associate of eminent men like Dr. Joseph Priestley, Colonel Isaac Barré, and Adam Smith. He numbered among his American friends Dr. Franklin, the Reverend Charles Chauncy, John Winthrop, Josiah Quincy, Jr., and Francis Dana. And he was a trusted confidant of the earl of Shelburne.

Many Englishmen of the time thought of Dr. Price as a noted moral philosopher and Dissenter clergyman. His reputation for the former was largely based on his *A Review of the Principal Questions and Difficulties in Morals, particularly those respecting the origin of our Ideas of Virtue, its Nature, relation to the Deity, Obligation, Subject-matter, and Sanctions* (1758). Price's stature as a philosopher has not been given as much recognition by later generations as has been the case with some of his contemporaries. Some present-day students of his thought, however, consider him to have been a better thinker than most of them. [4] Because his moral philosophy underlay his political principles, a brief description of the former might be in order here.

Historically, Price revived the "rational intuitionism" that went back to René Descartes and the English rationalists Ralph Cudworth and Samuel Clarke. He tried to stem the tide of British empiricism in eighteenth-century English thought. He refuted the empiricist position that the knowledge of truth, including moral judgments, was derived from simple ideas rooted in sense perception. He also denied Humean skepticism, which argued that knowledge is merely based on particularistic notions derived from man's senses and imagination, that man cannot truly know the reality of things. Dr. Price contended that man's reasoning faculty enables him to know reality and that man's moral perceptions are *a priori* cognitions of eternal, absolute moral laws detectable by the intellect and binding on man as a free moral agent. Reason is the faculty by which man acts as a free moral agent. It is central to man's discernment between right and wrong.

> There are undoubtedly some actions that are ultimately approved, and for justifying which no reason can be assigned; as there are some ends, which are ultimately desired, and for choosing which no reason can be given. . . . The powers of the imagination are very narrow; and were the understanding confined to the same limits, nothing could be known, and the very faculty itself would be annihilated. Nothing is plainer than that one of these often perceives where the other is blind . . . and in numberless instances knows things to exist of which the other can frame no idea.[5]

Reason perceives the relations between ideas we already possess. It apprehends self-evident ideas by intuition, not by sense experience. To observe merit in an action, argued Price, is to perceive it as a right action. He believed "right" closely related to "obligation." An action's intrinsic rightness promulgates an intuition of obligation, irrespective of rewards and punishments. Man, as a rational creature, should follow the dictates of good reasoning rather than instinct or emotion. There is a place for reward and punishment. Men are aware of the consequences of their actions. Yet virtue itself is "the object of the chief complacency of every virtuous man; the exercise of it is his highest joy."[6] Price was anticipating Kant's notion of the "categorical imperative." Like many eighteenth-century moralists, Price believed in a moral universe in which there were harmonious laws of nature perceivable by man's intellect. The natural and moral laws of the universe were in accord with the grand designs of the Creator. Moral truths could be knowable through intuitional perception. Reason, not sensation, was the means of making moral judgments. Man acts as a free moral agent and is no subject of deterministic forces.

Price's moral philosophy, therefore, was the foundation for his political principles, especially his ideas of civil liberty.

> His political thought came directly out of his moral philosophy; therefore political freedom rested upon moral foundations; and both were of Divine origin. This belief gave depth and stability to Price's thoughts. Long after the social contract theory was ridiculed by English utilitarians, Price's reasons for claiming freedom as an inalienable right would still be valid. Though he could never be a theocrat, politics were not a secular matter for Price, even when he insisted upon religious freedom and inveighed against state churches. Divine law and God's plan transcended denominational definitions. Price brought God into the affairs of man, or rather, he refused to render lip service to God while excluding Him from the world.[7]

Such principles largely accorded with what was to be called the "American character." It is striking that most of the American people, who inherited strong legacies of religious dissent and disapprobation toward authoritarian government, have long cherished beliefs more akin to the moral philosophy of Richard Price than to the cold, impersonal deism which infuses the Declaration of Independence. The deity of most Americans traditionally has been a personal God who blesses righteous nations and punishes those who abandon His ways. He is the God of "The Battle Hymn of the Republic" who judges nations with "His terrible swift sword."[8]

The first edition of *Observations on the Nature of Civil Liberty* came out in London in mid-February 1776. By that time the American conflict was swiftly taking on the character of an ideological struggle between a British government determined to preserve authority and unity in the British Empire and American patriots who were swayed by the thunderous arguments of Thomas Paine's *Common Sense* in favor of American independence. Dr. Price recognized that all the issues and quarreling of recent years were being transcended by a central principle which historically had excited men throughout the British world—that of human freedom. He viewed freedom as the most fundamental issue of the whole crisis. And he was convinced that the British government had neither the moral nor practical resources to defeat the Americans' objectives—whether they be along the lines of a settlement urged by the Whig Opposition in Parliament or even separation from the mother country. His treatise approaches the American crisis from three distinct vantage points—the critical issue of human liberty which pervades the whole imperial crisis, the wisdom of a British policy which seeks to settle the matter by force of arms, and an alarming calculation of the national debt followed by estimates of how much the war will threaten the government's fiscal stability.

In Part I of the *Observations* Price elevates the imperial crisis to the plane of his moral philosophy and takes the position that the issue of liberty is the major question of the struggle, that the crisis has the most profound ramifications for Englishmen and Americans alike. Regarding liberty in general, he is consistent with the principles of his longstanding philosophy. As man is a free moral agent, his acts of goodness both glorify his Creator and contribute to the dignity and freedom of his fellowmen. Man's liberty is of four kinds. Physical liberty is the freedom of man to be morally responsible for his actions. Moral liberty is the freedom to act in accordance with one's rational discernment of right and wrong. Religious liberty allows man freely to follow the dictates of his conscience in finding and doing the will of God. And, as the main thesis of the first part of his treatise, Price acknowledges civil liberty as the freedom of people to govern themselves under laws made with their assent and intended for their general welfare. Governments may vary in their forms from country to country. But they should share the common goal of promoting the general liberty of their peoples. For liberty "is the foundation of all honour, and the chief privilege and glory of our nature." [9]

Governments are merely the creatures of free peoples. They are to serve rather than to be served. Hence, sovereignty resides in a free people. When people are distant from their seats of government, it is necessary that they elect representatives of their will to speak for them in the halls of government. This point gives Dr. Price occasion to digress into his idea of a "United States of Europe" in which elected representatives of the various nations of the Continent constitute a "Senate" to represent the will and promote the liberties of European peoples. Such a grand design, he argues, will surely diminish the scourges of authoritarianism and war which have plagued Europe from time immemorial. He also agrees with the principles of Montesquieu in advocating systems of checks and balances in governments to reduce the abuse of power and to sustain popular liberty.

Having in mind the arguments which consider popular sovereignty as an invitation to mob tyranny and anarchy, Price insists that the freedom of a people is far more sacred than the authority of government to maintain law and order. The abuses of liberty are far less dangerous than governments' abuse of power. "If licentiousness has destroyed its thousands, despotism has destroyed its millions."[10] Parliaments are not omnipotent in themselves. They are given a trust and authority derived from the will of a free people. Each citizen is an individual with dignity and freedom, in accord with the laws of God and nature, and is therefore entitled to the respect of government. The principles used to uphold the Divine Right of Kings are not in agreement with the laws of God and nature because they assume that the mass of men are low vassals without true freedom and not to be trusted. "As moral liberty is the prime blessing of man in his private capacity, so is *civil* liberty in his *public* capacity."[11]

Price then addresses himself to one country's assertion of authority to rule another country. It is an implicit reference to the moral dilemma inherent in British imperial authority in America. "From the nature and principles of civil liberty . . . it is an immediate and necessary inference that no one community can have any power over the property or legislation of another community, that is not incorporated with it by a just and adequate representation. Then only . . . is a state free, when it is governed by its own will."[12] It is morally wrong when the government of one nation imposes its will on the government of another people, as is the case with British rule in Massachusetts Bay. The "right of conquest" is inconsistent with the moral laws derived from God and nature and, therefore, the law of nations. Nor can compacts which formalize such wrongs be sanctioned by the higher laws of moral right and human liberty.

It is therefore morally wrong for nations to have and maintain empires where a diversity of people and circumstances are subjected to the singular will of an authority which cannot and will not uphold common justice and liberty. "These are situations totally different; and a constitution of government that may be consistent with liberty in one of them, may be entirely inconsistent with it in the other." [13] When one free state has an empire subordinate to its will, then it is "an empire consisting of one state free, and the rest in slavery." [14]

In Part II of his pamphlet Dr. Price applies his moral arguments to the nature of British imperial rule and especially to the American question. In so doing he believes that he is striking at the very heart of the great issues dividing Great Britain and the colonists. If the moral laws which uphold human liberty are superior to the compacts of men, so are they superior to the numerous precedents, charters, and statutes upon which Englishmen are justifying British rule in America. On such moral grounds Dr. Price takes issue with all the major arguments currently being used to defend the policies of the North ministry.

Against the argument that British policy is just, Dr. Price raises the question of how such a "just war" can be reconciled to the British constitution and its legacy of liberty. The defense of the Declaratory Act of 1766, for example, is to contradict a basic principle of Englishmen's rights—the right of crown subjects to be represented in the bodies which make their laws. The government's cause cannot be just when it denies the American people a right which both moral law and English history sanction. That the war be justified in the name of "imperial unity" is to betray a liberty which Englishmen themselves cherish. "If in order to preserve its unity, one half of it must be enslaved to the other half, let it, in the name of God, want unity." [15] The arguments on such points like British sovereignty, Britain's right of supremacy in the imperial system, the mother country's historic rights, her sacrifices in the recent war, and virtual representation are secondary to the cardinal issue of liberty—in other words, the right of the Americans to govern their affairs. There is also the practical aspect of the matter. Can Britain expect to rule America when it is evident that the latter's growth and strength eventually are going to exceed those of the mother country? And is it realistic to think that the Americans will accept indefinitely the authority of a Parliament whose corruption already has disenchanted so many Englishmen? Great Britain cannot exercise parliamentary authority in America without building an imperial popery that will be a mockery of British justice. If Englishmen truly want justice, admonishes Price, let the Americans go in peace to enjoy the freedom cherished by both peoples.

In reply to the argument that the war is defensible on constitutional grounds, Dr. Price retorts that "we are not maintaining but violating our own constitution in America. . . . [We are denying] the right of a people to give and grant their own money."[16] Americans are presently fighting for principles over which Englishmen themselves had defied King Charles I. "This is a war undertaken not only against the principles of our own constitution, but on purpose to destroy other similar constitutions in America; and to substitute in their room a military force. . . . It is, therefore, a gross and flagrant violation of the constitution."[17]

Against the contention that the war is being waged in the public interest, Dr. Price is plainspoken. Is it not more likely that the government's interest solely is being served by its policies? Is not public interest a moot question here? Can it not be that the ignoble objective of power is motivating official policy in hopes of sustaining some narrow British interests at the expense of America? The war's cost in British blood and treasure will surely prove that such power is not worth the cost. And is it not true also that British policy is being made for the sake of sheer vengeance by men in government who dismiss the Americans as ungrateful insurgents? The charge of American ingratitude has little substance to it. To the contrary, they have long borne British wrongs with great forbearance until driven into armed defiance. Since the Trade Act of 1733 and especially since the post-1763 acts they have shown much patience and willingness to settle differences in a fair and just manner. But the British government pressed them too far and now leaves them with no recourse but armed resistance. America is a young and growing nation of hardy, independent yeomen who value their God-given freedom. Their resolution to fight for it is made evident by their unity from New England to Georgia. Arguments about the war being in the interest of the British people are absurd. Has not England taken up arms to defend the very same principles for which the Americans are now fighting? Is not the war inflicting severe damage on British trade and currency? How are British creditors now going to get redemption of American debts long owed to them? And, ominously enough, is there not a serious possibility that a European coalition will rise against Britain? Rather than being in the public interest, writes Price, current British policies are leading the country to the brink of disaster.

Dr. Price then refutes the argument that the war is being fought for "the honour of the nation." It is begging the question, he argues, for the British government to stand on a point of national honor when it unleashes war and destruction against another people 3,000 miles away on their own soil and before their very homes. An abstraction like national honor has too often been used by the governments who declare war rather than the people who endure it. There is a crucial difference between rulers' notions of national honor and those of the people. If Great Britain seeks true honor, let her make peace with America. "Prudence, no less than honour, requires us to retract." [18] Englishmen have praised the Dutchmen who fought Spain and cheered the Corsicans who defied France. Are not the Americans fighting for the same reason—their simple desire to be free? Britain must come to its senses, see the error of its ways, and find true honor by making peace with the Americans, asking only for their gratitude and commerce.

In his last rebuttal against arguments current in English opinion about the rightness of the war, Price makes an unwelcome appraisal of the popular idea that British chances for military success are good. To the contrary, he insists, they are dim. Circumstances are overwhelmingly against the prospects for the kind of victory sought by the government and expected by the English people. Does not common sense make it evident that a British army of thirty to forty thousand men cannot conquer a half-million Americans who are fighting on their own ground and near their own homes and families? Are Englishmen being honest with themselves in thinking that His Majesty's forces are dealing with a small band of fanatics when American families from Boston to Charleston are fasting and praying for the success of their cause? There also is the grave chance that jealous European powers, ever ready to strike against England when the opportunity presents itself, will ally with the Americans—if this happens, British hopes of military victory will be dashed.

Dr. Price concludes with an admonition that Great Britain might well provoke the displeasure of the God of nations upon herself. With the lamentations of an Old Testament prophet, he is moved to speak of British shame in another distant part of the world.

> Turn your eyes upon India. There more has been done than is now attempted in *America*. There Englishmen, actuated by the love of plunder and the spirit of conquest, have depopulated whole kingdoms, and ruined millions of innocent people by the most infamous oppression and rapacity.—The justice of the nation has slept over these enormities. Will the justice of Heaven sleep? Are we not now execrated on both sides of the globe?[19]

He appeals for peace in America on terms similar to those recently urged by Lord Shelburne in the House of Lords. Britain should take the initiative toward establishing peace. All those acts of Parliament which had provoked the crisis should be repealed. The government must acknowledge America's right to self-government and regulate imperial commerce affecting the Americans only with their approval. America should be exempt from British taxation. Britain simply would have to bear the main burdens of imperial debts herself. Like Shelburne, Price is hopeful that such liberal concessions would make possible the preservation of some sort of union between the two countries. Existing notions of Parliament's full sovereignty in the British Empire must be abandoned. There should be a federation of the British and American peoples with both equally represented in a reformed parliament, a body whose authority over strictly American affairs is limited.[20]

Such a plan proposes no grand scheme like that of John Cartwright or Granville Sharp. It is a simple, practical plan not much different from the proposals of British officials who made up the Carlisle Peace Commission in 1778. Had it been offered in 1774, it doubtless would have been taken seriously by American leaders. Most Americans then would have preferred to keep old ties with the mother country and would have been willing to accept a settlement short of complete separation.

Part III of the pamphlet is an appendix which includes Price's extraordinary tables and estimates on Great Britain's national debt at the outset of the American Revolution. He probably obtained much of his information from Shelburne. His calculations show that the national debt of Britain by midsummer of 1775 stood at £135,943,051, with an annual interest cost of £4,440,821. Price estimates that the debt would rise to the alarming figure of about £200,000,000 before the war ended. His estimation, unsettling as it was to many Englishmen in 1776, proved to be conservative, as it fell about £11,000,000 short of the actual debt figure at the war's conclusion.[21]

Dr. Price was surprised at the prompt and wide attention which the *Observations* received—in England, in America, and on the Continent. His pamphlet raised many more eyebrows than did the publications of other pro-American British Radicals during the two years before the Declaration of Independence, especially in his own country. His calculations on the national debt hit London like a thunderbolt. They probably made interesting reading in the Bourbon courts of France and Spain also. During the weeks following the *Observations*' initial publication it sold over 60,000 copies and went through five editions. Forty editions were published during its first two years. Price won praise from the few Englishmen who agreed with him. But he incensed most of his countrymen with his charges that they were sanctioning a betrayal of British freedom. Whether acclaimed or denounced, the pamphlet was the talk of London. Horace Walpole remarked that it caused "a great sensation."

Understandably, treasury officials and those holding government securities were stunned by Price's description of the national debt and "the danger to which they were exposed by ruinous measures of the Court."[22] Walpole considered this to be an important reason why it was the first pamphlet of its kind on the imperial crisis to make such a big impression. Recognizing their importance, the *Annual Register* published Price's tables and estimates in its own pages.[23]

Walpole also noted that the government turned loose many of its "hirelings" to castigate the pamphlet in a flood of progovernment publications. The government was defended by a number of able writers, including John Shebbeare, who wrote *An Essay on the Origin, Progress and Establishment of National Society*, and James Macpherson, who published his *The Rights of Great Britain Asserted against the Claims of America*. Dr. William Markham, archbishop of York, spoke for most of the Anglican establishment when he criticized the *Observations* as an invitation to social unrest and anarchy. In June 1777, Dr. Price wrote to one of his American friends, Arthur Lee, then an American agent in France, "I have drawn upon myself a torrent of opposition and abuse; but the satisfaction I feel in the consciousness of having endeavored to promote the cause of liberty and justice makes me abundant amends."[24]

Irrespective of the great controversy which the *Observations on the Nature of Civil Liberty* provoked in 1776, it certainly was one of the most eloquent and forceful pamphlets written by an Englishman during the American conflict. Its literary quality was considerable. Dr. Price skillfully interwove his moral philosophy with a splendid analysis of the issues underlying the crisis. His emotional appeal to men's propensity for self-respect and freedom had a universal quality that attracted lovers of liberty in his own time and in the generations afterward. In an age which had many great spokesmen for the principles of liberty, Price may rightfully be considered one of the most gifted and most important. His moral arguments for human freedom sustained the hopes and spirits of men who sought the sanction of "Nature's God" and "the opinions of mankind" in their struggles for freedom. He was a good, humble man of peace who, like many men of true greatness, lived nobly and well among people who valued the day-to-day goodness of his works. Unlike a man who inspires thousands with rhetoric or conquest, he was one whose manly example and great ideas sustained people who lived placidly in Newington Green and, as fortune was to have it, men who were creating a new nation across the Atlantic. "Unless he has the rare qualities of a Franklin, and some good fortune, a person such as Price is hardly likely to catch public fancy and win a hero's laurels in a revolutionary age."[25] Yet Dr. Priestley, who knew Price and his works very well, was moved to rank him with Franklin, Washington, Lafayette, and Paine.[26]

At a time when Americans were about to raise their banners in the name of independence, Price's principles struck at the soul of the imperial struggle by transcending long-debated issues and raising the fundamental question of what Anglo-American civilization was about—human freedom. His ideas added fresh meaning to the British constitution and anticipated the central theme of the Declaration of Independence. They defined national honor and greatness as the freedom and well-being of a nation's people. Only with these could a country truly enjoy liberty, prosperity, progress, and live peaceably with other nations, all to the glory of God and the improvement of humanity.

Finally, Dr. Price, at a time when Englishmen had not yet thought much about the problem of reconciling the principles of their constitution with their vastly enlarged empire, questioned the morality of empires. Imperialism implied the subjugation of people and the abridgement of their freedom. Civil liberty, as he conceived it, was irreconcilable with imperialism. Like John Cartwright and other Radicals, Price was a part of the anti-imperialist legacy that would rise to the surface of English life during the following century.[27] Regarding the American question in early 1776, he believed that its solution could be found only in British recognition of the Americans' freedom to fashion their own affairs. If the mother country could not bring herself to such a realization, then, as Dr. Price saw it, American independence was the only solution. "In the ultimate analysis, he saw in the American Revolution . . . a vivid, widely drawn illustration of the existence and virtue of philosophical liberty."[28]

NINE

Diverse Acquiescence
in Radical Opinion

MOST British Radicals, for a variety of motives described in an earlier chapter, supported the ideas of Cartwright, Sharp, Burgh, Macaulay, and Price because of their antigovernment stands. The diversity of their antigovernment opinions, however, indicates that they could easily disagree on specific questions of imperial reformation just as they often disagreed on the extent of parliamentary reform and other issues directly related to home affairs. Nevertheless, this chapter will demonstrate how the pro-American Radical spokesmen of 1774–76 had a considerable influence on the manner in which English Radicalism reacted to the events of the American war until it came to an end in the first years of the following decade. Writings like the *Political Disquisitions* and Mrs. Macaulay's *Address* helped to promote organized forms of dissent from the British government's American war policy which kept the issue before the public and eventually contributed to the pressures that led to peace negotiations in Paris. This influence may be seen in the activities of John Horne Tooke and his Constitutional Society, Christopher Wyvill's county association movement, and the parliamentary reform crusade of the Society for Constitutional Information.

When the impetuous John Horne Tooke read Cartwright's *American Independence the Interest and Glory of Great Britain* after the war started in 1775, he remarked, "If England possessed a half dozen men of his character and firmness in the different counties, they would have put a stop to the American war." [1] Shortly after the actions at Lexington and Concord were reported in London, his Constitutional Society met on June 7 and approved his proposal that the membership donate money to the families of Americans killed in those engagements. Several City newspapers described the meeting at King's Arm Tavern in Cornhill and included an announcement distributed by the society.

> At a special meeting this day of several members of the Constitutional Society, during an adjournment a gentleman [John Horne Tooke] proposed that a subscription should be immediately entered into by such of the members present who might approve the purpose, for raising the sum of £100 to be applied to the relief of the widows, orphans, and aged parents of our beloved American fellow subjects, who, faithful to the character of Englishmen, preferring death to slavery, were for that reason only inhumanly murdered by the King's troops at or near Lexington and Concord, in the province of Massachusetts on the 19th of last April; which sum being immediately collected it was thereupon resolved that Mr. Horne do pay tomorrow into the hands of Mssrs. Brownes and Collinson, on account of Dr. Franklin, the sum of £100 and that Dr. Franklin be requested to apply the same to the above-mentioned purposes. . . .[2]

Phrases like "preferring death to slavery" and "inhumanly murdered" were Horne Tooke's and they got him into trouble with the authorities. After the Americans were declared rebels in August, several officials in the government decided that an example had to be made out of Horne Tooke. He was not arrested and prosecuted, however, until 1777. His trial, ironically, began at the Guildhall on July 4. The charge against him was seditious libel against the crown. The proceedings ended with conviction, a fine of £200 and one year's confinement to King's Bench Prison. When the unrepentant Horne Tooke was released in the summer of 1778, he promptly began to collaborate with Dr. Price in compiling a statistical study of the costs of the American war. It was completed in 1780. The fiscal calculations were Price's, while their exploitation for antiwar propaganda was chiefly Horne Tooke's.

Published anonymously, the shocking pamphlet of Price and Horne Tooke was entitled *Facts: Addressed to the Landholders, Stockholders, Merchants, Farmers, Manufacturers, Tradesmen, Proprietors, of Every Description and Generally to All the Subjects of Great Britain*. Prolific columns of figures were included to demonstrate the government's waste and extravagance in prosecuting the war. Using rhetoric characteristic of his earlier polémics, Horne Tooke urged a prompt reduction of government spending, deplored the current burden of taxation in Britain and noted the current decline of British trade. He argued that the war was having terrific demoralizing effects on the country. An entire chapter was devoted to an attack on the King's Civil List. Lord North was made to appear totally incompetent in handling public revenues. The crown was accused of irresponsible use of the royal prerogative in the administration of imperial policy. Horne Tooke wrote that Parliament was so saturated with corruption that it lacked the moral fiber and legislative competence to settle the American mess. The British nation was confronted with a major crisis at home as well as in America, he argued, and there was no choice but to make constitutional reforms in Britain and the empire alike. "The corrupt influence of the Crown is risen to such a height that it will not be sufficient merely to clip the wings with which it was mounted; they must be seared to prevent their putting forth again. We are now arrived at a period when either corruption must be thoroughly purged from the Senate, or the nation is finally and irrecoverably undone." [3]

Several of Horne Tooke's associates in the Constitutional Society read an early draft of the pamphlet. The earl of Shelburne also looked at it and, though much impressed by the calculation of the war debt, did not like its tone and warned Horne Tooke that no good would be accomplished by its publication under present circumstances. But Horne Tooke, egged on by his society friends, went ahead and published it anyway. Even more than his inflammatory charges against Parliament and the government, the revealing estimation of the government's fiscal situation shocked many Britons at a late period in a frustrating war which had spread into a European conflict. The pamphlet was a fiery contribution to the growing public disillusionment with the government and its war policy. It helped to foment the pressures that eventually, forced Lord North's resignation and the beginning of peace negotiations in 1782. The pamphlet also combined the ideological, political, and economic ramifications of the American conflict. It was the Constitutional Society's—or John Horne Tooke's—last major stab against an American policy it had opposed since 1771. The career of Horne

Tooke in both the Bill of Rights Society and the Constitutional Society was evidence of the extraordinary ideological and political encouragement which the Radical imperial reformists of 1774–76 gave to antigovernment agitators during the American crisis, men who played leading roles in the Radical reform societies of the time.

More important than the influence which the Radical imperial reformers had on Radical opinion or activities in the early war years was the effect they had on internal pressures for peace and reform after the critical events of 1778. After the American victory at Saratoga precipitated European intervention in the conflict, the prospects of an exhaustive war, militarily and financially, caused many Englishmen to lose their earlier enthusiasm for disciplining the recalcitrant Americans. If Radical arguments for imperial reformation still have little appeal to most Britons, there was no question about their wanting an end to the war itself. Widespread disillusionment with the policies of the North ministry by 1779 gave Radical proponents of peace and reform their long-awaited chance to win the country's attention. Or so they thought at the time. As events proved, most Englishmen were willing to settle for peace without reforms—at least the kinds of reforms being urged by Radicals. Be that as it may, two quite important developments occurred in 1779–80 which testified to the influence which Radical spokesmen on imperial reform were beginning to have on English Radicalism—the rise of Christopher Wyvill's association movement and the establishment of the Society for Constitutional Information. The appearance of these two movements brought into play several important principles described in earlier chapters. There was the general demand for parliamentary reform which, in effect, meant an expansion of British liberty. The notion of greater legislative responsibility to the nation was implicit. Public opinion was to count for much more in the way the country was to be governed. And there was recognition of the need to organize people and opinion to achieve such objectives. Price, Cartwright, Sharp, Macaulay, and Burgh might be considered early theorists and strategists who set the stage for a Radical reformism in England that lasted down to the Reform Bill of 1832. Their cases for America served to amplify the case for Radical reform in their own country.

The rise of the county association movement in 1779–80 was chiefly the work of Christopher Wyvill and a few colleagues who had become sorely disenchanted with the war and its ruinous effects in England.[4] Wyvill was the "inspiration and driving force" of the Yorkshire Association, a county organization supporting peace and reform. Founded in 1779, it inspired the rise of similar organizations throughout the country.[5] Wyvill advocated reforms that would make Parliament more responsible to a broader base of the British nation and would create the machinery for a more strict accounting of how public revenues were spent. His view on the extent of parliamentary reform was more restrained than that of many London Radicals. He wanted the county associations to avoid partisan politics and entanglements which might obstruct his reform program. When he decided to collaborate with London Radicals and Rockingham Whigs in 1780, he did so as a matter of expediency at a critical juncture when prospects for public support seemed good.[6] But the fortunes of the county association movement were mainly determined by the conservative, yet disenchanted, gentry who were the pillars of such organizations out in the country.

Despite Wyvill's early hopes for the achievement of his Radical reform aims, he found that the great majority of his country supporters were not as anxious for extraordinary reform as they were for an end to the war and some piecemeal reforms to correct abusive expenditure of public money by politicians. These people were rural men of property. Caring little for the abstruse issues of the war, they wanted peace and economy which could bring things back to normal in the placid English countryside they loved. They were prepared to follow Wyvill into an alliance with Radical groups and Whig politicians in a united cause for peace. Their efforts were part of the pressure which influenced the British government to start negotiations in Paris in 1782. When the end of the war was in sight, the county associations began to disintegrate—so did Wyvill's plans for parliamentary reform. Wyvill had to cast his lot with Major Cartwright's Society for Constitutional Information in London.

The brief careers of Christopher Wyvill's Yorkshire Association and its many counterparts in the country were imposing evidence that organized opinion had great potential. They confirmed the

great significance of James Burgh's proposals in the *Political Disquisitions*. The associations showed that effective organization,
energetic leadership, and clearly stated objectives representing the
wishes of a large number of people were capable of having decisive
influence on the government in London. If the association movement in 1779–80 did not achieve Wyvill's personal aspirations, it
realized the desires of most of the gentry who filled its ranks. Such
organization was to have tremendous importance in nineteenth-
century Britain. As for Wyvill, his endeavors, so greatly frustrated
in 1780, succeeded in causing many of his contemporaries to re-
appraise the constitution of the period.[7]

Major Cartwright, later called "the father of the Society for
Constitutional Information," provided the leadership which
brought together fifteen reformers in April 1780 to form the charter
membership of that organization while the associations were active
in the country. They shared the beliefs that Parliament was unrepresentative and that the American debacle made parliamentary reform imperative. A number of men among the original membership
were prominent Radicals, though not all of them, despite their
support of reform, might be considered Radicals in the proper
sense. There were Cartwright, Sharp, and Price—each of them Radicals and imperial reformers at the outset of the war—and other
Radicals such as Capell Lofft, Dr. John Jebb, Thomas Brand Hollis,
Thomas Day, John Sawbridge, and Christopher Wyvill, who was
also working in the Yorkshire Association at the time. Distinguished people like Sir William Jones, Richard Sheridan, the play-
wright and M.P., and the reform-minded duke of Richmond were
also in the group. The society's membership expanded to sixty-one
by the end of the year. This body came to be made up of members
who were well intentioned, liberal, patriotic men of property who
supported the society's declaration of purposes initially stated in
April 1780. They opposed the American war, advocated parliamentary reform, and made plans for distributing reform propaganda, some of it to be written by themselves.[8] Again, it is clear that
Burgh's *Political Disquisitions* was understood by a rising generation of reformers. Unlike the county associations, the Society for
Constitutional Information survived the time of the American Revolution and was an important organ through which Radical propaganda was distributed until its dissolution in the repressive atmos-

phere of the 1790s. The society and the career of its leader, John Cartwright, formed an important chapter in a movement which culminated in the great parliamentary reforms of the nineteenth century.

During the society's first audit dinner in December 1780, a long list of toasts was given in which "America in our arms" and "the Irish Volunteers" were hailed along with addresses to parliamentary reform and liberty.[9] To the members the American conflict was a test to determine whether or not the colonists would successfully defend the principles of British liberty. The issue of parliamentary reform would be a test for determining the future extent of liberty in England. The news of Yorktown and the subsequent accession of the Rockingham-Shelburne ministry were causes for expecting the realization of their fondest hopes in both America and England. The end of the war, of course, did not bring parliamentary reform, but the American Revolution continued to be an inspiration to their cause long after 1783. They long reminded their countrymen that the loss of America was rooted in the corrupt and unrepresentative structure of parliamentary politics. "Had your representatives acted as faithful servants, you would not have lost America and your West India islands, nor have had many branches of useful commerce almost annihilated; and if you continue much longer supine, you will certainly lose all that remains, and suffer the ruin of your country to be completed."[10] Their arguments were neglected by an indifferent public and practical-minded politicians who thought them to be too doctrinaire and oblivious to political realities.[11]

To sum up, the writings of Cartwright, Sharp, Burgh, Macaulay, and Price at the outset of the American war helped to crystallize domestic and imperial issues which, in turn, generated a growing British Radical contention that the American crisis was a dramatic manifestation of the ill effects which the old structure of politics had brought on the country. The failures and humiliations which the war itself brought to Great Britain seemed, at least to most British Radicals, to confirm the necessity for reforming Parliament and expanding liberty in British life. Dr. Price's *Observations on the Nature of Civil Liberty* was praised as a masterpiece comparable to Paine's *Common Sense*. Burgh's *Political Disquisitions* became the Radicals' bible for parliamentary reform. Whether in behalf of America or of reform at home, Burgh and Catharine Macaulay both promoted ideas for organizing public opinion which had an important effect on Radical reformers by 1780. And when the Americans in 1776 declared their basic aim to be national independence, most British Radicals supported such a cause—a gesture which, oddly enough, Dean Tucker, one of their severest critics, had urged since January 1774.

TEN

Whig Politicians on
Radical Ideas

HOW did the great men of the Whig Opposition react to such novel
ideas about the British Empire? To answer this question is not only
to place Radical thinking within the perspective of contemporary
British opinion as a whole but also to demonstrate some of the basic
differences between English reformists and the politics of the old.
Whig ascendancy on the eve of the American Revolution.

In the last weeks of 1773 before news of the Boston Tea Party
reached London, many British politicians were more concerned
about taxes at home and the dissolution of the present Parliament
than about troubles in America. Few Englishmen, in office or out,
cared much for affairs in distant colonial provinces—an indifference which might not gratify devotees of American revolutionary
mythology but which, nevertheless, was true. Most British politicians thought the Americans, despite their value in trade, to be
outright nuisances. They had little patience with Americans'
liberty-mad bickering over a threepence tea duty, and there were
occasions when some of them probably admitted that separation
from America would be a blessing for England.

The news about the incident in Boston Harbor, however, stung
the temperaments and pride of the king, his government, Parliament, and the mass of Englishmen. Some mischievous colonials had
thumbed their noses at two objects about which Britons felt
strongly—the authority of Parliament and private property. When
the politicians met at Westminster in early 1774, their anger was
reenforced by angry public opinion. The voices of Radicals and
worried merchants who had large investments in colonial trade

were drowned out by demands for reprisals. Seldom in eighteenth-century England did Parliament enjoy such a popular endorsement of the actions it was about to take by way of the Coercion Acts. Parliamentarians who had long regarded America with apathy began to raise fundamental questions about empire and their policy in America. "Is America any longer to be dependent on this country? How far is it connected? In what degree? In what manner? It might be a greater question whether the colonies should not be given up?" [1]

The crisis provoked divisions in Parliament reminiscent of the old Tory and Whig duels early in the century. The great majorities in both Lords and Commons fully supported His Majesty's government in its determination to discipline the insolent Bostonians. The *Annual Register* described these politicians as an alliance of "Tories" and "Court Whigs." The opposition was delineated as miscellaneous Whigs who were convinced that Parliament had lost its independence from the crown and that the houses' acquiescence to the ministry's American policy put the principles of 1688 to shame. [2]

The history of the debate between prominiistry and Whig politicians on the imperial question from 1774 to the end of the war is familiar to students of the period. We need not dwell on the attitude of the so-called Tories toward the opinions of British Radicals. But the Whig Opposition is another matter. Some additional perspective on Radical ideas about the British Empire, as well as the character of both Radicals and Opposition Whigs, might be found if we take a look at the reaction of Whig politicians to Radical proposals for solving the American quandary. Such an objective can be achieved by appraising the opinions of Whig leaders whose views represented the broad scope of Whig thinking on the crisis of empire. Because his views so eloquently represented the position of most of the Rockingham Whigs, this group's attitude toward the Radicals' ideas will be viewed through the fertile mind of Edmund Burke. Charles James Fox, who joined this connection on account of the American question, also warrants some special attention. Shelburne's ideas provide some of the most intriguing examples of thinking close to that of the Radicals. And it is necessary to examine the opinions of the greatest British statesman of the time, the earl of Chatham.

Though this study essentially is concerned with Radical ideas on the imperial question, it must be remembered that it was men like Burke, Fox, Shelburne, and Chatham who were best known in the colonies as "the friends of America." Their speeches were reported in American newspapers. Until American independence was declared, they were regarded by many colonists as the best hopes for redress of grievances. For after all, they were men in positions to do something in the Americans' behalf if no more than publicly to oppose the government's colonial policy. But most of the English public saw them as unpatriotic prophets of doom who sympathized with lawless rebels. Many Englishmen believed their attacks on the influence of the crown to be an absurd ploy to hamper the government's ability to deal with the American situation effectively. Even Chatham received criticism from a public with whom he had been very popular a few years before. It might be argued that the Whig Opposition was no more acceptable to national opinion in the early war years than were Radicals. This view poses a few questions which should be answered in this chapter. What did the great men of the Whig Opposition think of the Radicals' ideas of empire? How did they agree and disagree? What did the American Revolution mean to each of them and how did they think it would affect the future of Great Britain?

Chatham stood far above most English politicians by virtue of his extraordinary analysis of the great issues of the time, the strength and eloquence of his oratory, and his aspirations for British greatness. His imperial nationalism caused him to assume a personal responsibility in upholding the vital interests of Great Britain both at home and abroad. He was a man of impeccable integrity untouched by the give-and-take of political patronage so prevalent in the eighteenth-century Parliament. Ambitious and proud, he possessed an arrogant willfulness often demonstrated by his uncompromising determination to have his way in day-to-day politics and national policy-making. Even his closest colleagues found it difficult to get along with him. Chatham thought grandly, and the tenacious pursuit of his aspirations for Britain made him impatient with lesser politicians and contemptuous of partisan politics. To him the business of politics was to promote national unity and prosperity toward the grand objectives of British power and greatness. He distressed both potential allies and enemies by going over the heads of crown and Parliament and appealing to the British people to win enthusiasm for his objectives. To cautious politicians he would say, "Not men but measures."[3]

Chatham was familiar with the spectrums of British opinion on many subjects, and his acquaintance with Radical thinking was no exception. Some Radicals, especially those of the City, claimed him as one of their own. He was on friendly terms with a number of Radical figures described in previous chapters. Thomas Hollis was his neighbor near Pitt's farm at Burton Pinsent in Dorsetshire. They first met in 1756 and soon became intimate friends. On many occasions until Hollis's death in 1774 they had long conversations about farming and politics. Chatham was a subject in many of the letters exchanged between Hollis and Jonathan Mayhew of Boston. Catharine Macaulay's *History of England* was both read and praised by Chatham. He once quoted her during a speech in the House of Lords, and it must have been very pleasing to the lady historian when the great Chatham criticized the Tory bias in Hume's *History of England*. Dr. Price was another of Chatham's Radical friends, though Chatham respected him more as an economist and theologian than as a political writer. Chatham's only speech in the House of Lords between 1771 and 1774 was in May 1772, when at Price's request he spoke in support of the Feathers Petition. He endeared himself to Price and many other Dissenters when he gave his oratorical powers to the cause of religious freedom. "I am for this bill, my lords, because I am for toleration, that sacred right of nature and bulwark of truth and most interesting of all subjects to fallible man."[4]

Like many Radicals, Chatham was well read in the political literature of reformist Whigs of the past. He also deplored "corruption" and the growing influence of the court in the early years of George III's reign. He had his own grand notions of British liberty but no elaborate plan of domestic reform. He believed that American rights, like those of Englishmen at home, were rooted in the principles of Englishmen's rights upheld by seventeenth-century jurists and the Glorious Revolution. Though he was the grand statesman of his time, his achievements in home affairs never matched his accomplishments as a war leader. He was not the sort of man who cared much about the day-to-day business of running government. His followers during much of the decade before the American war, along with those of Shelburne, numbered only around a dozen men. Caroline Robbins ventures to describe him as "a Churchill rather than a Gladstone." [5]

In order to understand Chatham's views on America and his attitude toward Radical notions of empire, it is necessary to appreciate fully the intensity of his feelings about Great Britain's future union with America as a key to the former's position in the world. His achievements as a war leader against France and Spain made him look upon the British triumph as his own handiwork. After 1763 he was determined that Great Britain's vast empire would facilitate British security, prosperity, and liberty. He recognized that such objectives demanded general unity and harmony among the peoples of the British Empire. He could not forgive the politicians whose blunders wrecked his dreams. When the American crisis exploded in 1774–76, Chatham, like the Radicals, cast full responsibility for the debacle upon a corrupt, misguided set of court politicians. He agreed with much of Burgh's *Political Disquisitions*. It was a reverberating critique of men whom Chatham despised for thwarting his imperial nationalism. Very few Radicals themselves were capable of matching Chatham's fiery denunciations of the government's American policy.

Chatham's position on the issues of Parliament's authority in the British Empire and taxation had some rather extraordinary, far-fetched qualities. They demonstrated how far he was willing to go to preserve Anglo-American unity. If there were differences with the arguments of Radical spokesmen, there was still a common motive of accommodating the Americans. Chatham argued that Parliament's authority in the empire was supreme in the regulation of trade. "I assert the authority of this Kingdom over the colonies to be sovereign and supreme, in every circumstance of government and legislation whatsoever." But he contrived grounds on which to share the Americans' opposition to tax measures like the Stamp Act with an anachronistic concept from feudal times which stated that taxation was not legislation but rather a kind of free gift of people to government. "Taxation is no part of the governing or legislative power." [6] And in the same vein, "I will as soon subscribe to Transubstantiation as to Sovereignty (by right) in the colonies." [7] Chatham therefore supported the Rockingham Whigs' repeal of the Stamp Act on his own grounds that the colonial assemblies were the rightful legislators of internal tax laws, that Parliament had no authority to pass such measures for colonies. But he opposed the Declaratory Act by reasoning that such an assertion violated the colonial right of self-taxation.[8] He would never compromise with the Rockinghamites on this issue and therein was one of the reasons why Chathamites and Rockingham Whigs could not unite against the North ministry.[9]

On the subject of reforming the parliamentary system, Chatham, despite his contempt for the men who dominated Parliament at the outset of the American Revolution, did not share the Radicals' enthusiasm for their notions of parliamentary reform. His concept of representation was in the mold of the old Whig oligarchy, and he had serious reservations about increasing the electorate. He would have been quite satisfied with the old parliamentary system dominated by a clear majority of Chathamites who would follow him without reservation.

Despite some critical differences over Parliament's place in the empire and over parliamentary reform, it is likely that most British Radicals would have supported Chatham if he had been in power around 1774–76.[10] Both parties wanted a settlement with the Americans and a weakening of court influence. And it is probable that the Radicals would have been pleased to accept Chatham's plans for the future of the British Empire's connection with America.[11]

In early 1775, when several Radicals had already proposed a reformation of the imperial system, Chatham made his famous proposals in Parliament that suggested the creation of a kind of quasi-federal union with America. He had consulted with Dr. Franklin on the subject. In an effort to allay the worsening tensions in America, Chatham offered a plan that would pacify the colonists and preserve Anglo-American unity. He recommended that Parliament acknowledge lack of authority to tax the Americans for revenues and also repeal the Coercion Acts. Parliament would still have the right to regulate trade in the empire and provide for its defense. He implied that Great Britain might recognize the Continental Congress as a legitimate body for raising colonial money to help finance America's defense. It was no grand scheme like that of Radicals such as John Cartwright, and it was largely inspired by Chatham's desire to save his dreams for Britain's future. But there is no reason to believe English Radicals would have opposed it.

During the last years of his life Chatham was a sick, broken man whose world fell apart with the American War of Independence. Unlike the British Radicals, he refused to take the Declaration of Independence as America's final word to the mother country. To the very end he vainly persisted in his efforts for some kind of reconciliation. In his last speeches before the House of Lords he poured out his hopes that America, which he considered the key to Britain's future greatness and power, could somehow be persuaded to retain an extraordinary connection with Great Britain. He continued to defend the principles of American rights and to denounce the politicians who were shattering his dreams. These points formed the essence of his last speech in the House of Lords in 1778, when he suffered his fatal stroke.[12] Whereas the Radicals accepted the Declaration of Independence and were inspired by America's success, Chatham thought the American Revolution was an unmitigated disaster and a tragic blow to his personal aspirations for the future of his country.

Shelburne's ideas, though more subtle and sophisticated, were not far removed from those of Chatham. Like the Great Commoner, William Petty, earl of Shelburne, was something of a maverick in the parliamentary politics of the time. He was one of the most gifted and innovative men in the House of Lords. His ideas were far in advance of his time and he had many more attachments to British Radicalism than Chatham. At Bowood he received some of the most cultivated and liberal-minded people of the day, including Jeremy Bentham, David Garrick, Mirabeau, Dr. Franklin, and Radicals such as Dr. Price, James Burgh, Sergeant Glynn, Colonel Isaac Barré, and Sir William Jones. Dr. Priestley, who was the librarian at Bowood for several years, was closer to Shelburne than were most Radicals. Because of his unconventional ideas and his own contempt for political faction, Shelburne was unpopular with most of his contemporaries in Parliament. He was a peer of considerable ability, but his virtues were offset by his "obsequious manners, suspicious temper, cynical judgement of others' motives."[13]

His ideas about the imperial question were brilliant, imaginative, and utterly incomprehensible to most of his colleagues in the House of Lords. He proved to be more a splendid theorist and innovator than an effective politician. He warmly supported parliamentary reform, religious emancipation, and the principle of American rights. Bentham once said that he was the "only minister he ever heard of who did not fear the people." [14]

Shelburne was not a great devotee of Chatham the man, but they shared many views on current questions. Both men carried a following in Parliament that seldom went above a dozen men. Shelburne included among his group Colonel Barré, John Dunning, the City Radical James Townsend, and Shelburne's half-brother Thomas Fitzmaurice. [15] Both Shelburne and Chatham venerated the Revolution of 1688 and the principles of British liberty. They lamented "corruption" and crown influence as the sources of ill-conceived American policies. Shelburne was close to Chatham in his efforts to preserve the union of Great Britain and America after the latter's death in 1778. [16] His brilliant diplomacy at the end of the war initially sought to salvage some sort of commercial union with America reminiscent of Chatham's principles. [17] Like his Radical acquaintances, Shelburne saw the American Revolution as a sequel to the Revolution of 1688 in which the colonists were fighting for their liberties as good Englishmen. The war was "the native off-spring of ministerial ignorance, obstinacy and want of principle." [18] The government's position toward the colonists was "a piece of metaphysical refinement." [19]

Shelburne's concept of the British Empire combined his own pragmatism with the idealism of a quasi-federation of Britain and America not unlike that of Chatham. His willingness to make concessions to the Americans was rooted in expediency, and his hopes to sustain British liberty in the empire won him the trust of many Radicals. Like most Englishmen, he greatly valued the British Empire for its enormous economic and strategical benefits. Unlike Chatham, he was not as strongly attached to the old mercantilism as were most of his contemporaries. He thought that American complaints about the Trade Acts had substance. He did not think that the mercantilist principle of colonial subserviency could be reconciled with the rights of Englishmen. He opposed the Declaratory Act on the expedient ground that Parliament, theoretically sovereign in the British Empire, should not legislate internal taxes on the colonies.

Shelburne's ideas on change in the British Empire represented not an anti-imperialism, as was true of many Radicals, but rather a "new imperialism." Such thinking was traceable to the influence of both Dean Tucker and Adam Smith. Shelburne had known Smith since 1758, but Josiah Tucker seems to have had more influence on Shelburne when the latter was in the House of Lords in 1762–63. When Shelburne was trying to push the treaty with France through the House of Lords, the dean counseled him against keeping places like Guadeloupe and Martinique because of the expense required to govern and defend them. Both Tucker and Smith convinced Shelburne that the old mercantile system was bad economics, especially in America. Shelburne accepted the argument that colonies were worth no more than the industry and trade they could develop both for themselves and Great Britain. The prosperity of the empire must be promoted to minimize the sacrifices of wealth for administration and defense. Shelburne believed that the old mercantilism could be modified to alleviate American complaints and also to preserve an empire with both political and economic freedom to promote the imperial federation conceived by himself. Because of his hopes for such a federation he never could have agreed with Dean Tucker's arguments for American independence. But both men recognized the need for new adjustments in imperial economics years before the outbreak of the American war.[20]

Shelburne shared Chatham's wartime despair and anxieties over the prospect of American independence. In early 1778 he wrote Chatham that peace with America on the basis of some kind of reconciliation was imperative. He hoped for a federal union in which both peoples would have the same friends, same enemies, one purse and one sword. Two nations with a common constitution, a common language, and mutual interests could surely find some basis for reconciliation. If a union of the two countries was not maintained, Great Britain, not America, would be the greatest loser. "The moment that the independence of America is agreed to by our Government, the sun of Great Britain is set, and we shall no longer be a respectable people."[21] Ironically, Chatham was spared from seeing the loss of America formalized, while Shelburne was the architect of the diplomacy that recognized the United States of America in 1782–83. Underestimating America's desire for separation in 1782, he kept alive his hopes for preserving a commercial union until he was forced to recognize hard reality. He had some consolation in realizing the justice of the Americans' cause and its implications for American liberty. Fearing what the effects of a British military victory in the colonies could have meant for both Englishmen and Americans, he described himself before the House of Lords "as a friend to liberty, as a reverer of the English constitution, as a lover of natural and political justice—he would be much better pleased to see America forever severed from Great Britain, than restored to our possession by force of arms, or conquest."[22]

Shelburne's radicalism became more pronounced because of the American debacle. As a politician he was pragmatic and independent and unafraid to put Radical ideas into practice. Dr. Priestley, though he did not care for life at Bowood, was Shelburne's librarian from 1773 to 1780. He evidently influenced Shelburne's estimation of the imperial situation and domestic affairs. More than any of the other Radicals whom Shelburne knew, Priestley introduced him to men and ideas which anticipated the Victorian "world of utilitarian middle class politics," with its virtues of self-reliance, respect for property, and thrift.[23] It was during these years that Shelburne became one of the country's earliest and best-known supporters of causes that were eventually realized in nineteenth-century Britain— parliamentary reform, Catholic emancipation, repeal of the Test Act, and free trade.

As noted earlier, Shelburne had met Priestley through Dr. Price, whom Priestley had known since 1769. Their friendship became a warm one after Shelburne's support of the Feathers Petition in 1772. More attracted to Price for his humanity and economic expertise than for his antiwar principles, Shelburne drew a great deal of his information on the national debt in wartime from the studies of Dr. Price. Shelburne, as we have seen, was an early convert to the idea of a sinking fund. It also may be remembered that John Horne Tooke consulted with both Price and Shelburne while putting together the explosive *Facts* in 1780, something for which Shelburne never forgave Horne Tooke.[24]

Shelburne also knew James Burgh before the war and was intimately familiar with the *Political Disquisitions*. He was not capable of political activism in a movement espousing universal male suffrage, radical change in the parliamentary system, and other measures advocated by Burgh. But he went far in Burgh's direction, short of political democracy. Shelburne believed himself to have the restraint and discretion to implement many of Burgh's ideas if given a chance in high office. When he read Major Cartwright's *Take Your Choice!* in 1776, he expressed sympathy with Cartwright's cause despite the overwhelming obstacles to parliamentary reform. "It will not be easy to get any number of great men, though favorable in their opinions to such a scheme as yours, to be active and zealous in carrying it into execution; nor have I much hope that any great reformation will take place in this country till some calamity comes that shall make us feel more, and awaken us more, to reflection."[25] It is possible that Shelburne's ministry, had he been as able a politician as he was an innovator, might have secured something in that direction after the war, but like the Reform Bill of 1832, it would have had no dramatic effects. Nevertheless, Shelburne was the most eminent figure in English politics with strong ties to Radical theorists during the American crisis.

While most of the followers of Bedford and George Grenville were "Court Whigs" during the war, the Rockingham Whigs were the largest of the Opposition groups in Parliament. They were not a party in the modern sense. Most of them were peers and M.P.s who were connected with Rockingham by way of common views on singular issues, and such factors as patronage and family relations. It has been estimated that there were about twenty hard-core Rockinghamites. In the spring of 1774 when Parliament debated the Coercion Acts this connection numbered from forty to fifty men. Together with the followers of Chatham and Shelburne, they constituted only about 10 percent of the total membership of Parliament.[26] Most of the Rockinghamites came from the country. Independent, cautious, and usually disinterested in imperial affairs, they were described by Burke as men of "honest, disinterested intentions, plentiful fortunes, assured rank, and quiet homes."[27] Among them were the dukes of Portland, Devonshire, Manchester, and Richmond and the earls of Fitzwilliam and Effingham. In the

House of Commons Rockingham had the support of able figures like William Dowdeswell, David Hartley, George Savile, and, of course, the great Burke and the extraordinary Fox, the latter coming over to the Rockinghamites on the American issue. Their political philosophies ranged from the cautious conservatism of Rockingham to the radicalism of Richmond. Their attitudes toward Radical ideas on the British Empire and parliamentary reform varied. They shared the Radicals' conviction that the eighteenth-century constitution was threatened by the growing influence of the court.[28] Most of the Rockinghams despised Wilkes but were alarmed by the court's manner of reacting to the case. The majority of the Rockinghamites had little interest in the American colonies until the imperial crisis raised serious questions about the influence of the crown and its threat to the political interests of the Newcastle-Rockingham forces. They also feared the economic consequences in England of a bad American policy. Like Chathamites and Radicals, they were convinced that George III's efforts to "be a King" were overt threats to Parliament's independence. The Declaratory Act of 1766 was a Rockinghamite ploy to assert Parliament's authority in both Britain and the colonies.

After passage of the Coercion Acts in 1774, the Rockingham Whigs' position on the American question took on some features that endured through most of the war period. They were adamant in upholding the principle of Parliament's sovereignty in the British Empire while arguing the inexpediency of asserting such an authority in the American case. Most of them favored the preservation of the old imperial system, a position which won them much support from merchants. They sought such long-range objectives as conciliation with America and general peace and prosperity in the empire. They were determined to restore Parliament's independence from the court—that is, the revival of the Whig oligarchy under the eighteenth-century constitution.[29]

The practical implications of their opposition to the government's American policy made both the Rockinghamites and the Chathamites popular among radicals on both sides of the Atlantic. But the Rockinghamite position on the principle of parliamentary sovereignty made it difficult for Chatham and the Radicals to support them on theoretical grounds. As enunciated by Burke, the

Rockingham contention rested on the right of Parliament to legislate on all matters domestic and imperial. Exceptions to the principle, as on the issue of American taxation, were to be made on the bases of expediency and Britain's long-range interests. The Rockinghams took the position that the Americans themselves had not challenged Parliament's authority except when their rights and interests were abused by imprudent court policies. It was, in essence, not a pro-American policy. Most Rockinghamites, as a rule, were not greatly interested in America. They simply wanted peace which would enable England to prosper and benefit from her ties with the colonies.[30]

Lord Rockingham himself was one of the great peers of his time and a representative of the old Newcastle oligarchy. He was distinguished, perhaps, by the support he enjoyed from Burke and Fox, while, at the same time, he had a following composed of those Whigs who opposed the crown. Donoughue comments that Rockingham "has shone in history with the reflected light of other men: the friend of Savile, the patron of Burke, the ally of Fox. . . . He raised his prejudices to the dignity of principles. . . . Defeat in America, not Rockingham's leadership, brought his party back into power in 1782."[31] Yet he was a great conciliator of the cliques and differing opinions among his followers. He had no doubts about Parliament's authority in the empire. But he argued that that authority, in America's case, should be applied with caution and flexibility.[32] Both British and American Radicals, however, criticized him for making the American issue secondary to that of restoring the position of the Whig oligarchy.

As to the radical reform of Parliament, Rockingham's attitude during the association movement of 1779–80 was one which favored measures to restore the old parliamentary politics of Newcastle's day. "The grievances we feel and the cause of our misfortune, arise from the corruption of men when chosen into Parliament. Cut off the ways and means of corruption, and the effect must and will naturally cease."[33] Burke's economical reform proposals at the end of the American war suited Rockingham's purposes. The Radicals' proposals for parliamentary reform would only promulgate greater corruption of politics by the court. "Abstract principles, theoretically right, will furnish matter for disputation in the schools of Utopia, till time is no more. But poor old England may pine away and die for want of medicines, deemed alight ones, and which nevertheless may check for disorder, and may give time for wisdom, sobriety and attention to re-establish her present miserable, broken constitution." [34]

It is very seldom that a political point of view, such as that of the Rockingham Whigs, is so well defined and eloquently presented as was the case in the principles of the "philosopher in action," Edmund Burke. For this reason, a description of the Rockingham Whigs' attitudes toward the Radicals' ideas will be presented through the mind of this great man. Burke's biographer, Sir Philip Magnus, writes, "Burke's political outlook was not shared by all Englishmen, but it was the outlook of the dominant and most characteristic section of the English people. The instinctive political empiricism of the average Englishman . . . bears . . . the impress of the character and personality of Edmund Burke." [35] It is easy to think of Burke as the great philosopher of pragmatic conservatism whose principles were a systematic refutation of radical change and politics. It is important to note that, during the great imperial crisis, he was essentially "a politician and a party man" who tried to gain support for solving the American question through a flexible pragmatism that would bring peace and conciliation. [36] His writings and oratory in Parliament were both prolific and brilliant. The fundamental ideas of Burke and the major distinctions between his position on the imperial question and that of the Radicals may be viewed in his *Thoughts on the Cause of the Present Discontents* (1770), his two famous speeches on conciliation with America in March and November, 1775 and *A Letter to the Sheriffs of Bristol* (1777).

Burke was distinguished from his political associates by sheer genius and his conviction that effective political organization of the Whig Opposition was imperative for any successful engagement of gigantic issues such as the American question.

> Party is a body of men united, for promoting by their joint endeavors the national interest, upon some particular principle, in which they are all agreed. For my part, I find it impossible to conceive, that any one believes in his own politics, or thinks them to be of any weight, who refused to adopt the means of having them reduced into practice. It is the business of the speculative philosopher to mark the

proper ends of Government. It is the business of the politician, who is the philosopher in action, to find out proper means towards those ends, and to employ them with effect.[37]

Oddly enough, this classic statement on political parties could have found considerable support from Radical organizers like Major Cartwright and Christopher Wyvill. Perhaps Burgh and other Radicals, who were beginning to recognize the possibilities of political organization, were more appreciative of what Burke was saying than were the latter's own colleagues in Parliament.

Like the Radicals, Burke had his own notions about the natural rights of man and the British constitution. But he hardly shared their beliefs about the wisdom of popular government or political democracy. "Honesty and justice," the essence of liberty, were best assured through a Whig oligarchy faithful to the principles of 1688. The best govern best. And the best government, argued Burke, was the aristocracy of the politically experienced and prudent, men tempered in the tradition of public responsibility. But in the end the result was to be general prosperity and liberty. "To govern according to the sense and agreeably to the interests of the people is a great and glorious object of government. This object cannot be obtained but through the medium of popular election; and popular election is a mighty evil. . . . They are the distempers of elections, that have destroyed all free states."[38] He rejected Radical ideas about parliamentary reform because he thought that more democracy would only accentuate the crown's ability to manipulate opinion and elections. Such Radical reformism was "the greatest of all evils, a blind and furious spirit of innovation, under the name of reform."[39]

More than any other political figure of the time, Burke eloquently denounced the influence of the court which, along with both Whig politicians and Radicals, he believed to be the cause of domestic and imperial discord.

The power of the Crown, almost dead and rotten as Prerogative, has grown up anew, with much more strength, and far less odium, under the name of Influence. . . . There is . . . a peculiar venom and malignity in this political distemper beyond any that I have ever heard or read of. In former times the projectors of arbitrary government attacked only the liberties of their country; a design surely mischievous enough to have satisfied a mind of the most unruly ambition. . . . But the scheme of the junto under consideration [the King's Friends] not only strikes a palsy into every nerve of our free constitution, but in the same degree benumbs and stupifies [sic] the whole executive power; rendering government in all its grand operatives languid, uncertain, ineffective, making Ministers incapable of attempting, and incapable of executing, any useful plan of domestic arrangement, or of foreign politicks [sic]. It tends to produce neither the security of a free Government, nor the energy of a Monarchy that is absolute.[40]

Like others in the Whig Opposition who lamented the government's American policy, Burke thought the imperial disaster to be a direct result of the blindness, incompetence and obstinacy of a clique surrounding the crown. He thought Charles Jenkinson, who was the secretary at war in 1778–82, to be the chief scoundrel. "I have great reason to suspect that Jenkinson governs everything. . . . To follow Jenkinson, will be to discover my Lord Bute, and my Lord Mansfield, and another person [the King] as considerable as either of them."[41]

Burke was impatient with long, legalistic arguments over Parliament's supremacy under the constitution and in the British Empire. He was an avowed defender of the Revolution Settlement. He had no doubts about Parliament's right to legislate on imperial affairs. Like Rockingham, he clearly upheld the principle of the Declaratory Act. Yet he recognized the complexities of the taxation issue and saw no way out of it but through discreet pragmatism. Theoretically, Parliament might have the right to tax the colonies. In wartime taxation might be imperative. But he scoffed at the abstract arguments over taxes and representation between the government's apologists and pro-American spokesmen. He admonished Parliament, "You are not bound to exercise every right you possess. Your prudence should regulate the exercise of your power."[42] In his famous speech on reconciliation with the colonies on 22 March 1775, Burke told the House of Commons that neither "metaphysical arguments," nor punitive measures against America could bring about what all responsible Englishmen wanted.

The proposition is peace. Not peace through the medium of war; not peace to be hunted through the labyrinth of intricate and endless negotiations; not peace to arise out of universal discord, fomented from principle, in all parts of the empire; not peace to depend on the juridical determination of perplexing questions, or the precise marking the shadowy boundaries of a complex government. It is a simple peace, sought in its natural course and in its ordinary haunts. It is peace sought in the spirit of peace and laid in principles purely pacific. I propose, by moving the ground of the differences and by restoring the *former unsuspecting confidence of* the colonies in the mother country. . . .[43]

Preservation of the British Empire and the mercantile laws, yes. But the use of coercion was as impractical as it would be disastrous. The discreet balance between parliamentary authority and colonial liberty must be maintained with practicality and magnanimity. The British government should be satisfied with the regulatory advantages to be had in trade, not in burdensome taxes that animate colonial resentment.

Burke looked upon the British Empire as an "aggregate of many states under one common head." A thin, delicate line existed between the liberty of the parts and the governing body of the whole. Common sense and statesmanship were required to sustain a harmonious relationship between the two. As for the case of America, Burke concluded that the colonists were in a predicament not unlike that of Englishmen in 1688.

Whoever goes about to reason on any part of the policy of this country with regard to America upon the more abstract principles of government, or even upon those of our ancient constitution, will be often misled. . . . This commerce must be secured by a multitude of restraints very alien from the spirit of liberty; and a powerful authority must reside in the principal state in order to enforce them. But the people who are to be the subjects of those restraints are Englishmen, and of a high and free spirit. To hold over them a government made up of nothing but restraints and penalties, and taxes in the granting of which they can have no share, will neither be wise nor long practicable. People must be governed in a manner agreeable to their temper and disposition; and men of free character and spirit must be ruled with, at least, some condescension to this spirit and this character. The British colonist must see something which will distinguish him from the colonists of other nations.[44]

It was both foolish and inexpedient for Parliament or the court to cry "revolt" or "treason" when some of the colonists asserted themselves against the will of the mother country. It is inevitable that liberty precipitate diversity and conflicting opinions. Only prudence and magnanimity can prevent irreconcilable differences. England, argued Burke, could not expect affection and loyalty from colonists burdened with laws and restraints to serve the selfish interests of one part of the British Empire at the expense of the other parts.[45]

Burke's patience with the Americans during the tense months of 1774–75 did not extend to the also temperamental Dean Tucker. The latter's publication of *The True Interest of Britain* provoked a verbal feud between the two that led to some angry public exchanges. Differences of opinion over the Americans prompted Burke's remarks in the House of Commons on 19 April 1774 to the effect that the dean was seeking the favor of the North ministry in hopes of securing a bishopric. Tucker angrily denied the charge and retorted that Burke and his friends in the House were encouraging the outrageous behavior of the colonists in Massachusetts Bay. When a friend encouraged Burke to make amends with the indefatigable divine of Gloucester in March, 1775, Burke replied, "If the Dean of Gloster [*sic*] becomes my friend it will shine in my history. But we must keep our wicked jests to ourselves."[46] A few days later on March 22 when he presented to the Commons his famous "Speech on Moving the Resolutions for Conciliation with the Colonies," Burke included a jibe at Tucker's proposal for American independence. "It is nothing but a little sally of anger, like the frowardness of parish children, who, when they cannot get all they would have, are resolved to take nothing."[47] Dean Tucker promptly responded to Burke's speech by taking him to task for casting the American upstarts as oppressed martyrs of British injustice. He scoffed at the Whig spokesman's defense of the Bostonians' conduct in the name of a "fierce spirit of liberty." In *A Letter to Edmund Burke* the dean argued that the "oppressed" Americans had shown their hypocrisy with their charges of British "oppression." Colonial intolerance toward people in their own midst, he alleged, long had been a notorious fact. New England Puritanism possessed a legacy of intolerance. The "manners" of southern gentility were betrayed by allowance of slavery. Rather than standing as pillars of British liberty, the colonial legislatures were filled with men who "are either lawyers, or smatterers in law" excelling in chicanery on such things as debts to English creditors, taxation, smuggling or Parliament's authority. All of which was more reason to get rid of the Americans.[48] Throughout the period of 1774–76, however, Burke scoffed at the dean's arguments, insisting that common sense and cool heads in England and America could bring about some sort of settlement that required no resort to extremities. When both sides began the exchange of blows, he maintained that the Americans were left with no choice but to hold their ground until British leaders saw the light of reason.

When America declared its independence, Burke stuck to his old arguments. But he refused to be swayed into ideological enthusiasms encouraged by Radical publications such as Dr. Price's *Observations on the Nature of Civil Liberty*, as he made evident in his *A Letter to the Sheriffs of Bristol*. Burke defended his decision to follow Rockingham out of Parliament until the government changed its American policy. The Americans were good Englishmen, he insisted, and were fighting for their self-respect and the only kind of freedom that Englishmen could live in—that liberty which is "the vital spring and energy of the state itself."[49] But he did not carry his reasoning to the philosophical conclusions of Dr. Price. Burke refused to deal in abstractions on liberty and would not endorse the concept of popular sovereignty. Like other Rockingham Whigs, he believed in government by virtuous aristocracy for the general good.

Burke, like most of the Rockingham Whigs, was prepared to accept a peace on the basis of American independence after Saratoga and the French intervention—a position much opposed by Chatham and Shelburne. For his part, Burke hoped that some kind of tie with America under Parliament might be salvaged even after 1778. Unlike Shelburne, however, he did not think it a likely prospect. When the government's position steadily deteriorated in 1779–80 and Rockingham's vacillation prevented the rise of an effective Whig Opposition, he, along with Fox, took the lead in the House of Commons in urging a change of government and peace with America. When the county association movement gained momentum, he was among the conservative Whigs who backed "economical reform" but opposed the ambitious program of Wyvill.

The reaction to the Yorkshire Movement in 1780–81 spelled out Burke's position toward Radicals who wanted to change a political structure embarrassed by humiliation in America. When Shelburne submitted a motion in the House of Lords to shorten parliaments in 1780, Burke said, "This Bill, I fear, would precipitate one of two consequences. I know not which most likely, or which most dangerous; either that the crown by its constant state power, influence and revenue, would wear out all opposition in elections, or that a violent and furious popular spirit would arise. I must see, to satisfy men, the remedies; I must see, from their operation in the cure of the old evil, and on the one of those old evils, which are inseparable from all remedies, how they balance each other, and what is the total result."[50] He did not think that parliamentary reform, at least the kind urged by the Radicals or Lord Shelburne, would end current political corruption or bring government that would be much better than the system such reformers were criticizing. He agreed with the association men that the present evils of war, court influence, and fiscal scandal necessitated political action. But he rejected their radicalism, thinking their petitioning tactics to be both wrong and futile. While the associations were barraging Parliament with petitions, Burke was working on his Civil Establishment Bill. If these groups could assist Whig efforts to bring down the North ministry, he would have considered their existence worthwhile. But effective, desirable reform must be the business of able, responsible politicians, who would cure the body politic without using a remedy worse than the illness. While Fox received the plaudits of Radicals for his position on the war and reform in 1780–81, Burke earned their contempt. He, at least, had some satisfaction in getting his Civil Establishment Bill through Parliament in 1782 after the county associations had disintegrated into impotence. "I cannot indeed take upon me to say I have the honour to follow the sense of the people. The truth is, I met it on the way while I was pursuing their interest according to my own ideas."[51]

Neither by temperament nor reason, then, could Burke accept the ideas of people like Burgh, Price, or Macaulay. Radicalism was too prone to abstract nonsense and naïve notions about human nature. To place a nation and its institutions at the disposal of theories and popular whim was dangerous to the very liberty Radicals espoused. He dismissed Catharine Macaulay as a "republican virago."[52] To Burke the utopian ideas of Radicalism offered no more acceptable solutions to the intricacies of British domestic troubles than they did with the hard realities of the American question.

This sentiment of a philosopher thinking about the nature of man was also the attitude of an experienced politician who knew that statutes by themselves did not guarantee social harmony or political virtue. Burke condemned the rationalism out of which grew eighteenth-century radical optimism. Speaking as a conservative, from observations of government at work rather than as an a priori political metaphysician, Burke wrote, "Indeed, all that wise men even aim at is to keep things from coming to the worst. Those who expect perfect reformations, either deceive or are deceived miserably."[53]

Charles James Fox emerged as the most ebullient pro-American apologist among the Rockingham Whigs during the war. He became a hero to Radicals who read his speeches in the House of Commons. In 1777 Burke described Fox as "one of the pleasantest men in the world as well as the greatest genius this country has ever produced."[54] Good-natured and open-minded, he charmed men in and out of Parliament. "Without possessing Burke's intellectual distinction, he was a much greater parliamentarian: vigorous, persevering, and with a clear and lucid mind, which could simplify and resolve complex problems; excelling alike in set speeches or in debate; and able to win both personal affection and political loyalty."[55] Equally well known, however, were his extravagance, dissolute habits, and political opportunism which were to bring to him many frustrations—as well as to many people who placed their hopes in him.

Fox's career shows him to have been a man of striking paradoxes.[56] He spoke in behalf of Colonel Luttrell against Wilkes in his first great speech on the floor of Commons in 1769. He accepted a post as an admiralty lord in the North ministry in 1770. He spoke against the Feathers Petition in 1772. When the American crisis worsened in 1773–74, however, he joined the Rockinghams in their position on the imperial question.

During the war he remained in the House of Commons when Burke and other Rockinghamites stayed away. His pro-American oratory was magnificent, and his position on the imperial crisis remained consistent throughout the conflict. Radicals were pleased with his arguments that the government's conduct threatened both British and American liberty. "I rejoice that America has resisted. Three millions of people so dead to all the feelings of liberty, as voluntarily to submit to be slaves, would have been fit instruments

to make slaves of the rest."[57] When America declared its independence, Fox was one of the first men in the House of Commons to
urge its recognition by the British government or some kind of conciliation that would produce the same effect. After the Battle of
Saratoga, he joined Burke in the House of Commons with appeals
for peace negotiations while Rockingham remained at home in
Yorkshire. Whereas Burke's arguments made him unpopular with
the Radicals, Fox's polemics won their admiration. Fox had not
committed himself to irretrievable positions on the abstract points
of the taxation and representation questions. He had not isolated
himself from his parliamentary associates as Chatham had. In 1778
he urged withdrawal from America and going at the throat of
France. He succeeded Chatham and Wilkes in the skills of "high-
class rabblerousing" as the country turned against continuation of
the war in 1779–80.[58] Fox fully supported the Yorkshire Petition
in 1780 and spoke in favor of parliamentary reform. He became a
warm friend of Radicals ranging from Wilkes to Dr. John Jebb.
Many Radicals, including Major Cartwright and Wyvill, placed
great hopes in his contributions to the cause of Radical reformism
in the waning months of the war. But ambition prevailed over principle in 1783 when Fox stunned his followers by forming a coalition government with Lord North. Radical hopes in Fox were
dashed.

In all justice to Fox, he was sincere in his good intentions toward Radicals and their various causes. Given the appropriate circumstances, he probably would have tried to satisfy many of their
reform appeals. Yet he was essentially a political maverick who
could not follow any party or cause unless its members were
prepared to be led by him. His attitudes on the great imperial and
domestic questions enabled him to win the confidence of many Radicals. But parliamentary politics offered too many temptations to
the ambitious Fox. His ties with the Radicals ebbed and flowed, just
as they did with politicians in office.[59]

The deaths of Chatham and Rockingham left Shelburne in a
position to become the architect of British peace negotiations in
1782. He earnestly probed for agreements that would produce a
federal union of Great Britain and America based on the "principle
of equal and honest reciprocity." Along with his chancellor of the
exchequer, Pitt the Younger, he fought for his American Intercourse

Bill which would revive the old Anglo-American trade and build a mutual interdependence of the two nations politically, economically, and strategically.[60] His scheme was generous and imaginative. When the Americans refused to negotiate until Britain recognized their independence, Shelburne gave in. He still tried to get some sort of commercial accord, to drive a wedge between the American and French diplomats in Paris, and to rebuild British naval primacy. His long-range objective was an Anglo-American harmony that might be the basis for some kind of union in the future. His goals doubtlessly appealed to Radicals like Dr. Price who were interested in such matters. But Shelburne was undone by his weak political position in 1783. His policies were blasted by the Fox-North coalition.

Peace with America was followed by an economic nationalism in Parliament unopposed even by Fox. A commercial policy as displeasing to Americans as before the war was successfully pushed by Lord Sheffield, William Eden, Lord North, and the crown. In effect, this meant a continuation of the old mercantile policy toward what remained of the British Empire in the West and toward foreign countries.[61] British Radicals who were pleased with America's success were dismayed by the policy of their own government once again. Their American friends were not surprised. Before and during the war, American radicals thought British political leadership to be obstinate and narrow. Many of them even were skeptical about men like Chatham and Rockingham in the Whig Opposition, suspecting that they used the American question to further their own political designs.[62]

With the exceptions of Chatham and Shelburne and the more radical-minded figures among the Rockinghams—Richmond, Abingdon, and Sir George Savile—the political Whigs stood on a forum quite distinct from that of the Radicals, who wanted fuller realization of the ideological implications of the Revolution of 1688 by extending a political voice to a larger number of Britons. If the Rockingham oligarchs wanted to free Parliament from the influence of the crown, the Radicals wanted to free Parliament from oligarchy. Burke and most Whig politicians had little faith in the Radical idea that better and more responsible government would come from a democratization of Parliament and the electoral system. Radicals had greater faith in human nature and thought that an expansion of the electorate would bring more virtuous government. While Burke's Civil Establishment Bill was designed to revive Parliament's independence from the court, the reformism of Major Cartwright and Wyvill was directed toward making Parliament more accountable to the British public. Therein lay Radical hopes for greater social justice, opportunity, education, and tolerance.

As for the American question, most of the Whig politicians thought of the American situation in the light of the English political situation. Solutions to the American problem were to be worked out on clearly expedient grounds with no more ambition than to preserve the old imperial system. Abstract qualms over liberty appealed to only a few of them. The American Revolution was an unnecessary disaster that confirmed their belief that the crown had gone too far and that it was time to reassert the hard-won position of Parliament under the Whig oligarchy. They had the consolation of the crown's humiliation in 1782–83. British diplomacy toward America after the war was evidence of their lack of enthusiasm for the ideological principles upon which the Republic was founded. Indeed, many Whigs who had opposed the war were among the most spiteful politicians who opposed Shelburne's generosity toward the Americans.

The Radicals, on the other hand, were jubilant over the American victory for reasons both ideological and political. If their reform endeavors in England failed, the birth of the American Republic promised to be an inspiration to their own causes in the future. Unfortunately for Cartwright's efforts for parliamentary reform in the years after 1783, most Englishmen were content with old ways and not yet prepared for supporting radical breaks from the past. Such complacency was disillusioning to Radicals who were moved by desires to improve the lot of the very people who gave them little attention. The repressions of the French revolutionary years were a severe blow to the Radicalism of Burgh, Price, Cartwright, and the others. In time, the Industrial Revolution brought another chapter in radical reformism.

ELEVEN

~~~~~~

British-American Radical Connections

THE American radicals whose decisions and actions set the stage for independence were aware of the sympathy given their cause by the British Radicals. Though the British Radicals' American audience was largely confined to the remarkable group of patriot leaders like John Adams and Thomas Jefferson, the ideas of Englishmen such as Burgh and Price were an encouragement, even inspiration, to the Founding Fathers of the Republic. American leaders in the Congress and the colonial assemblies appear to have overestimated the influence of the Radicals in England on the eve of the war, however. But the American patriots' principles—similar to those of their British Radical friends—enjoyed considerable support in the colonies and this was critical in the eventual success of the American Revolution. It is clear that the ideas of British Radicals as described in the preceding chapters had a much greater short-range influence in America than in England. But it is impossible to measure the extent of British Radical influence among the general populations of the colonies at the outset of the war. Still, the ties between these English friends of America and the leaders of the Revolution are so visible to posterity that it is possible to reach some conclusions about the British-American radical connection. How much, for example, did these Englishmen contribute to the American radical frame of mind that came to defy the might of the British Empire?

It is evident that Burgh's *Political Disquisitions* made a strong impression on American patriots. Burgh sent copies of his volumes to his old friend Dr. Franklin and also to John Dickinson and John Adams. The Philadelphia printer Robert Bell published the *Political*

Disquisitions in 1775, about sixteen months after the initial appearance of the first volume in London. Many members of the Continental Congress subscribed to the Bell editions in 1775–76, including Thomas Jefferson, James Wilson, Christopher Gadsden, Roger Sherman, Benjamin Rush, John Hancock, Robert Morris, and Silas Dean.[1] All five Americans connected with the drafting of the Declaration of Independence were familiar with Burgh's volumes. General Washington, one of the first subscribers to the Bell editions, probably read them shortly after taking command of the Continental Army. They came to be part of his library at Mount Vernon.

Burgh's views on English political life were shared by Benjamin Franklin, his longtime friend from the coffeehouse gatherings in London. He obtained much of his information on America from Franklin. Franklin once told Burgh that less corruption and more economy in the British government would reduce the mother country's need of American revenues, that many colonists' anger over the tax laws was rooted in their awareness of the ignoble uses being made of their money. When writing to Dr. Price after the Revolutionary War, Franklin expressed his satisfaction that many Englishmen finally had come to recognize the need of economical reforms in their government, something understood by Burgh and Price himself before the war.[2] Franklin respected Burgh and his ideas. Because Franklin himself was one of the most venerated men in the Continental Congress, it is likely that his endorsement of the *Political Disquisitions* made Burgh's ideas attractive to American radicals who welcomed criticism of their adversaries in England.

John Adams read Burgh's first two volumes while writing his own *Novanglus* in late 1774. Burgh was one of his favorite writers on English affairs.[3] In a letter to Burgh, dated 28 December 1774, Adams expressed hope that the *Political Disquisitions* might have some effect on the politicians in London. "We now see plainly, that every trick and artifice of sharpers, gamblers, and horse-jockies, is to be played off against the cause of liberty in England and America; and that no hopes are to be left for either but in the sword. . . . I cannot but think those *Disquisitions* are the best service that a citizen could render to his country at this great and dangerous crisis."[4] Writing as a revolutionary in the winter of

1774–75, Adams thought that Burgh's books should be read by every literate American. Thus Burgh's ideas received the plaudits of a man who was one of the great British imperial statesmen of the prerevolutionary decade and who, by 1775, was one of the most influential colonists to have lost faith in the old imperial system.[5]

Jefferson knew the *Political Disquisitions* "intimately." He and Burgh agreed on many of the moral and political issues which came out of the colonists' quarrel with the mother country. There is a good deal of Burgh in Jeffersonian political thought. Jefferson shared Burgh's dim view of the English aristocracy. Even the ancient centers of English learning at Oxford and Cambridge were, in Jefferson's words, mere "seminaries of vice."[6] Neither of the two men liked great cities. They shared romantic notions about the simplicities and virtues of agrarian democracy. Some of the great principles of Jefferson's party in the 1790s were echoes of ideas written into the *Political Disquisitions*. When writing to Thomas Mann Randolph in 1790, the author of the Declaration of Independence urged the young law student to include the *Political Disquisitions* on his reading list.[7]

As with the ideas of other British Radicals, it is impossible to measure with any accuracy the influence which Burgh may have had on colonial opinion outside the circles of American Radical leadership. Burgh's views about civic virtue, representative government, and the abuse of political authority possibly contributed, some have argued, to the development of "the American mind."[8] The *Political Disquisitions*' moral intonation and invective against British leaders likely pleased colonial readers. Colonists would have been flattered to read an Englishman's appraisal of Americans as being more virtuous than their fellow subjects in England. Burgh's volumes could have catered to their prejudices against Old World authority and corruption. Such newspapers as the *Pennsylvania Packet*, *Maryland Journal*, and *Baltimore Advertiser* recommended the *Political Disquisitions* to the colonial reading public. The books, however, were a bit expensive by contemporary standards. It is doubtful that they were purchased by many people outside the well-to-do segments of colonial society. The Handlins claim that the volumes had a "wide-spread influence upon the revolutionary generation—not only the leaders, but even the common fold. . . .

[Their] phrases were familiar in the town meetings of western Massachusetts. . . ."⁹ Such a conclusion presumes a great deal about the reading habits of the colonial American. Yet it might have been possible for sizable audiences to have heard Burgh's ideas expounded from a few colonial pulpits or in the tirades of agitators.

American editions of John Cartwright's *American Independence the Interest and Glory of Great Britain* appeared in Philadelphia and New York in 1775–76. Very few historical materials exist to tell us what even American radical leaders thought about it. Under the circumstances of the time, however, it is likely that they dismissed the proposal of an Anglo-American confederation as impractical, visionary, and beyond the comprehension of contemporary British leadership. Be that as it may, there were men in the Second Continental Congress who were familiar with the imaginative proposals of this obscure English naval lieutenant, and the pamphlet's tone may have made some contribution to American leaders' own ideas about settling the imperial quandary. Long afterward, in June 1817, John Quincy Adams wrote to the then elderly and well-known agitator for parliamentary reform to thank him for a copy of his 1774 pamphlet. Perhaps Adams was being generous to the old reformer, perhaps he accurately understood his father's recognition that the Revolution was not something inevitable—nevertheless, he complimented the seventy-seven-year-old Major Cartwright by acknowledging him as "the rare, I had almost said the only, example of an Englishman who understood and openly stated the real merits of that great question, upon which the continual union, or the severance of Great Britain and her colonies depended, but from which all, or the infinitely greater part of the nation shrank, or averted their eyes. Had the principles of that paper been those of the British government and people, they and the North Americans should yet have been one nation."¹⁰

Granville Sharp's *The People's Natural Right to a Share in the Legislature* appeared both in Ireland and America in 1775–76. Anthony Benezet, the Quaker antislavery reformer of Philadelphia, was responsible for the edition which appeared in Philadelphia. Dr. Franklin had known Sharp since 1773 and doubtlessly encouraged members of the Congress to look at the pamphlet.¹¹ Like Cartwright, Sharp's defense of America provided encouragement and welcome propaganda to American radicals. The stress which both Cartwright and Sharp put on annual parliaments and equal representation, curiously enough, came to be realized in America in 1776 when the new state constitutions stipulated that officeholders must be residents of their districts.[12]

Evidence that Catharine Macaulay's *History of England* was popular among American revolutionaries was shown by its presence in the libraries of colonial homes, societies, and universities from Boston to Charleston. Each volume which appeared between 1763 and 1771 was widely advertised in American publications. The volumes were popular among students at Harvard, Yale, and Rhode Island colleges.[13] Several American leaders commented about their value and expressed their compliments to the author by personal correspondence.

Dr. Franklin, who knew Catharine Macaulay during his years in London, read her first two volumes by 1765. In a letter to a City newspaper on 20 May 1765, he expressed his distress at the ignorance of American affairs shown by the editors of London's newspapers. He advised them to pay more attention to "that honest set of writers" in England, including Mrs. Macaulay, whose knowledge of America enjoyed the admiration of "us coffee-house students in history and politics."[14] Like many men who came to form American radical leadership in the Revolution, Franklin ranked "the historian in petticoats" with the Livys, Rabins, Robertsons, and Humes.

Thomas Hollis, Mrs. Macaulay's good friend, sent a copy of the second volume to Reverend Mayhew in Boston in 1765. After reading it, Mayhew wrote Hollis, "It appears to me to be a very just and excellent history of those wretched times; written with a spirit of liberty, which might shame many great men (so-called) in these days of degeneracy, and ty-r-anny [*sic*] and oppression."[15] He evidently spoke for many of Mrs. Macaulay's New England readers. In 1770 John Adams expressed his delight with the *History* in a letter to the author. "It is calculated to strip off the gilding and false lustre from worthless princes and nobles, and to bestow the reward of virtue, praise, upon the generous and worthy only. No charms of eloquence can atone for the want of this exact historical morality; and I must be allowed to say, I have never seen a history in which it is more religiously regarded."[16]

Catharine Macaulay was one of Thomas Jefferson's favorite

historians.[17] Especially interested in Stuart history, he expressed the opinion current among Virginia's gentry that the *History of England* accurately presented the Stuart era as a "critical period" which had been succeeded by "unrealized hopes" raised by the Glorious Revolution.

When she called upon the peoples of the British Isles to join hands in popular opposition to the British government's American policy in 1775, the celebrated Mrs. Macaulay doubtlessly was the most popular Englishwoman in the colonies. The first American edition of her *Address to the People of England, Scotland and Ireland on the Present Crisis of Affairs* appeared in New York after hostilities had begun in Massachusetts Bay. The pamphlet was read by most American radicals, including members of the Continental Congress. In November 1775, Richard Henry Lee sent her a letter of gratitude and expressed hopes that her appeal to public opinion in Great Britain might make her countrymen more conciliatory to the American cause. Lee gave her a detailed description of the recent engagements near Boston. He also advised her that the current American invasion of Canada had good prospects for success and that her anxieties over the Quebec Act might be relieved.[18] General Washington also had read the *Address* sometime in 1775 and was "most impressed" by it. It is likely that many American leaders in the Congress entertained hopes that such a pamphlet as Mrs. Macaulay's might have some effect on English public opinion. Their awareness of Radical criticisms of the government in the City of London, the activities and propaganda of the Radical societies and a potential public displeasure with the prospect of an expensive British military campaign may have given them reason to think that persons like Mrs. Macaulay might be instrumental in swaying many Englishmen against an American conflict when they saw that the costs of war would give diminishing returns to the mother country. Such an assumption proved wrong in 1775–76. But, as Mrs. Macaulay herself correctly understood, public opinion in Britain did count for something, as was borne out by public pressure against the war after 1778.

Richard Price's timely *Observations on the Nature of Civil Liberty* was published in America and in several European countries in 1776, when the colonial assemblies and Congress were making their critical decisions for independence. Its American reception was obviously enthusiastic. Price's words were an eloquent moral encouragement to American leaders who recognized that His Majesty's government had already condemned them as rebels and traitors. Jefferson read the pamphlet during or shortly after his writing of the Declaration of Independence. He was sending copies of the *Observations* to his friends during the summer of 1776.[19] Most of the men of Independence Hall either read it or were familiar with its contents. One of Jefferson's friends who received a copy wrote that it had "clear and explicit reasoning" and that it should benefit the American cause by alleviating the scruples and doubts of some colonials over the wisdom of their risky adventure.[20]

The welcome reception which British Radical writings enjoyed among American radicals in 1774–76 indicates that the two groups had a strong connection. The tie was strengthened by personal friendships, frequent correspondence, the exchange of ideas, and a mutual readiness to circulate each other's propaganda. Underlying such a bond was a common ideology traceable to the English liberal Whig past, which was borne out by their general agreement on the nature of the British constitution, the existence of a court conspiracy which menaced British liberty, and a mutual recognition that the English political structure needed to be reformed.

Prominent Americans who were among the leadership of the American Revolution gravitated to the society of British Radicals on their visits to England during and after the war. This is especially demonstrated by Benjamin Franklin's long residence in England. He was the strongest personal tie between British Radicals and their American counterparts. The preceding pages indicate that he was on more intimate terms with the leading figures of British Radicalism than any other American of his time. As an agent for Pennsylvania, Franklin lived in London during sixteen of the eighteen years before the war. He moved through the circles of British officialdom and London society and was the best-known American in England. British officials who cared little for America found him irritating and boring. But he delighted the men of Saint Paul's Coffeehouse. His friendships with the Honest Whigs gave cause for his later recollection of this period as the happiest time of his life. Over a period of many years he and Dr. Price regularly attended the fortnightly meetings of Honest Whigs on Thursday evenings at Saint Paul's Coffeehouse and, after March 1772, at the London Coffeehouse on Ludgate Hill.

Dr. Franklin also was a frequent visitor in the homes of Honest Whigs. He was very close to the Prices and often attended Dr. Price's services. He visited Theophilus Lindsey's chapel on Essex Street in 1774. Bishop Shipley and Shelburne were the two most prominent Englishmen with whom Franklin was on cordial terms. He made numerous visits to Shipley's home at Twyford, where he enjoyed the company of the bishop's family. In 1771 he visited Dr. Priestley in Leeds while journeying through Yorkshire. This extraordinary man was a well-traveled and knowledgeable American whose years in England made him invaluable to American leaders who sought to be well informed in English affairs. Many of the acquaintances between British and American radicals originated through Dr. Franklin.

It is curious that British Radicals like James Burgh were ahead of Franklin in doubting the British government's ability to resolve the American question. Even when James Otis and Daniel Dulany were challenging the extent of Parliament's authority in the colonies, Franklin's own views marked no radical departure from traditional constitutional notions about the relationship between the mother country and America. During the crises of 1765–66 and 1767–70 he remained optimistic enough to think that conciliation was possible.[21] Not until Parliament passed the Coercion Acts in 1774 did he seriously question continuation of the old imperial ties. After this he became more American than British in his thinking about the British Empire. His growing conviction in 1774–75 that the British government was incapable of resolving its differences with the colonies on grounds satisfactory to America doubtlessly was strengthened by the advice of his friends in British Radical circles. When Franklin left England for Philadelphia in early 1775 his departure was personally distressing to his old friends. Dr. Price wrote Josiah Quincy, Jr., "I have lost by his departure a friend that I greatly loved and valued. He talked of coming back in the beginning of next winter; but I do not much expect to see him again."[22]

Franklin kept in touch with his English friends despite the war. From both Philadelphia and Paris he corresponded with Dr. Price, something for which the latter could have easily gotten into trouble.

Franklin's friendships with many of these Englishmen were important channels through which American leaders got their information on British Radical opinion. It is probable that men in the Congress who much respected Franklin were prone to overestimate the influence of Radicals in England and to view British affairs through the minds of people like Price and Mrs. Macaulay.

Dr. Benjamin Rush, another Philadelphian and a member of the Congress in 1775–76, also had social and political ties with the Honest Whigs. He completed his medical studies at the University of Edinburgh in 1768 and then came down to London for additional training at Saint Thomas's Hospital in 1768–69. He seems to have been acquainted with republican politics while at Edinburgh and he easily moved into Honest Whig company through Dr. Franklin's introductions. It is not known whether he met Granville Sharp, who was in the midst of the Jonathan Strong case. Rush's own humanitarian projects, including his antislavery work, in later years were similar to those of Sharp in England.

Josiah Quincy, Jr., one of the Boston Quincys and a rising star among Boston patriots on the eve of the Revolution, came over to London during the autumn of 1774 to plead his city's case before Lord North and Lord Dartmouth in hopes of getting the Coercion Acts suspended. His stay in London during the winter gave occasion for his meeting numerous English Radicals about whom he had heard. Franklin brought him into the company of the coffeehouse Whigs. Quincy went down to Bath to visit Catharine Macaulay. He visited the home of Burgh shortly before his departure for America in the spring of 1775. He seems to have been especially befriended by Dr. Price. Quincy failed to achieve his mission to the British government, and the London climate possibly aggravated a severe case of tuberculosis which took his life before he could reach home.

The Lee brothers, Arthur and William, of Westmoreland County, Virginia both had extraordinary careers in another branch of English Radicalism, City politics, during the years before the Revolution. Like many of colonial Virginia's sons, Arthur Lee had been sent to England for his education. He attended Eton and the University of Edinburgh during the 1760s. He was caught up in the frenzy of the Wilkes affair while studying law at Lincoln's Inn and the Middle Temple. When he began his law practice in the City he became an outspoken apologist both for Wilkes and for American complaints with the government. As noted earlier, he was mainly responsible for getting a pro-American clause into the Middlesex Petition in 1769. During the early 1770s he wrote a number of Wilkesite attacks on the North government under the name of Junius Americanus. In 1770 Massachusetts Bay's House of Representatives appointed the Virginian as that colony's agent in England. Lee's activities in English Radicalism reached a climax during the heat of the Boston crisis in 1774 when he wrote a scathing attack on the government in *An Appeal to the Justice and Interests of the People of Great Britain*. He wrote a sequel the following year with his *Second Appeal*. Like many Wilkesites, Arthur Lee was a firebrand in his criticisms of the British government. When war began in America he left England and served the American cause as an agent in France by encouraging French intervention.

William Lee came to London in 1768 and entered into a business partnership with Stephen Sayre, another American, and one Dennys de Berdts. He followed his brother into City politics and soon earned his own reputation as a Wilkesite. He became an associate of Sawbridge, Townsend, and other City Radicals who were then rising to positions of influence. Both William Lee and Stephen Sayre were elected as sheriffs of the City in 1773. In 1775 William Lee became the only American ever to be elected as a City alderman. When the American Revolution started, he joined his brother as an American agent in France.

Friendships between British and American radicals after the war were no less warm and cordial than before. The former respected their American friends even more. For men like Franklin, Washington, and Adams had become great statesmen who had created a republic and were dealing directly with the great powers of Europe. At the same time, figures like John Adams and Thomas Jefferson who came to England after the war could always expect their warmest welcomes from Dr. Franklin's old friends.

When John Adams came over from France in 1785 to the court of Saint James he soon came to know Bishop Shipley, Thomas Brand Hollis, Granville Sharp, Dr. Priestley, and other Radicals. Both he and Mrs. Adams came to love Dr. Price. They regularly attended Price's chapel services in Hackney and had their grandson, William, christened by him.[23] Jefferson arrived in London from the court of France in 1786 to assist Adams in his frustrating negotiations with the British government and was introduced to English Radicals who already admired him as one of the American Revolution's legendary figures. Jefferson dined with the Prices at least twice.[24] There is no evidence that he met Major Cartwright, though they later corresponded. Jefferson subscribed to the unhistoric notion of Cartwright and his friends in the Society for Constitutional Information that British liberty was traceable to the ancient liberties of the early medieval Anglo-Saxon race.[25]

Only one of the figures described in the earlier chapters ever visited America after the war. This was the indefatigable Catharine Macaulay. She had married William Graham in 1778 and, along with her pro-American sympathies, had given most of her friends cause to ostracize her. She finished her final three volumes of the *History of England* in Binfield by 1783. She considered the American victory something of a personal triumph. Her enthusiasm for the Republic's success made her eager to visit America and meet its heroic founders. In late 1784 the *Annual Register* and *Gentleman's Magazine* announced to the English public that Mrs. Graham and her husband had departed the country, the latter offering a quip that her chief mission was to frame a new code of law for the Americans.

The lady historian arrived in Boston in late 1784, finding herself to be as well known in America as in England and certainly more popular. The Grahams spent the winter in Boston, where they were received by their warmest American friend, Mercy Warren, the "first lady of the American Revolution." Their meeting was the climax of a friendship that started with their correspondence in about 1763. Mrs. Macaulay had a greater influence on the American patriot than any other woman of her time.[26] The "first lady of the American Revolution" and the first lady of British Radicalism had much in common. Both were outspoken feminists, well read in history and well educated in contemporary politics, and both had brothers who were prominent in radical politics, James Otis and John Sawbridge.[27] Mrs. Warren claimed that she was even more impressed by her English friend than during their correspondence over the past twenty years. The Grahams spent part of the winter of 1784–85 at the Warrens' home, Milton House, outside Boston. Mercy Warren was one of the few people who, at least in public, defended the Grahams' marriage, most likely because of her long friendship with the lady historian and apologist for American liberty.[28] She confessed to her Boston friends that Mrs. Graham was talkative and opinionated but that her faults were offset by her being "a lady of the most extraordinary talent, a commanding genius, and brilliance of thought."[29]

After meeting the leading citizens of Boston, the Grahams traveled south in the spring of 1785. They stopped in New York, where they met Richard Henry Lee and numerous other celebrities of American liberty. Lee arranged for the Grahams to be received at Mount Vernon, where Mrs. Graham was delighted to meet her favorite hero of the Revolution. The Grahams were the guests of General Washington and his wife for ten days in June 1785. Washington evidently was pleased to be the subject of his guests' admiration. He was impressed by Mrs. Graham's erudition and her enthusiasm for the future of the Republic.[30] He showed her his library and the private papers he had accumulated during the war. Mrs. Graham probably considered the visit to Mount Vernon to have been the high point of her American travels. She frequently wrote to Washington until her death in 1791 and her letters were reciprocated by the first president of the United States. She saw the stately Washington as one who personified the classical heroes about whom she had read since her youth.

Colonial leaders' knowledge of British Radical publications and personal friendships with such Englishmen have shown that there was much correspondence between the two groups before, during, and after the Revolutionary War. In some cases such writing began when these Englishmen and Americans came to know each other by reputation and sent copies of their publications to one another, such as Burgh sending a copy of his *Political Disquisitions* to John Dickinson. The traditional ties which the Hollis family had with New England families and his own donation of books to colonial libraries made Thomas Hollis one of the best-known English Radicals in America until his death in 1774. The correspondence between Hollis and the Reverend Mayhew of Boston during the 1760s was considerable and provides some interesting insight into the way British and American radicals viewed the colonial crises of those years.[31] Dr. Price had many American friends whom he knew only through occasional correspondence, including such distinguished colonists as the Reverend Charles Chauncy of Boston's First Church, Professor John Winthrop of Harvard, Ezra Stiles, the president of Yale College, and others.[32] As described above, Catharine Macaulay and Mercy Warren corresponded over a period of twenty years before they met in late 1784.

The letters exchanged between all these people provide tangible evidence on several features of the British and American radical connection. On the one hand, information exchanged between the two groups enabled them to have invaluable and ofttimes accurate information about the situations on each side of the Atlantic—Radicals like Dr. Price were among the most knowledgeable Englishmen of the time on American affairs. On the other hand, both groups were prone to arrive at conclusions from such correspondence which did not accurately represent the broad spectrum of opinion in their respective countries. British Radicals seem to have overestimated the support which American revolutionaries had even during the war without fully appreciating the fact that many colonists' reaction to events was passive. As shown above, American leaders themselves seemed to have overestimated British Radical influence in England at the outset of the war.

There also were various indirect channels of opinion between British and American radicals about which something should be said. Not the least of these were colonial newspapers which publicized British opinion dissenting from the government's American policy. Thirty-eight newspapers were published in the mainland colonies by 1775. Their reporting on antigovernment opinion in England concentrated mainly on the great Whig politicians, especially the speeches of men like Chatham and Burke. The Wilkes affair received enormous attention, and its influence on colonial attitudes has been noted. Aside from public announcements about the publication of colonial editions of British Radical writings, however, very little material appeared in American newspapers about people such as Burgh or Price. At the same time, it appears that the wide colonial attention to the Wilkes case was a notable factor in encouraging Americans to believe that Wilkes' supporters represented a substantial part of English opinion. It is likely that colonial newspaper publishers were familiar with the writings of people like Burgh and the other English Radicals outside politics. Their publications' attention to antigovernment feeling in England encouraged some American leaders to think it more extensive than it actually was.[33]

H. Trevor Colbourn has made an extensive study of colonial libraries during this period, and he shows that they were rich in volumes on English Whig political thought—testimony to the fact that many of the Republic's founders were well read in history and in the liberal Whig political thought of the seventeenth and eighteenth centuries. Quite a number of these libraries included the writings of contemporary British Radicals, especially Catharine Macaulay's *History of England* and James Burgh's *Political Disquisitions*. Miscellaneous works, including broadsides, sermons, and pamphlets by British Radicals also were to be found. The colonial colleges, Harvard, Yale, the College of New Jersey, King's College, the College of Philadelphia, and William and Mary, had libraries where students had access to these works. Subscription libraries in large towns, Philadelphia, Boston, New York, made such literature available to the reading public. Some of the finest collections of contemporary English Radical literature were in the private libraries of Adams, Jefferson, Dickinson, Dulany, Richard Bland, James Wilson, Charles Carroll, George Mason, and George Washington. It is evident that Americans who sought to confirm their anti-British opinions readily turned to their copies of Macaulay and Burgh. They were people with a cause and they preferred to read history that espoused a cause. Such writers encouraged them "to prevent the spread of the poison of corruption to their own shores."[34]

Obviously the pamphlet was the most widely used means by which British Radicals exported their opinions to the Americans. This was the grand age of the political pamphleteer. The pamphlet was, as Bernard Bailyn describes it, a one-man show.[35] It was the splendid instrument of the individualist, the eccentric and the polemicist. It was an economical device through which men such as Cartwright could propose a grand scheme for imperial reformation and Price could make known his eloquent case for American liberty.

A recent study made on the publication of British pamphlets dealing with the American colonies between 1750 and the end of the American Revolution shows that most of them came out during the critical period of 1774 to 1777.[36] The most important Radical pamphlets, as already seen, appeared at this time. Also included were several important American works, such as John Dickinson's *Letter from a Farmer in Pennsylvania* and Thomas Jefferson's *A Summary View of the Rights of British America*. Like anti-American pamphlets printed in England during these years, the writings of the Radicals usually were published in London in initial editions of 500 copies, advertised in City newspapers from two weeks to a month, reviewed in the *Monthly Review*, issued by booksellers-publishers like John Almon, and sold in the bookshops of the City and Westminster at a cost of one shilling.[37] The British Radical pamphlets displayed a literary quality and erudition superior to their American counterparts, with a few exceptions. Colonial pamphlets tended to be more pallid, imitative, and sometimes crude.

The British Radical pamphlets which came out in the years 1774 to 1777 were usually reprinted in the colonies within a few months of their initial appearance in England. The Philadelphia printer Robert Bell published a number of them, as did numerous colonial printers in such other large towns as Boston and New York. The pamphlets of Cartwright, Sharp, Macaulay, and Price all appeared in Philadelphia when the Continental Congress was sitting in 1775–76. The delegates of the Congress obviously read or knew about them. A number of them, certainly Jefferson, mailed copies to constituents in their home provinces. It would be surprising that such writings, appearing at such a time and under such circumstances, did not give something to the frame of mind that was crystallized in the Declaration of Independence.

How did British and American radicals agree and differ on the thorny questions of taxation, representation, parliamentary authority, and the mercantile laws? Given the fact that they were connected by mutual sympathy and general principles, it is still true that no cohesive view developed between the two groups on many of the particulars of such problems—a circumstance which demonstrates the enormous difficulties which the British government confronted at the time. It has been argued that not even the most capable British statesmanship could have found some sort of settlement with colonial leaders short of a major reformation of the imperial system.[38] Even had British forces won the war in 1777 the old constitutional and economic issues between London and colonial seats of government would have lingered on and plagued a mother country unprepared to abandon old notions of empire.[39] Such puzzling issues were bewildering even to most British Radicals, with the exception of people like Macaulay and Price who saw them as entirely secondary to the more important questions of liberty.

The position of American radicalism by 1774 on the largely integrated issues of taxation, representation, and parliamentary authority evolved from a long series of hair-splitting engagements between colonial spokesmen and British officials during the preceding decade. Numerous American pamphlets between 1764 and 1774 argued that Parliament's jurisdiction in the British Empire was limited. Richard Bland's *The Colonel Dismounted* (1764) insisted that the "internal" affairs of the colonies fell under the legislative jurisdiction of colonial assemblies, though Parliament still had the right to legislate on matters of "external," or imperial, importance. In accordance with the ancient principle of legislative action by consent of the represented, taxation of the colonists was consistent with British liberty only when authorized by colonial assemblies.[40] This position conceived of a parliamentary sovereignty by degree of jurisdiction. James Otis's *The Rights of the British Colonies Asserted and Proved* (1764) and *A Vindication of the British Colonies* (1765) contended that a due respect for colonial liberty could be assured only when colonial assemblies responsible to their constituencies possessed the sole authority to tax them. Parliament's imposition of taxes on the colonists denied the crown's American subjects the ancient right of taxation by their own consent. The unqualified sovereignty of Parliament in the empire, therefore, was inconsistent with British liberty.[41] By 1774 American radicals generally accepted this idea of federated sovereignty distributed among Parliament and the colonial assemblies. This idea left no place for the principle of virtual representation. Nor would these American leaders have been more accommodating with the kind of reformed Parliament sought by British Radicals. Parliamentary reform in England was a moot question to American radicals because, reformed or not, it still would not be an American Parliament and should have no general sovereignty over colonial affairs.

If the broad ranks of British Radicalism had been obliged to resolve such questions, they would have merely added to the confusion. City Radicals with political or commercial ties at stake in the quandary appear to have been divided on particulars. Some of them accepted the principle of federated sovereignty for Parliament as argued by Chatham and Shelburne. Others went along with the idea of an imperial Parliament possessing a "sleeping sovereignty," a notion urged by Rockingham and Burke. As we have already seen, Honest Whigs such as Burgh, Price, and Cartwright supported the principle of federated sovereignty as an assurance of American liberty and rights. At the same time, they were interested in parliamentary reform—an objective which, though it might not work out an accommodation on particulars, would make Parliament more representative, more just, and more conciliatory toward the Americans. A reformed Parliament which conceded to American arguments would not be dismantling the British Empire. Too many bonds between England and America existed, and arguments that the two peoples would drift apart—economically, diplomatically, or culturally—did not stand up to reason. Most important to Radicals like Macaulay and Price, a British satisfaction of American complaints and due recognition of colonial liberty made all other issues secondary. Such views, however, could not be understood by the British government or public. They were suggesting a concept of empire which eighteenth-century Englishmen could not reconcile with their belief in imperial unity, authority, and economic regulation.

The question of the mercantile laws was not as complicated a matter. Of course, economic interest was an important consideration in the minds of British and American radicals who recognized that some of the mercantile laws were beneficial. Obviously London Radicals who had much at stake in colonial trade were reluctant to go along with some of the antimercantile arguments of New England manufacturers and shippers. At the same time, the Radicals whose writings defended America in 1774–76 recognized that even economic interest must bow to considerations of morality and liberty. Their ideas were at odds with the old mercantile imperialism and espoused an anti-imperialism which questioned the inequities and irrationalities of economic regulation as an infringement on American freedom. Despite Dean Tucker's unpopularity among these Radicals, there were critical grounds upon which they agreed. John Dickinson wrote some of the best material on this subject in America, including his *The Late Regulations Respecting the British Colonies* (1765). He argued that mercantile restrictions on American trade were, in the long run, disadvantageous both to Britain and America.[42] He was not only agreeing with Tucker but also arguing, as did such English Radicals as Burgh, that the very nature of imperialism was an undue restriction upon the ancient liberties of Englishmen.

The connection between British and American radicals at the outset of the Revolution, notwithstanding the considerations which brought them together in 1774–76, had roots which went far deeper than the imperial issues of the time. They shared a uniquely British political tradition which went back to the liberal Whig principles of seventeenth- and early eighteenth-century Englishmen whom Caroline Robbins calls commonwealthmen. This legacy, along with conditions in the post-1763 British world, caused them to nurture a fresh, invigorating notion of liberty that was tempered by the Enlightenment and restrained by an old English practical-mindedness. Their mutual veneration for the achievements of the historic English constitution was no less than their admiration of the refined political theories of John Locke.

Such was the reservoir from which they drew their common ideology of liberty by 1776—an ideology which set contemporary notions of the natural rights of man within the framework of their moral and political concepts of what British liberty was about.[43] They shared a pragmatic idealism. They knew history and tried to learn its lessons. Many of them were men of science and applied its principles while fashioning ideas and institutions that might bring a wider, fuller realization of human liberty. They sought no utopias or gods to replace the old. Most of them understood the complexities of human nature and recognized that the achievement of their objectives would still leave future generations with the task of reconciling the problem of authority and freedom. These were men of tolerance and restraint—their ideology never lost touch with their sense of humanity. On both sides of the Atlantic they studied each other's writings, which "brought comfort, information, and an enhanced awareness of common history and common purpose."[44] Together they were "the enemies of complacency in one of the most complacent eras in England's history."[45]

Together, radicals on both sides of the Atlantic admired the British constitution, with its unique equilibrium of monarchy, aristocracy, and democracy, as mankind's noblest instrument for the promotion of freedom. They agreed that the constitution had gone wrong when English politicians started giving only lip service to the Revolution of 1688. They resented the complacency of the Whig oligarchy and its reluctance to promote the promises of the Revolution's principles. Circumstances forced each of the two groups to find different formulas to realize their common aspirations of liberty. "Geography sets the stage for the drama of history," writes Sir George Clark. Only a few British Radicals like James Burgh and Catharine Macaulay went so far as to embrace the republican principle of popular sovereignty as the rightful foundation of the constitution. Most of them clung to the traditional idea that the constitution and Parliament were integrated as the embodiment of the sovereign body politic. Composed of king, Lords and Commons, Parliament was the historic basis from which British liberties came forth. Radicals like John Cartwright sought the restoration of a balanced constitution through parliamentary reform. They wanted a better constitution by way of a better Parliament. American radicals, on the other hand, cast aside this notion of the constitution and adopted the principle of popular sovereignty to justify their revolution and then to frame their written constitutions. Whereas the natural rights of Englishmen were to be realized by the traditional principle of parliamentary sovereignty, they were to be realized in America on the basis of popular sovereignty. This encouraged an American idealism which lasted long after the Revolution itself. Europeans found it "rigid, moralistic and self-righteous."[46] British Radicals, however, were confident that the American Revolution would be a blessing to the Old World rather than a scourge.[47]

Their common notions of liberty also caused British and American radicals to share a common alarm over the existence of a court conspiracy in England to resurrect the ghost of Stuart despotism at the cost of British freedom. Radical writings encouraged this fear on both sides of the Atlantic. Colonial apprehensions had been precipitated by the post-1763 principle of imperial responsibility. Jonathan Mayhew's fears of the creation of an American episcopacy reflected a New England suspicion that the Anglican church might be used to extend the prerogative in the colonies. Colonial displeasure with official arbitrariness, the presence of British troops, and the growing efficiency of British administration after 1763 all seemed too reminiscent of Continental despotism. Writs of assistance and incidents like the Boston Massacre reenforced colonial apprehensions. The British Radicals' fears were aroused by the Wilkes affair and the intransigence of the government's American policy. Reports of incidents in America, the war itself, and the trial of John Horne Tooke seemed to confirm their suspicions.

The conspiracy was attributed to the ambitions of the king, the schemes of Lord Bute, the influence of certain great families at court, and especially those politicians known as the "King's Friends." Whig interpretations of this period by British and American historians during the nineteenth century reenforced the notion of a concerted design to revive the royal prerogative. Though the Namier school has disproven its existence, belief in such a conspiracy has died hard. Whether such a plot was real or not, it is a fact that British and American radicals thought it to be a hard reality and an ominous threat to liberty. Both groups agreed with Burgh's conclusion that it was rooted in English political corruption. They saw America as a refuge from an English political system gone wrong. Men like Burgh and Cartwright entertained notions of American moral supremacy because of its "provincial virtues— rustic and old-fashioned, sturdy and effective—challenged by the corruption at the center of power, by the threat of tyranny, and by a constitution gone wrong."[48]

In sum, the British Radicals were the strongest ideological connection which the leadership of the American Revolution possessed in the European world of the late eighteenth century. They were sources of inspiration to each other. They read each other's writings and their common heritage enabled them to enjoy a mutual understanding and sympathy. Both groups honored the constitution and liberties of England while seeking to realize human freedom on a new and larger scale. They believed that the imperial crisis resulted from political conditions in England which were eroding liberty in both the colonies and the mother country. British Radicals who viewed the imperial questions of 1774–76 in this light recognized that the American problem demanded innovative solutions which complacent Englishmen were unable to accept. The mistakes which led to the disasters of 1775–76 were a springboard for American independence and the reinvigoration of a liberal Whiggism inspired by the principles of both 1688 and 1776. The few figures who spoke for the broad spectrum of British Radicalism at the outset of the American Revolution represented the most advanced thinking in England on the subject of empire. They were among the most informed, sensitive, and active Englishmen of the time in engaging the American problem and recognizing what needed to be done by the mother country. They advertised conditions in America, aroused English attention to colonial complaints, and propagated their notions of how the problem should be resolved. At the same time, they inaugurated a parliamentary reform movement which anticipated one of the most important chapters in English life during the next century.[49]

CONCLUSION

JOSIAH TUCKER's proposal for American independence was an idea more extreme than any of those urged by British Radical spokesmen in 1774–76 and, as the course of events proved, the dean of Gloucester found satisfaction in his accurate analysis of the American crisis. After the Continental Congress declared national independence to be America's basic war aim in 1776, he could at least have agreed with the Radicals on several points. The bold enterprise of the Americans would, sooner or later, succeed. The British government's resort to force in hopes of preserving the old colonial system in the rebellious colonies was futile. The logical thing to do was to initiate peace negotiations as soon as possible and learn how to get along with the Americans in some sort of new relationship. Neither the British government nor public was prepared to accept such advice until forced to do so several years later.

Englishmen had certainly not heard the last of Tucker. He continued to chastise the government throughout the war years. He deplored the fact that British leaders were making war on thirteen colonies far from English shores over some hypothetical differences about Parliament's authority. He insisted that the North ministry was still in a position to negotiate a settlement after the actions near Boston in 1775 and, in lieu of the certain futility of current policy, the government had no other choice. Britain, he warned, would gain nothing by a long, costly war which would only harden the Americans' determination to resist until they had their way.[1]

When the American quarrel was expanded into another great eighteenth-century European conflict in 1778, the dean's criticisms of the British government were aired in one of his most earnest antiwar pamphlets, *Cui Bono?*, a compilation of public letters addressed to the French Minister of Finance Jacques Necker. Speaking as a "citizen of the world," he shows his distress over the events which have brought on another war between the British and

French, warns against the dangers of American revolutionary ideology, and laments the British government's blindness to the necessity for a negotiated peace.[2] Neither Britain nor France, claims the dean, can gain from continued fighting. No two nations in Europe have more reasons for getting along with each other. "If France should grow the poorer, she must be so much the worse customer to England; if richer, probably so much the better."[3] The court of France is warned of the dangers to which it exposes itself by its flirtation with poisonous revolutionary ideology and the strains which intervention in America will bring on the French treasury. To his own government the dean expresses his despair that six years of failure seem to have taught British leaders nothing. Arguments that victory is still possible, that the national honor is at stake, are empty absurdities. Fears that American independence will bring economic disaster to England simply do not stand up to good reasoning. Trade between the two countries should flourish more than ever before. England's buying power will insure a vast market for American exports while the volume, quality, and cheapness of British goods should quickly revive American buying habits from the mother country. "Were America this moment to lay herself at our feet, and to submit to a *carte blanche*, provided we would take her again into favour,—it is evidently our interest not to accept of such a present."[4]

Tucker had his own ideas on the structure of a settlement with America, its major principles including proposals to restore Anglo-American trade and insure the well-being of Americans who had never abandoned their loyalty to the crown. The four New England provinces, which he believed to be the major trouble-makers, should be given their independence. Maryland, Virginia, and the Middle Colonies also are to be turned loose. Because of their large Loyalist populations, Georgia and the Carolinas are to maintain some kind of tie with Britain—along with a newly created state for Loyalists between the Connecticut and Hudson rivers including Long Island, Staten Island, and a portion of the old New York province. After a lapse of ten years, the legislature of each state can institute whatever form of government it pleases. Tucker speculates that a breach would develop between the independent and Loyalist states and this should be to the commercial advantage of Great Britain. He also suggests some international readjustments consistent with his ideas of a world of suppliers and customers to promote international prosperity after the war. East Florida and Gibraltar should be returned to Spain in return for Puerto Rico. Minorca should go to Austria in order to bring that Continental state into the world of maritime commerce. Such an international scheme of trade can benefit Britain and stimulate a European economic order to discourage future wars.[5]

When he learned about Yorktown in late 1781, Dean Tucker was not surprised at an event he had been expecting since the war started. He saw it as a blessing for Great Britain and, when Lord North's government fell in early 1782, he wrote to his friend Lord Kames,

> I look upon it to have been a very imprudent act to have settled any distant colonies at all whilst there remained an inch of land in Great Britain capable of further cultivation; afterwards, to have been very foolish and absurd to have engaged in their disputes either with the French or the Spaniards, and to have espoused their quarrels; and lastly, to have been the height of madness to have endeavored to conquer them after they had broken out in open rebellion. They were always, from first to last, a heavy weight upon us, a weight which we ourselves ought to have thrown off if they had not done it for us.[6]

When British peace commissioners were negotiating with the Americans in Paris in 1782, Dean Tucker speculated on the effects of the American victory on British policy in Ireland and India. He was pleased with the Rockingham-Shelburne concession of autonomy in home affairs to Ireland. But this was a small step and much remained to be done. Though the Irish now had access to ports in America, Africa, and the Levant and could export their woolens and glass, their commercial activities were still unduly restricted to serve selfish British interests. He was convinced that the final solution to the Irish problem lay in a union of Britain and Ireland, something preferable to overt separation. Tucker clung to his long-held ideas about India and became even more convinced that the East India Company's position in India would bring a curse to England. Not even Pitt the Younger's India Bill in 1784 changed his mind.

> If Great Britain had been unable to maintain her authority over a couple of million people at a distance of only three thousand miles, he was at a loss to understand how men could be so "infatuated with

party rage" or "blinded with the hopes of filthy lucre" as not to realize that a handful of proprietors and directors could not continue their "destested [*sic*] usurpations over the lives, liberties, and properties of thirty millions at the distance of ten thousand miles."[7]

Much of Dean Tucker's reasoning should have appealed to English Radicals, especially Dr. Price. Their principal differences over the meaning of the American Revolution, however, kept them far apart in their antiwar motives. Dean Tucker was unrelenting in his hostility to American revolutionary ideology and those Englishmen who subscribed to it. The dean's most comprehensive statement of his Old Whig politics was his *Treatise Concerning Civil Government*, first published in 1781. He presented himself as a sort of "Old Oligarch" who feared the American Revolution in much the same manner that Burke feared the French Revolution in 1789. Alarmed over the implications of American revolutionary ideas, Tucker wrote a scathing denunciation of John Locke's political philosophy. He scoffed at the social contract theory and dismissed the doctrine of natural rights as metaphysical nonsense. The ideological principles of the American revolutionaries were pregnant with doctrinaire fanaticism which could haunt traditional European civilization. There were Englishmen in the country whose sympathy with such principles was encouraging the notion that England be placed at the mercy of mobs.

> In one word, let the impartial world be the judge, whether the Americans, in all their contests for liberty, have even once made use of Mr. Locke's system for any other purpose, but that of pulling down, and destroying; and whether, when they came to erect a new edifice of their own on the ruins of the former,—they have not abandoned Mssrs. Locke, Molineux, Priestley, and Price, with all their visionary schemes of universal freedom, and liberty of choice.[8]

When Burke was writing his *Reflections on the Revolution in France*, Dean Tucker might easily have been tempted to remind the earlier apologist for America that his conduct in the House of Commons in 1775 may well have inspired the deeds of the National Assembly at Versailles in 1789.

Neither Cartwright, Sharp, Burgh, Macaulay, nor Price would have quarreled with the anti-imperialist tone in Tucker's arguments. But none of them considered such an extreme step as complete separation from America to be either necessary, desirable, or inevitable. Not until the Americans declared national independence in the summer of 1776 did Radical spokesmen conclude that such a step was preferable to other solutions—a conclusion made when they recognized that the conduct of the British government left the Americans no other choice. From 1776 onward to the end of the conflict, Radicals such as Mrs. Macaulay and Dr. Price made no effort to conceal their best wishes for the American cause.

James Burgh died on 26 August 1775 before he could have known that the quarrel would lead to the creation of a new republic. The *Political Disquisitions*, however, became a major catechism of English Radicalism. Radicals who supported the American Revolution and the cause of parliamentary reform owed more to Burgh's volumes than any other publication of the period. His republican principles probably made a major contribution to the political education of the American Founding Fathers, who went about the business of creating a republic on the foundation of British concepts of liberty. His influence was felt in both the ideology of the Declaration of Independence and the various American constitutions. One historian has argued that James Madison drew from Burgh's ideas on politics and monetary principles when writing some of the *Federalist* papers.[9]

None of the English Radicals so personified the zeal for Burgh's case on parliamentary reform and its connection with the American Revolution as did John Cartwright. Still in the Royal Navy as a lieutenant at the outset of the war, he received a personal request in February 1776 from his old commander, Lord Admiral Howe, to serve on the admiral's staff in the coming naval campaign off the coast of North America. Cartwright was forced to choose between the dictates of conscience and personal loyalty to a man whom he held in the highest regard. With much distress, he sent a letter to Howe on February 6 expressing his painful decision to refuse the request because of his opposition to the war. "Thinking as I do on the most unhappy contest between this kingdom and her colonies, it would be a desertion from my principles were I to put myself in a situation that might probably cause me to act a hostile part against them."[10] To which Howe replied on February 12, "Being persuaded that men of character will ever act . . . upon principles that do them honour, he must respect those of Mr. Cartwright too much to be desirous of lessening his satisfaction in them, were he even qualified for such an undertaking." [11]

Though Cartwright's decision cost him his naval commission and a promising future in the Royal Navy, he did not turn his back on public service for his country. He accepted an appointment as major in the Nottinghamshire militia and won a reputation as an able, respected militia officer. His commanding officer, Lord Percy, publicly praised him. Major Cartwright also was given the freedom of the city of Nottingham while the country was fighting a war he publicly opposed. Cartwright held on to his father's estate in Nottinghamshire, combining his farming and militia duties with his crusade for parliamentary reform. The events of 1774–76 convinced him that the old Whig oligarchy was hopeless. "My patience and forbearance with the whole crew of ministers are now worn out. . . . I am not only angry with the ministers, but with the opposition too. . . ." [12] His *Take Your Choice!* appeared in 1776 as an important sequel to the *Political Disquisitions* and his reputation as a parliamentary reformer soon spread about London. He became a familiar figure among the Radicals of the City such as Dr. John Jebb, Granville Sharp, and others who were to join him in founding the Society for Constitutional Information in 1780.

It was ironic that Major Cartwright's ideas for imperial reform in early 1774 included principles which formed the substance of British peace offers to America after the Battle of Saratoga. The ideas of William Pulteney in 1778, for example, were "revivals of Cartwright's schemes." [13] In 1778 the Carlisle Commission, which included Admiral Howe, offered plans for a settlement along similar lines. Cartwright's conviction that an imperial policy which betrayed a longstanding corruption and incompetence of both court and Parliament animated a life of agitation for parliamentary reform which earned him the title of "father of parliamentary reform." His recognition of an American "nation" which underlay his proposals for imperial reformation has received the confirmation of eminent historians like L. H. Gipson.

The rupture of the British Empire . . . had its source fundamentally in the fact that America now embodied a mature and powerful

English-speaking community with a mind of its own. . . . British
statesmen as a group were responsible for the breach, to the extent of
their failure to realize that the old system of imperial control was no
longer applicable to a society so highly cultivated, so extended, and
so numerous.[14]

Granville Sharp had some experiences during the war similar to
Cartwright's. In July 1775 he considered his employment as assistant to the secretary of the Ordnance Office to be incongruous with
his opinions about the American crisis and requested a leave of ab-
sence until hostilities were ended.

I cannot return to my ordnance duty whilst a bloody war is carried
on, unjustly as I conceive, against my fellow-subjects; and yet to re-
sign my place would be to give up a calling, which by my close atten-
dance for near eighteen years, and by my neglect of every other
means of subsistence during so long a period, is now become my only
profession and livelihood.[15]

He was given a leave of two months. When peace did not come, he
secured a second leave of three months and then a third for six
months through the winter of 1775–76. In July 1776 the Ordnance
Department was forced to give him a choice between resumption of
his duties or resignation. Having to decide between employment
with its regular income and his personal principle, Sharp chose to
be a conscientious objector to the war and resigned his place. For-
tunately, however, his two brothers in London respected Sharp's
action and agreed to provide him financial support while encouraging him to go on with his philanthropic causes.[16] Sharp was given a
means of livelihood by his brothers and sisters throughout his reform career.

After his departure from the Ordnance Office Sharp threw himself into several causes for liberty. His reputation as a champion of
the Negro caused many London blacks to turn to him when in need.
Some four hundred received help from him at one time or another.[17] He became one of Major Cartwright's companions in the
cause of parliamentary reform and was a charter member of the
Society for Constitutional Information. Cartwright once wrote of
Sharp as "a man of singular good sense, active worth and piety. . . .
[He has the] purest and most genuine love of mankind, a generous

ardour in the sacred cause of public freedom, and a truly Christian faith, hope and charity." [18]

Sharp also spent much of his time during the war in activities on America's behalf. His work for parliamentary reform was partly inspired by hopes that the Americans would be encouraged to make peace with a government that represented a reformed Parliament and would agree to form some kind of union with the mother country.[19] During the period before Saratoga when the American cause seemed to be in doubt, some Americans in England secretly contacted Sharp and asked his assistance in communicating with influential officials about prospects for a settlement acceptable to Philadelphia. Sharp obligingly went to the Colonial Office to see Lord Dartmouth about the matter and also urged Dartmouth to consider a peace plan based on American legislative autonomy. Nothing came of the interview and nothing is known of Dartmouth's reaction to Sharp. Sharp talked to General James Oglethorpe and the duke of Richmond about his ideas for a settlement shortly afterward. They soon found that a compromise settlement became a moot question when the news of Saratoga reached England. Sharp accepted the imminence of American independence but continued to hope that the Americans might be willing to cooperate in the creation of a confederation like that proposed by his friend Major Cartwright a few years earlier. During the summer of 1781 he again tried to be a peacemaker by arranging a meeting between an American agent and two prominent Englishmen, the duke of Grafton and Bishop John Hinchcliffe. When the latter two men backed out at the last moment, Sharp tried to persuade Thomas Secker, the archbishop of Canterbury, to take their place. This also failed and the meeting never came off.

After the war Sharp accepted Benjamin Franklin's request for his help in reconciling American Anglicans to the Church of England. Sharp went to the archbishop of Canterbury and asked that the church agree to the ordination of American bishops, priests, and deacons. The archbishop influenced Parliament's legislation in 1784 allowing the church to ordain priests and deacons. Because of doubts about the American Anglicans' omission of the king's name in their Book of Common Prayer and some unorthodox passages in the edition, the mother church was reluctant to establish an American episcopacy. Sharp eventually succeeded in changing the archbishop's mind in 1787 and the way was open for the church's ordination of the first bishops of the Protestant Episcopal Church of America.

Catharine Macaulay's pro-American sympathies and marriage to William Graham severely damaged her position in English society, and her notoriety forced her to live a reclusive life in Berkshire after 1778. She finished the last three volumes of the *History of England* by late 1783. The Grahams's warm reception in America in 1784–85 must have reassured the lady historian when she found herself famous in American revolutionary circles. The couple returned home in 1785 and the English public heard little from her until shortly before her death in 1791. When Edmund Burke attacked the pro-French revolutionary sentiments in Dr. Price's *A Discourse on the Love of Our Country* in 1789–90, she rose to the latter's defense by writing a scathing criticism of Burke's opinions in her *Observations on the Reflections of the Right Hon. Edmund Burke*. She reiterated her belief in popular sovereignty and chastised Burke's lack of faith in popular government. She expressed her belief that the French Revolution would produce "men of true virtue" like Washington and Franklin to lead Frenchmen in their quest for liberty and democracy.[20]

The *Observations on the Nature of Civil Liberty* carried an import which made Dr. Price one of England's best-known and most controversial dissenters against the American war. His pamphlet was cheered by City Radicals, who gave him the freedom of the City, while his calculations on the government's finances bewildered people throughout the country. But Price was distressed by his critics' fierce accusations that he was disloyal to his country. Burke took him to task for his notions of popular liberty. John Wesley accused Price of attempting to inflame the Americans against a British government which was unjustly charged with oppression.[21] Price, however, remained adamant in his opposition to the war; and his other publications were to keep him in the center of controversy. He continued to receive letters from American friends like Franklin, Winthrop, Chauncy, and Arthur Lee and, when he could, passed on to them news about affairs in England. American agents even gave him a secret code number, 176, and depended on him for information of value to them. Dr. Price's prestige in Philadelphia was evident when, in the autumn of 1778, the Congress, in need of his fiscal advice, offered to make him a citizen of the United States and authorized inviting him to America as a consultant to Congress. Deeply moved, Dr. Price gratefully declined such honors by virtue of his wife's bad health, his obligations to his congregation, and other circumstances which forbade a man at his stage of life to make such a change.[22]

In early 1777 Dr. Price saw that the war was fulfilling his expectations. Disturbed by the great criticism he had brought on himself and believing that he was misunderstood by his critics, he decided to publish another pamphlet, *Additional Observations on the Nature and Value of Civil Liberty, and the War with America*.[23] He reiterated his philosophy of civil liberty and presented a fresh analysis of the war situation. He wrote of his distress that the government was not prepared to alter its position or to foresee new dangers. He showed more recent calculations proving that the government's fiscal situation was weakening. He also included his estimates of the French government's fiscal status and warned that the Bourbons still had the financial capacity to intervene in the conflict. The Battle of Saratoga took place shortly after Price's warnings, and his worst fears were justified. Before he knew of the Franco-American alliance in early 1778, he responded to criticism of him by Burke and Archbishop Markham in another pamphlet called *The General Introduction to the Two Tracts on Civil Liberty, the War with America, and the Finances of the Kingdom*.[24] Again he restated his principles of liberty and his case against the war. He expressed his regret at Burke's criticisms when there was need for unity among English opponents to the conflict. He still thought a compromise peace was possible if the British government would repeal the Coercion Acts and other laws that had provoked the fighting. Perhaps an autonomous America would be willing to enter some kind of cooperative union with England if the mother country showed its willingness for reconciliation. The ominous prospects shown by government finances and the growing danger of a major European war made British initiatives for peace even more necessary.[25] The warnings were prophetic of the events of 1778–82. The French were in alliance with America while Dr. Price was writing what was the last of his public admonitions against the war before its outcome was decided.

During the last years of the conflict Dr. Price received honors in America comparable to those of revolutionary leaders. In April 1781 he and General Washington were awarded the LL. D. degrees by the Yale Corporation. Price was made a fellow of the American Academy of Arts and Sciences in January 1782. He was elected to membership in the American Philosophical Society three years later.[26]

Few Englishmen welcomed the success of the American Revolution and the birth of the Republic as did Price. On New Year's Day 1783 he wrote to Dr. Rush of Philadelphia and expressed his heartfelt belief that the American Revolution would begin a new era in the history of mankind. "I think it is one of the most important revolutions that has ever taken place in the world. It makes a new opening in human affairs which may prove an introduction to times of more light and liberty and virtue than have yet been known."[27] He thought and wrote extensively about the United States for the rest of his life. Englishmen, Irishmen, and Americans read with great interest his appraisal of the Revolution and advice to the leaders of the Republic in his *Observations on the Importance of the American Revolution, and the Means of Making It a Benefit to the World.*[28] Price thought that the birth of the United States of America marked humanity's brightest hope for liberty, justice, progress, and human improvement.[29] He offered suggestions to American leaders on numerous subjects which might contribute to the stability and growth of the American Union—the public debt, peace, liberty, civil rights, religious freedom, education, dangers to the Union, debt and internal strife, the unequal distribution of property, the problems of trade, banking and credit, the taking of oaths, and the dilemmas of the Negro trade and slavery. The last words of the pamphlet were an admonition to the young nation which eloquently spoke for Dissenting Englishmen of the eighteenth century.

> Should the return of peace and the pride of independence lead them to security and dissipation—Should they lose those virtuous and simple manners by which alone Republics can long subsist—Should false refinement, luxury, and irreligion spread among them; excessive jealousy distract their governments; and clashing interests, subject to

no strong controul [*sic*], break the federal union—The consequence will be, that the fairest experiment ever tried in human affairs will miscarry; and that a Revolution which had revived the hopes of good men and promised an opening to better times, will become a discouragement to all future efforts in favor of liberty, and prove only an opening to a new scene of human degeneracy and misery.[30]

Price's concern for the Union's stability was commensurate with the thinking of American leaders at the Mount Vernon Conference in 1785 and at the Annapolis Conference the following year. Many of the men who framed the federal Constitution of 1787 had read Price's timely volume. As in 1776, his interest and encouragement were welcome. It is no overstatement to argue that his place in the history of American constitutional thought is both credible and important.[31]

Price lived long enough to welcome the beginning of the French Revolution and also to receive honors from its leaders. During the autumn of 1789 he was invited to deliver a sermon before the Society for Commemorating the Revolution at the Old Jewry Meeting House in honor of the one-hundredth anniversary of the Glorious Revolution. His address was the text for his last important pamphlet, *A Discourse on the Love of Our Country*. It praised the English, American, and French revolutions as victories of freedom over oppression. Once again he became the object of Burke's criticism, as is evident in the *Reflections on the Revolution in France*. Dr. Price's description of patriotism was a fitting commentary on himself and other English Radicals who had defended the American Revolution. The true love of one's country, he argues, is not a narrow, blind patriotism but a devotion to right and goodwill for all men. The true patriot is a citizen who seeks to enlighten his fellow citizens, to promote both private and public integrity, to venerate religion and liberty, and to be willing to defend a country where such principles are honored.

> Our regards, according to the order of nature, begin with ourselves; and every man is charged primarily with the care of himself. Next come our families, and benefactors, and friends; and after them our country. We can do little for the interest of mankind at large. To this interest, however, all other interests are subordinate. The noblest principle in our nature is the regard to general justice, and that good-will which embraces all the world.[32]

Such was the spirit in which the Honest Whigs addressed their countrymen on the great questions of their time. Their opinions were informed and their intentions were honorable. These reformists venerated the constitution no less than other eighteenth-century Englishmen. Unlike most of their generation, however, they saw in it broad, fertile possibilities for a grand extension of liberty and equity. They thought of the Glorious Revolution as an event with ideological potential yet to be fulfilled. They were convinced that England's failure to adapt to the extraordinary conditions of the post-1763 period was rooted in a corrupt, incompetent, and unrepresentative political structure that needed to be reformed. The keystone of their program was parliamentary reform—an achievement that was prerequisite to more representative, virtuous government. They aspired to a Parliament which would zealously serve a prosperous, progressive nation of liberty-loving farmers, tradesmen, and merchants. Like most Englishmen, they respected tradition and property. They believed in the virtues of religion and social responsibility. Their reform causes were emblazoned with a sense of humanity. They had much faith in human nature and the ability of men to resolve great problems with sound reasoning and goodwill.

Such men were distressed by the attitudes which most Englishmen had toward their fellow subjects in the colonies—a mercantilist frame of public mind which regarded the colonies as dumping grounds "for thieves, bankrupts, and prostitutes, for which we received tobacco in return." [33] They thought of the imperial crisis as a confrontation between unjust, unreasonable notions of authority and principles of liberty to which colonists were no less entitled than Englishmen who had never left their native soil. They rejected all the official and popular arguments that abandonment of the old imperial system would ruin the mother country. Old bonds and common interests among Englishmen and Americans were too strong to allow for one people to be oblivious to the injury of the other. Their aspirations for the peoples of the colonies were rooted in schemes for imperial reformation which would transform the old mercantile system into a union of free, prosperous, harmonious British peoples. Such a creative rationalization of empire showed them to be among the most liberal and enlightened Englishmen of their age.

The practical soundness of their various proposals about the British Empire was, in the long run, borne out by the subsequent history of the empire, however unrealistic those proposals were in the short run. Tucker's case was remarkably accurate. Anglo-American trade doubled in the fifteen years after the end of the American Revolution. The eventual acceptance of free trade, partly anticipated in his principles, brought England a golden age of economic primacy in the world. Though nineteenth-century Englishmen and Americans did not like to admit it, they shared many common interests. Victorian Britain's economy was much dependent on America, while the spectacular growth of the Republic took place under the guardianship of British power. If neither people shared much affection for the other, their respective national interests, as foreseen by Tucker, came to have decisive effects which benefited both parties. America's rise in the world occurred under the shelter of the Pax Britannica.

Sharp's historical arguments on Irish and American legislative rights were among the host of debates over Parliament's authority which took place in the decade before 1776. His intent, however, was to see justice done for peoples in the British Empire. He recognized that justice could not occur when distance and bureaucracy make it impossible to administer a faraway peoples' affairs with flexibility and effective responses to local problems. This rationale made good sense to the utilitarians of Lord Durham's day, and the principle of home rule became a cornerstone of the dominion system. Cartwright's scheme of imperial union as an instrument for spreading British civilization and liberty around the world foresaw the idealism which captured the imaginations of Victorian imperialists. The British Commonwealth of Nations and the American Republic eventually were reunited in common causes to defend principles of British civilization against their adversaries in the twentieth century. Dr. Price was one of those eighteenth-century Anglo-American apostles of liberty who recognized that the freedom and integrity of the individual is the chief end of British civilization, that the old ideas of empire were incongruous with such a principle. His concept of liberty influenced the Founding Fathers of the Republic and was reflected in the anti-imperialist arguments of nineteenth-century Americans and Little Englanders.

James Burgh's case for parliamentary reform was a forceful

argument that inspired activities for such a cause down through the time of the French Revolution. However, it required the stability of a post-Napoleonic European order and the challenges unleashed by the Industrial Revolution to bring about a cautious acceptance of parliamentary reform. Both he and Catharine Macaulay recognized the values of organization and propaganda in mobilizing popular pressures for change—a recognition which played an important role in the history of nineteenth-century reform movements.

Because the ideas of these spokesmen were antigovernment in tone, British Radical opinion, as a whole, supported them for reasons as diverse as the Radical movement itself. But it was a support given by a small segment of English opinion. Most of the Whig Opposition agreed with the antigovernment sentiments of these imperial reformists but shared very little enthusiasm for their ideas of changing the colonial system. They were little more enlightened than most Englishmen about ideas of empire and they certainly did not accept schemes of domestic reform which would threaten the old Whig oligarchy—they were no more willing to surrender the Whig ascendancy to the mobs than they were to the court. American radicals recognized that they could not achieve their objectives in lieu of existing political realities in England, and they resorted to revolution. But they acknowledged and appreciated British Radical endeavors in their behalf, drawing inspiration and encouragement from them.

If the British government could have been prepared to offer the Americans a settlement based on principles suggested by these Radical theorists in 1774–76, it is likely that they would have been accepted, a war would have been avoided, and American self-determination would have evolved to its eventual achievement in one form or another. But king, Parliament, and people clung to old habits of thinking which could not be changed by the oratory of Chatham, the genius of Burke, or the innovative ideas of Radical reformers. When the government sent the Carlisle Commission to America in 1778 to offer a settlement reminiscent of reform proposals suggested in 1774, it was too late for any kind of solution short of complete American independence.

The American radicals who came to dominate colonial assemblies by 1775, in the last analysis, were asking a great deal from the mother country. It would have been extraordinary if the British government had magnanimously granted the colonists their wishes. It is no small matter to expect people, including governments, suddenly to abandon traditions and attitudes rooted in the successes of past experience. Most men are creatures of habit. They stubbornly hold on to prejudices which make a complex world understandable. Each generation sustains comforting, reassuring mythologies which add a sense of security and purpose to the times. The concept of mercantile empire was the means by which the mass of eighteenth-century Englishmen understood the place of colonies in the British world and this concept seemed to justify the great amounts of blood and treasure expended for the defense of the British Empire. If history has judged King George III and Lord North as dimsighted, stubborn men who blundered away most of the British-American Empire, it can well be argued also that they stood on principles of imperial unity and responsibility which were both understood and supported by the great majority of the crown's subjects, including a large number of American subjects. The king and his ministry had no villainous designs to tyrannize either America or their own country. Most of the great minds of England believed their policy to have been the correct one in 1774–75, including Edward Gibbon who was then writing the first volume of *The Decline and Fall of the Roman Empire*. "I am more and more convinced that we have both the right and the power on our side, and that, though the effort may be accompanied with some melancholy circumstances, we are now arrived at the decisive moment of persevering or of losing forever both our trade and empire."[34] In his apology for the king, John Brooke writes, "When the most learned historian of the age was wrong about America we should not be too hard on King George."[35] Men like Chatham and Burke in the Whig Opposition accurately recognized that the king's policy would not work. But it was the king who had his way because his government had the overwhelming support of Parliament and the nation. Neither the grand designs of Chatham, the political genius of Burke, the eloquence of Fox, nor the innovative schemes of Shelburne could prevail against the temper of the times. In such a world the British Radical spokesmen of 1774–76 were voices in the wilderness with a remarkable anticipation of what lay in the future for Anglo-American civilization.

No one can justly deny that these Radical spokesmen were credits to their civilization and that their ideas were enlightened, honest, and quite prophetic. But if they had been given a more popular Parliament in 1774–76 they would have been sorely distressed to see a reformed Parliament that would have backed the king to the hilt. The notion that a more representative Parliament would have been a more virtuous, enlightened legislature did not stand up to the practical realities of human nature and contemporary public understanding. Burke and the Rockingham Whigs understood this. They had no illusions about the problems posed by innovative schemes for human improvement. There were no simple ways to solve complex human problems. As for the American enigma, they saw that American leaders were as cantankerous and narrow as the king and his ministers. They sought to achieve the best in a bad situation by settling the American mess by the dictates of practical necessity—whether in 1774 when conciliation was possible or in 1782 when American independence was the only practical step to take. If Rockingham had been a more effective leader or Chatham a less stubborn politician, the Whig Opposition might have affected parliamentary opinion enough to force the king to change his government and its American policy sooner than he did.

Dean Tucker's realism accurately recognized that Great Britain was confronting a surging American interest so distinct from its own that the agonies of separation were preferable to those which would surely come from a maintenance of the old ties. One might briefly reflect on the course of history if nineteenth-century British governments would have had to cope with American expansion to the Pacific and the dilemmas of slavery. At the same time, their posterity might justly honor Englishmen like Major Cartwright, Sharp, Burgh, Mrs. Macaulay, and the good Dr. Price whose idealism represented a British aspiration to refurbish the ancient constitution with fresh concepts of liberty and justice. They understood that Englishmen should not expect the Americans to accept the humiliations and wrongs they themselves would not have tolerated. British civilization was not far from the threshold of an age when the resolution of human problems would be formed by the pragmatic integration of Burkean political philosophy with the principles of Benthamite utilitarianism. This was not, however, without a humane desire to build a better way of life for all subjects of the British crown. There was much substance in Dr. Price's belief that governments and other human institutions must help to improve society while preserving human liberty and animating the better qualities of man's nature.

NOTES

The Crisis of Empire

1. David L. Keir, *The Constitutional History of Modern Britain since 1485*, 9th ed. (New York: W. W. Norton & Co., 1969), p. 292.
2. L. H. Gipson, *The British Empire before the American Revolution*, 15 vols. (New York: Alfred A. Knopf, 1936–70), 11: 1–6.
3. G. H. Guttridge, *English Whiggism and the American Revolution*, 2d ed. (Berkeley: University of California Press, 1966), p. 61.
4. Ibid., p. 58.
5. Keir, *Constitutional History*, pp. 363–64.
6. John Brooke, *King George III* (New York: McGraw-Hill Book Co., 1972), pp. 162–63.
7. Dora Mae Clark, *British Opinion and the American Revolution* (New Haven: Yale University Press, 1930), p. 242.

On the Eve of the American Revolution

1. Some important studies on British Radicalism at the outset of the American Revolution are the result of research done in the past quarter century, including Lucy Sutherland, *The City of London and the Opposition to Government, 1768–1774: A Study in the Rise of Metropolitan Radicalism* (London: University of London, Athlone Press, 1959); Ian R. Christie, *Wilkes, Wyvill and Reform* (London: Macmillan & Co., 1962); George F. E. Rudé, *Wilkes and Liberty* (Oxford: Clarendon Press, 1962); Simon Maccoby, *The English Radical Tradition* (London: Charles and Adam Black, 1966). Dora Mae Clark's *British Opinion and the American Revolution* remains quite valuable also.
2. Pauline Maier, "John Wilkes and American Disillusionment with Britain," *William and Mary Quarterly*, 20 (1963): 375–77, 395.
3. Herbert Butterfield, *George III, Lord North and the People, 1779–1780* (London: G. Bell & Sons, 1949), p. 262.
4. Rudé, *Wilkes and Liberty*, p. 192.
5. I think they give an accurate estimation of Wilkes. For example, *see* Sutherland, *The City of London and the Opposition to Government*, pp. 12–15.
6. *See* O. A. Sherrard, *A Life of John Wilkes* (New York: Dodd, Mead & Co., 1930), pp. 270–71 and Maier, "John Wilkes and American Disillusionment with Britain," pp. 373–74.
7. Zealous American radicals like Arthur Lee and William Palfrey were

devoted to both Wilkes and his cause. Consult Richard Henry Lee, *Life of Arthur Lee*, 2 vols. (Boston: Wells & Lilly, 1829), 1: 185–86; and George M. Elsey, ed., "John Wilkes and William Palfrey," *Publications of the Colonial Society of Massachusetts*, 34 (1943): 427–28. Benjamin Franklin thought Wilkes to be a rake, "an outlaw . . . of bad personal character, not worth a farthing." *See* John Bigelow, ed., *The Works of Benjamin Franklin*, 12 vols. (New York: G. P. Putnam's Sons, 1904), 4: 149.

8. Dora Mae Clark, *British Opinion and the American Revolution* (New Haven: Yale University Press, 1930), p. 165.

9. Ibid., p. 166.

10. A. Francis Steuart, ed., *The Last Journals of Horace Walpole during the Reign of George III from 1771 to 1783*, 2 vols. (London: John Lane, 1910), 1: 466.

11. *Annual Register*, 18 (1775): 149.

12. Ibid., p. 272.

13. Sir John Fortesque, ed., *The Correspondence of King George III*, 6 vols. (London: Macmillan & Co., 1927), 3: 233. Opposition charges that the government intimidated City newspapers which criticized official American policy are described in Solomon Lutnick, *The American Revolution and the British Press* (Columbia: University of Missouri Press, 1967).

14. *See* Clark, *British Opinion and the American Revolution*, pp. 160–63. Founded in 1613, the Robinhood, by the time of the American Revolution, was a debating society for City tradesmen and others, including country gentlemen and politicians who cared to attend. The Middlesex Petition and Stamp Act were subjects of bitter debates among members. Such encounters gave occasion for frequent pro-American polemics like those of Will Chatwell. *Gentleman's Magazine*, 39 (1769): 289–91.

15. Christie, *Wilkes, Wyvill and Reform*, pp. 33–34.

16. George S. Veitch, *The Genesis of Parliamentary Reform*, 2d ed. (Hamden, Conn.: Archon Books, 1965), p. 29.

17. *Annual Register*, 12 (1769): 75.

18. Minnie Clare Yarborough, *John Horne Tooke* (New York: Columbia University Press, 1926), pp. 41–42.

19. George Otto Trevelyan, *The Early History of Charles James Fox* (New York: Harper & Brothers, 1904), p. 440.

20. Yarborough, *John Horne Tooke*, pp. 79–81.

21. Fred J. Hinkhouse, *The Preliminaries of the American Revolution as Seen in the English Press, 1763–1775* (New York: Columbia University Press, 1926), p. 201.

22. Yarborough, *John Horne Tooke*, p. 78.

23. This society statement is quoted from Christie, *Wilkes, Wyvill and Reform*, p. 49.

24. Charles Francis Adams, ed., *The Works of John Adams*, 10 vols. (Boston: Little, Brown & Co., 1856), 2: 325.

25. Hinkhouse, *The Preliminaries of the American Revolution*, p. 171.

26. Clark, *British Opinion and the American Revolution*, p. 156.

27. *See also* Joseph Priestley, *An Essay on the First Principle of Gov-*

ernment and on the Nature of Political, Civil and Religious Liberty (Printed for J. Johnson; London: 1771). A broad description of Priestley's principles may be found in John A. Passmore, ed., *Priestley's Writings on Philosophy, Science and Politics* (New York: Collier Books, 1965). Whereas Richard Price's concept of liberty was rooted in his moral philosophy, Priestley's ideas for expanding liberty anticipated the utilitarianism of Jeremy Bentham. Élie Halévy, *The Growth of Philosophic Radicalism* (New York: Macmillan & Co., 1928), p. 22.

28. In 1783 Dr. Kippis spoke for most Honest Whigs in urging a magnanimous peace with America and in reflecting on the historical significance of the American Revolution. "It is a revolution which is difficult, perhaps impossible, to parallel in the annals of mankind; and the effects of it will extend to both hemispheres. . . . It may be . . . hoped that the interests of justice, humanity, and liberty will acquire fresh strength, and be more widely diffused through the globe." Andrew Kippis, *Considerations on the Provisional Treaty with America and the Preliminary Articles of Peace with France and Spain* (Printed for T. Cadell; London: 1783), p. 30.

29. Hazlitt befriended American war prisoners held in England during the Revolution. William C. Hazlitt, *The Hazlitt Memoirs*, 2 vols. (London: George Redway, 1897), 1: 11–12.

30. Dr. Fothergill visited and preached in America in 1754–56. His published sermons made him a familiar figure to colonists during the Great Awakening of the mid-eighteenth century.

31. Day knew several Americans. He once had occasion to meet a Southern slave owner and lectured him on the evils of slavery. Day later recognized that the American Union might be endangered by the incongruities posed by the slavery dilemma. James Keir, *An Account of the Life and Writings of Thomas Day* (London: John Stockdale, 1791), pp. 39–40. Like Dr. Kippis, Day urged a generous peace with America at the end of the war. Thomas Day, *Reflections upon the Present State of England and the Independence of America* (Printed for John Stockdale; London: 1782).

32. Lord Teignmouth, ed., *Memoirs of the Life, Writings and Correspondence of Sir William Jones* (Philadelphia: William Poyntell & Co., 1805), p. 102. For Jones's opinions on America and reform, *see also* Garland Cannon, ed., *The Letters of Sir William Jones* (Oxford: Clarendon Press, 1970).

33. Bishop Shipley made himself conspicuous in the Anglican hierarchy when he publicly deplored the Coercion Acts in 1774. Jonathan Shipley, *A Speech Intended to Have Been Spoken on the Bill for Altering the Charter of the Colony of Massachusetts Bay* (Reprinted and sold by William and Thomas Bradford; London: 1774). Benjamin Franklin considered the bishop one of America's best friends during the Revolution. Jared Sparks, ed., *The Works of Benjamin Franklin*, 12 vols. (Boston: John B. Russell, 1837), 9: 229.

34. Caroline Robbins, *The Eighteenth Century Commonwealthman* (New York: Atheneum, 1968), p. 334.

35. William Paley, *The Principles of Moral and Political Philosophy* (Boston: Richardson & Lord, 1825). A recent treatment of Paley as a theologian, moral philosopher, and political thinker is D. L. LeMahieu, *The Mind of William Paley* (Lincoln: University of Nebraska Press, 1976).

36. *See* Anthony Lincoln, *Some Social and Political Ideas of English Dissent, 1763–1800* (Cambridge: Cambridge University Press, 1938).

37. Drafted at the Feathers Tavern in London in 1772, it called for a liberalization of subscription requirements to church dogma and discipline. It failed to carry sufficient support in Parliament after a lengthy debate. William Cobbett, ed., *The Parliamentary History of England*, 36 vols. (London: T. C. Hansard, 1813), 17: 245–97.

38. J. H. Plumb, *England in the Eighteenth Century, 1714–1815*, 12th ed. (Baltimore: Penguin Books, 1966), pp. 133–34.

39. Gordon S. Wood, *The Creation of the American Republic* (New York: W. W. Norton & Co., 1972), p. 609.

40. Bernard Bailyn, *The Ideological Origins of the American Revolution* (Cambridge: Harvard University Press, 1973), p. 95.

41. Lewis B. Namier, *England in the Age of the American Revolution*, 2d ed. (London: Macmillan & Co., 1963), p. 39.

42. Ibid.

43. J. H. Rose, A. P. Newton, and E. H. Benians, eds., *The Cambridge History of the British Empire*, 8 vols. (New York: Macmillan & Co., 1929), 1: 761.

Radical Spokesmen on Imperial Crisis, 1774-1776

1. Thomas R. Adams, "The British Pamphlets of the American Revolution for 1774: A Progress Report," *Proceedings of the Massachusetts Historical Society*, 81 (1969).

2. A recent example would be A. L. Burt, *The Evolution of the British Empire and Commonwealth from the American Revolution* (Boston: Heath & Co., 1956). This traditional interpretation has been challenged or amended by imperial historians who stress multiple causation, economic forces, or quantitative analyses.

3. Among the distinguished men who appeared at these meetings were Dr. Priestley, Dr. Kippis, Bishop Shipley, James Boswell the biographer, the duke of Richmond, William Watson, the physician at the Foundling Hospital, Matthew Maty, principal secretary of the Royal Society and principal librarian at the British Museum, Peter Templeman, keeper of the reading room at the British Museum, Sir John Pringle, president of the Royal Society, and Dr. Fothergill. Carl B. Cone, *Torchbearer of Freedom, the Influence of Richard Price on Eighteenth Century Thought* (Lexington: University of Kentucky Press, 1952), p. 54.

4. Oscar Handlin and Mary Handlin, "James Burgh and American Revolutionary Theory," *Proceedings of the Massachusetts Historical Society*, 62 (1961): 43.

5. Caroline Robbins, *The Eighteenth Century Commonwealthman* (New York: Atheneum, 1968), p. 365.

6. Bernard Bailyn, *The Ideological Origins of the American Revolution* (Cambridge: Harvard University Press, 1973), p. 41.

7. There is no recently published biography of Burgh but a scholarly study of the man as an academician, moralist, polemicist, and political writer is presented in Carla H. Hay, "Crusading Schoolmaster: James Burgh, 1714–1775" (Ph.D. diss., University of Kentucky, 1972).

8. Peter William Clayden, *The Early Years of Samuel Rogers* (London: Smith, Elder & Co., 1887), p. 11.

9. Burgh's numerous friendships are described in the *Dictionary of National Biography*. See Leslie Stephen and Sidney Lee, eds., *The Dictionary of National Biography* (London:1917), 3: 322.

10. Ian R. Christie, *Wilkes, Wyvill and Reform* (London: Macmillan & Co., 1962), p. 53.

11. Clayden, *Early Life of Samuel Rogers*, pp. 34–35.

12. Lord Edmund George Fitzmaurice, *Life of William, Earl of Shelburne*, 3 vols. (London: Macmillan & Co., 1876), 2: 236.

13. A good and comprehensive biographical portrait of Price and the influence he had on his time may be found in Cone, *Torchbearer of Freedom*.

14. Dr. Price's correspondence with distinguished Americans ranged over a long period of years, even during the American war. Among them were the Reverend Charles Chauncy of Boston's First Church, John Winthrop, Hollis Professor of Mathematics and Natural Philosophy at Harvard College, and Ezra Stiles, president of Yale College. *See* Charles E. Norton, "The Price Letters," *Proceedings of the Massachusetts Historical Society*, Series 2, 17 (1903): 262–378.

15. George Otto Trevelyan, *The American Revolution*, 4 vols. (London: Longmans, Green & Co., 1917), 3: 210.

16. Accounts of Cartwright's life and reform career may be found in Francis Dorothy Cartwright, ed., *The Life and Correspondence of Major Cartwright*, 2d ed., 2 vols. (New York: Augustus M. Kelley, 1969); John W. Osborne, *John Cartwright* (Cambridge: Harvard University Press, 1972). *Also see* George S. Veitch, *The Genesis of Parliamentary Reform*, 2d ed. (Hamden, Conn.: Archon Books, 1965); Simon Maccoby, *The English Radical Tradition* (London: Charles & Adam Black, 1966); Graham Wallas, *The Life of Francis Place* (New York: Longmans, Green & Co., 1898); John W. Osborne, *William Cobbett: His Thought and His Times* (New Brunswick: Rutgers University Press, 1966).

17. R. G. Adams, *Political Ideas of the American Revolution*, 2d ed. (New York: Facsimile Library, 1939), p. 57.

18. Cartwright, ed., *Life and Correspondence*, 2: 293.

19. It was not unusual for her contemporaries to have strong opinions about Catharine Macaulay. *See* G. B. Hill, ed., *Boswell's Life of Johnson*, 6 vols. (Oxford: Clarendon Press, 1934), 1: 517–18; R. B. Johnson, ed., *The*

Letters of Hannah More (New York: Dial Press, 1926), p. 80; G. F. R. Barker, ed., *Horace Walpole: Memoirs of the Reign of George III*, 4 vols. (New York: G. P. Putnam's Sons, 1894), 3: 121–22; Margaret George, *One Woman's Situation: A Study of Mary Wollstonecraft* (Chicago: University of Illinois Press, 1970), p. 10.

20. Richard S. Hooker, "The American Revolution Seen through a Wine Glass," *William and Mary Quarterly*, Series 3, 11 (1954): 60.

21. Lucy Martin Donnelly, "The Celebrated Mrs. Macaulay," *William and Mary Quarterly*, Series 3, 6 (1949): 204.

22. Hollis will receive little attention in these pages, though his career as a Radical propagandist had some important American connections in the generation before his death in 1774. *See* Francis Blackburne, ed., *Memoirs of Thomas Hollis* (London: 1780); Bernard Knollenburg, ed., "Thomas Hollis and Jonathan Mayhew: Their Correspondence, 1759–1766," *Proceedings of the Massachusetts Historical Society*, 15 (1949–50); Caroline Robbins, "The Strenuous Whig, Thomas Hollis of Lincoln's Inn," *William and Mary Quarterly*, Series 3, 7 (1950); David S. Lovejoy, "Henry Marchant and the Mistress of the World," *William and Mary Quarterly*, Series 3, 12 (1955); Thomas Hollis, ed., *The True Sentiments of America Contained in a collection of letters sent from the House of Representatives . . . to several persons of high rank in this kingdom* (Printed for John Almon; London: 1768).

23. Robbins, *The Eighteenth Century Commonwealthman*, p. 361.

24. W. E. H. Lecky, *A History of England in the Eighteenth Century*, 7 vols. (London: Longmans, Green & Co., 1906), 3: 414.

A Commonwealth of Nations: John Cartwright

1. Descriptions of Dean Tucker's life and writings may be found in Walter E. Clark, *Josiah Tucker* (New York: Columbia University Press, 1903) and R. L. Schuyler, ed., *Josiah Tucker: A Selection from his Economic and Political Writings* (New York: Columbia University Press, 1931). The latter includes the complete text of the important *The Elements of Commerce and Theory of Taxes*, never published until 1931. For a complete bibliography of Tucker's writings on theology, morals, politics and economics, *see* Paul L. Ford, "Josiah Tucker and His Writings," *Journal of Political Economy*, 2 (1893–94): 330–47.

2. Josiah Tucker, *The True Interest of Britain* (Printed and sold by Robert Bell; Philadelphia: 1776), pp. 15–17.

3. Ibid., pp. 49–51.

4. Vincent T. Harlow, *The Founding of the Second British Empire*, 2 vols. (London: Longmans, Green & Co., 1952–64), 1: 210.

5. Bernard Bailyn, *The Ideological Origins of the American Revolution* (Cambridge: Harvard University Press, 1973), p. 41.

6. John Brooke, *King George III* (New York: McGraw-Hill Book Co., 1972), pp. 107–09.

7. John Cartwright, *American Independence the Interest and Glory of Great Britain* (Printed by H. S. Woodfall and sold by J. Wilkie; London: 1774), pp. 10–11.

8. Ibid., p. 48.

9. Ibid., p. 3.

10. R. G. Adams, *Political Ideas of the American Revolution*, 2d ed. (New York: Facsimile Library, 1939), p. 57.

11. Julian Boyd, ed., *The Papers of Thomas Jefferson*, 18 vols. (Princeton: Princeton University Press, 1950–71), 6: 581–600.

12. Harold M. Baer, "An Early Plan for the Development of the West," *American Historical Review*, 30 (1925): 540.

13. Cartwright, *American Independence the Interest and Glory of Great Britain*, p. 27.

14. John W. Osborne, *John Cartwright* (Cambridge: Harvard University Press, 1972), p. 9.

15. Simon Maccoby, *The English Radical Tradition* (London: Charles & Adam Black, 1966), p. 3.

16. R. L. Schuyler, "The Britannic Question and the American Revolution," *Political Science Quarterly*, 38 (1923): 104.

17. R. R. Palmer, *The Age of the Democratic Revolution*, 2 vols. (Princeton: Princeton University Press, 1959), 1: 79.

18. Reginald Coupland, *The American Revolution and the British Empire* (London: Longmans, Green & Co., 1930), pp. 28–29.

"Home Rule" for Ireland and America: Granville Sharp

1. Granville Sharp, *A Declaration of the People's Natural Right to a Share in the Legislature* (Printed for B. White; London: 1774), p. v.

2. Ibid., p. 20.

3. Ibid., pp. 26–27.

4. David L. Keir, *The Constitutional History of Modern Britain since 1485*, 9th ed. (New York: W. W. Norton & Co., 1969), pp. 434–35.

5. Ibid., p. 435n. Keir, who also is familiar with the views of Grant Robertson and A. F. Pollard, suggests that the measures were "meant rather as a check on the Viceroy than on the Parliament."

6. Sharp, *A Declaration of the People's Natural Right*, pp. 77–78.

7. Ibid., p. 65.

8. *The Statutes-at-Large*, 6 George I, V, p. 280.

9. Sir Edward Coke, *Institutes of the Laws of England* (Philadelphia: Robert H. Small, 1853), I, Sec. 212, 141 a, b.

10. Daines Barrington, *Observations on the More Ancient Statutes* (London: J. Nichols, 1796), pp. 160–65.

11. William Blackstone, *Commentaries on the Laws of England* (New York: W. E. Dean, 1850), IV, Bk. 1, p. 71.

12. Quoted from Hooker by Sharp, *A Declaration of the People's Natural Right*, pp. 3–4.

13. Ibid., p. 2.
14. Ibid., p. 37.
15. Ibid., p. 34.
16. Charles F. Mullett, *Fundamental Law and the American Revolution, 1760–1776* (New York: Columbia University Press, 1933), p. 195.
17. H. Trevor Colbourn, *The Lamp of Experience: Whig History and the Intellectual Origins of the American Revolution* (Chapel Hill: University of North Carolina Press, 1965), pp. 54–55.
18. Eric Robson, *The American Revolution in Its Political and Military Aspects, 1763–1783* (Hamden, Conn.: Archon Books, 1965), p. 80.
19. E. C. P. Lascelles, *Granville Sharp and the Freedom of Slaves in England*, 2d ed. (New York: Negro Universities Press, 1969), p. 105.

Parliamentary Reform: James Burgh

1. James Burgh, *Britain's Remembrancer: Or, The Danger Not Over* (Re-printed by Benjamin Franklin; Philadelphia: 1747), p. 41.
2. Ibid. Also quoted by Bernard Bailyn, *The Ideological Origins of the American Revolution* (Cambridge: Harvard University Press, 1973), pp. 86–87.
3. James Burgh, *Thoughts on Education* (Reprinted and sold by Rogers and Fowle; Boston: 1749), p. 7.
4. James Burgh, *The Dignity of Human Nature* (Reprinted and sold by John W. Folsom; Boston: 1794), p. 21.
5. Ian Christie estimates that Volume I was initially published around January 1774; Volume II, in late 1774; Volume III, in late spring or early summer 1775. Ian R. Christie, *Wilkes, Wyvill and Reform* (London: Macmillan & Co., 1962), pp. 53, 56–57.
6. James Burgh, *Political Disquisitions*, 3 vols. (Printed and sold by Robert Bell and William Woodhouse; Philadelphia: 1775), 1: xii.
7. Ibid., 2: 408.
8. Ibid., 1: 3.
9. Ibid., 3: 192.
10. Ibid.
11. Ibid., 2: 287.
12. Ibid., p. 291.
13. Ibid., p. 304.
14. Ibid., p. 306.
15. Ibid., p. 307.
16. Ibid., p. 310.
17. Ibid., p. 328.
18. Quoted from Burgh's *Crito* by Herbert Butterfield, *George III, Lord North and the People* (London: G. Bell & Sons, Ltd., 1949), p. 259n.
19. Burgh, *Political Disquisitions*, 3: 428–29.
20. Butterfield, *George III, Lord North and the People*, p. 259.
21. Burgh, *Political Disquisitions*, 3: 433–34.

22. Ibid., p. 434.

23. Ibid., 3: 460.

24. *The Monthly Review*, 51 (1774): 344, 354–55.

25. Christie, *Wilkes, Wyvill and Reform*, p. 54.

26. Oscar Handlin and Mary Handlin, "James Burgh and American Revolutionary Theory," *Proceedings of the Massachusetts Historical Society*, 62 (1961): 49.

The Force of Public Opinion: Catharine Macaulay

1. This passage from Volume I of the *History* is drawn from a citation made by Lucy Martin Donnelly, "The Celebrated Mrs. Macaulay," *William and Mary Quarterly*, Series 3, 6 (1949): 177.

2. Bernard Bailyn, *The Ideological Origins of the American Revolution* (Cambridge: Harvard University Press, 1973), p. 41.

3. Donnelly, "The Celebrated Mrs. Macaulay," pp. 200–201.

4. Quoted in Donnelly, "The Celebrated Mrs. Macaulay," p. 181.

5. Catharine Macaulay, *An Address to the People of England, Scotland and Ireland on the Present Crisis of Affairs* (Reprint of the 3d English edition by John Holt; New York: 1775), p. 6.

6. Ibid., p. 11.

7. Ibid., p. 12.

8. Ibid., p. 10.

9. Ibid., p. 12.

10. Ibid., p. 15.

11. Donnelly, "The Celebrated Mrs. Macaulay," pp. 203–04.

A Question of Human Freedom: Richard Price

1. Carl B. Cone, *Torchbearer of Freedom, the Influence of Richard Price on Eighteenth Century Thought* (Lexington: University of Kentucky Press, 1952), p. 1.

2. Ibid., pp. 2, 15.

3. Ibid., pp. 52–68.

4. William D. Hudson, *Reason and Right: A Critical Examination of Richard Price's Moral Philosophy* (London: Macmillan Co., 1970), p. xi. Discussions of Price as a moral philosopher also may be found in W. H. F. Barnes, "Richard Price—A Neglected Eighteenth Century Moralist," *Philosophy*, 17 (1942); Frederick Copleston, *A History of Philosophy*, 8 vols. (New York: Image Books, 1964), 5, pt. 2; Cone, *Torchbearer of Freedom*.

5. This passage from Price's *A Review of the Principal Questions and Difficulties in Morals* is cited from Copleston, *History of Philosophy*, 5, pt. 2, pp. 165–66.

6. Price's words quoted in Copleston, *History of Philosophy*, 5, pt. 2, p. 166.

7. Cone, *Torchbearer of Freedom*, p. 26.

8. The reader might consult Max Savelle, *Seeds of Liberty* (New York: Alfred A. Knopf, 1948), especially his chapter on American patriotism. *See also* Max Savelle, *The Colonial Origins of American Thought* (Princeton, N.J.: D. Van Nostrand Co., 1964); William Warren Sweet, *The Story of Religion in America* (New York: Harper & Bros., 1950); Alan Heimert, *Religion and the American Mind* (Cambridge: Harvard University Press, 1968).

9. Richard Price, *Observations on the Nature of Civil Liberty, Principles of Government, and the Justice and Policy of the War with America* (Reprinted and sold by John Dunlap; Philadelphia: 1776), p. 6.

10. Ibid., p. 10.

11. Ibid., p. 12.

12. Ibid., p. 13.

13. Ibid., p. 17.

14. Ibid., p. 18.

15. Ibid., p. 22.

16. Ibid., p. 29.

17. Ibid.

18. Ibid., p. 50.

19. Ibid., p. 58.

20. This concept is also mentioned in Anthony Lincoln, *Some Political and Social Ideas of English Dissent, 1763–1800* (Cambridge: Cambridge University Press, 1938), p. 137.

21. Cone, *Torchbearer of Freedom*, p. 85n.

22. A. Francis Steuart, ed., *The Last Journals of Horace Walpole during the Reign of George III from 1771–1783*, 2 vols. (London: John Lane, 1910), 1: 529–30.

23. *Annual Register*, 20 (1777): 260.

24. Charles E. Norton, "The Price Letters," *Proceedings of the Massachusetts Historical Society*, Series 2, 17 (1903): 311.

25. Cone, *Torchbearer of Freedom*, p. 200.

26. *Gentleman's Magazine*, 61 (1791): 389–90.

27. R. L. Schuyler, "The Rise of Anti-Imperialism in England," *Political Science Quarterly*, 37 (1922): 456–58.

28. Lincoln, *Some Political and Social Ideas of English Dissent*, p. 102.

Diverse Acquiescence in Radical Opinion

1. Quoted from Minnie Clare Yarborough, *John Horne Tooke* (New York: Columbia University Press, 1926), p. 84.

2. Ibid., pp. 87–88.

3. Anonymous [Richard Price and John Horne Tooke], *Facts: Addressed to the Landholders, Stockholders, Merchants, Farmers, Manufacturers, Tradesmen, Proprietors of Every Description and Generally to All the Subjects of Great Britain and Ireland*, 3d ed. (Printed by J. Johnson; London: 1780), p. 11.

4. For a definitive treatment of the county association movement, *see* E. C. Black, *The Association: British Extraparliamentary Political Organization, 1769–1793* (Cambridge: Harvard University Press, 1963).

5. Other local associations appeared in the counties of Hertfordshire, Sussex, Huntingdon, Surrey, Cumberland, Bedfordshire, Essex, Somerset, Gloucestershire, Wiltshire, Dorset, Devonshire, Norfolk, Berkshire, Buckinghamshire, Nottinghamshire, Kent, Northumberland, Suffolk, Herefordshire, Cambridgeshire, and Derbyshire; also in the boroughs of London, Westminster, York, Bristol, Gloucester, Nottingham, Hereford, Reading, Cambridge, Bridgewater, and Newcastle-on-Tyne.

6. Ian R. Christie, *Wilkes, Wyvill and Reform* (London: Macmillan & Co., 1962), pp. 70–75.

7. Black, *The Association*, p. 130.

8. Francis Dorothy Cartwright, ed., *The Life and Correspondence of Major Cartwright*, 2d ed., 2 vols. (New York: Augustus M. Kelley, 1969), 1: 132–36.

9. Herbert Butterfield, *George III, Lord North and the People, 1779–1780* (London: G. Bell & Sons, 1949), p. 352.

10. Society for Constitutional Information, *Pamphlets* (Written by a member of the Society for Constitutional Information; London: 1782), p. 44. This volume of society pamphlets is located in the Department of Special Collections, King Library, University of Kentucky.

11. George S. Veitch, *The Genesis of Parliamentary Reform*, 2d ed. (Hamden, Conn.: Archon Books, 1965), pp. 74–75.

Whig Politicians on Radical Ideas

1. *Annual Register*, 17 (1774): 62.

2. Ibid., 19 (1776): 47.

3. G. H. Guttridge, *English Whiggism and the American Revolution*, 2d ed. (Berkeley: University of California Press, 1966), p. 35.

4. Quoted from Basil Williams, *The Life of William Pitt, Earl of Chatham*, 4th ed., 2 vols. (New York: Octagon Books, 1966), 2: 294–95.

5. Caroline Robbins, *The Eighteenth Century Commonwealthman* (New York: Atheneum, 1968), pp. 275–76.

6. Dora Mae Clark, *British Opinion and the American Revolution* (New Haven: Yale University Press, 1930), p. 263.

7. Williams, *Life of William Pitt*, 2: 32–33.

8. *See* O. A. Sherrard, *Life of Lord Chatham*, 3 vols. (London: The Bodley Head, 1958), 3: 197–98.

9. Guttridge, *English Whiggism and the American Revolution*, p. 71.

10. Williams, *The Life of William Pitt*, 2: 313.

11. In 1907 Basil Williams published an article which suggests that Pitt, sometime during the 1760s or 1770s, conceived a plan in which the House of Commons would be transformed into a federal legislature composed of representatives from Britain and all the colonies in the British

Empire. British M.P.s were to be subject to existing property qualifications, but colonial members were to be elected by colonial assemblies and exempt from such qualifications. Taxes in the colonies were not to exceed a rate of one pound on estates—no higher than threepence on the pound in peacetime or one shilling on the pound during war. The historic Navigation Acts were to be preserved. *See* Basil Williams, "Chatham and the Representation of the Colonies in the Imperial Parliament," *English Historical Review*, 12 (1907): 756–58.

12. William Cobbett, ed., *The Parliamentary History of England*, 36 vols. (London: T. C. Hansard, 1813), 19: 1012.

13. Leslie Stephen and Sidney Lee, eds., *The Dictionary of National Biography*, 23 vols. (London: 1917), 15: 1011.

14. Ibid.

15. Bernard Donoughue, *British Politics and the American Revolution: The Path to War, 1773–75* (London: Macmillan & Co., 1964), p. 130. The views of Barré and Dunning on the American question are described in Lewis B. Namier and John Brooke, *The History of Parliament: The House of Commons, 1754–1790*, 3 vols. (New York: Oxford University Press, 1964), 2: 53, 368.

16. A splendid history of Shelburne's efforts is in Vincent T. Harlow, *The Founding of the Second British Empire*, 2 vols. (London: Longmans, Green & Co., 1952–64), 1: Chapters 6–8.

17. Samuel Flagg Bemis, *The Diplomacy of the American Revolution*, 7th ed. (Bloomington: Indiana University Press, 1967), p. 254; Vincent T. Harlow, *The Founding of the Second British Empire*, 1: 308–10, 448–51.

18. Lord Edmund George Fitzmaurice, *Life of William, Earl of Shelburne*, 3 vols. (London: Macmillan & Co., 1876), 3: 120.

19. Ibid., pp. 1–2.

20. John Norris, *Shelburne and Reform* (London: Macmillan Co., 1963), pp. 32–33.

21. Fitzmaurice, *Life of William, Earl of Shelburne*, 3: 18.

22. Cobbett, ed., *Parliamentary History*, 21: 1035.

23. Norris, *Shelburne and Reform*, pp. 84–85.

24. Fitzmaurice, *Life of William, Earl of Shelburne*, 3: 96.

25. This remark by Shelburne is quoted in Norris, *Shelburne and Reform*, p. 87.

26. Donoughue, *British Politics and the American Revolution*, pp. 127–30.

27. Quoted by Guttridge, *English Whiggism and the American Revolution*, p. 74.

28. Donoughue, *British Politics and the American Revolution*, p. 132.

29. Ibid., pp. 144–45.

30. Ross J. S. Hoffman, *The Marquis: A Study of Lord Rockingham, 1732–1782* (New York: Fordham University Press, 1973), pp. 319–20.

31. Donoughue, *British Politics and the American Revolution*, p. 129.

32. George Thomas, Earl of Albemarle, *Memoirs of the Marquis of*

Rockingham, 2 vols. (London: Richard Bentley, 1852), 2: 80–81.

33. Ibid., p. 398.
34. Ibid., p. 409.
35. Sir Philip Magnus, *Edmund Burke* (London: John Murray, 1939), pp. 80–81.
36. Carl B. Cone, *Burke and the Nature of Politics*, 2 vols. (Lexington: University of Kentucky Press, 1957, 1964), 1: xv.
37. Edmund Burke, *Thoughts on the Cause of the Present Discontents* (Printed for J. Dodsley; London: 1770), p. 12.
38. Cobbett, ed., *Parliamentary History*, 21: 604.
39. Louis I. Bredvold and Ralph G. Ross, *The Philosophy of Edmund Burke* (Ann Arbor: University of Michigan Press, 1960), p. 166.
40. Burke, *Thoughts on the Cause of the Present Discontents*, pp. 71–72.
41. Thomas W. Copeland, ed., *Correspondence of Edmund Burke*, 9 vols. (Cambridge: Cambridge University Press, 1958–70), 3: 190.
42. Guttridge, *English Whiggism and the American Revolution*, p. 65.
43. Thomas H. D. Mahoney, ed., *Edmund Burke: Selected Writings and Speeches on America* (New York: Bobbs-Merrill Co., 1964), pp. 119–20.
44. Ross J. S. Hoffman and Paul Levack, eds., *Burke's Politics: Selected Writings and Speeches of Edmund Burke* (New York: Alfred A. Knopf, 1949), pp. 52–53.
45. Ibid., pp. 78–79.
46. Copeland, ed., *Correspondence of Edmund Burke*, 3: 132.
47. Mahoney, ed., *Burke: Selected Writings and Speeches on America*, p. 140.
48. Josiah Tucker, *A Letter to Edmund Burke* (Printed by R. Raikes, Gloucester, and sold by T. Cadell; London: 1775), pp. 9–23.
49. Edmund Burke, *A Letter to the Sheriffs of Bristol* (Printed by William Pine; Bristol: 1777), p. 58.
50. Cobbett, ed., *Parliamentary History*, 21: 604.
51. N. C. Philips, "Edmund Burke and the County Association Movement," *English Historical Review*, 76 (1961): 263.
52. Cone, *Burke and the Nature of Politics*, 1: 206–07.
53. Burke's remark is quoted in Cone, *Burke and the Nature of Politics*, 1: 212.
54. Namier and Brooke, *History of Parliament*, 2: 457.
55. Ibid.
56. George Otto Trevelyan, *The Early History of Charles James Fox* (New York: Harper & Brothers, 1904), p. 243.
57. Lord John Russell, ed., *Memorials and Correspondence of Charles James Fox*, 2 vols. (Philadelphia: Blanchard & Lea, 1853), 1: 104–05.
58. Robbins, *The Eighteenth Century Commonwealthman*, p. 322.
59. George Otto Trevelyan, *The American Revolution*, 4 vols. (London: Longmans, Green & Co., 1909), 1: 139.

60. Charles R. Ritcheson, *Aftermath of Revolution: British Policy Toward the United States, 1783–1795* (Dallas: Southern Methodist University Press, 1969), pp. vii–viii.

61. Ibid., pp. 4–6.

62. Alison G. Olson, *Anglo-American Politics, 1660–1775* (Oxford: Oxford University Press, 1973), pp. 180–82.

British-American Radical Connections

1. A comprehensive list of American subscribers to the Bell editions is described in Carla H. Hay, "Crusading Schoolmaster: James Burgh, 1714–1775" (Ph.D. diss., University of Kentucky, 1972), Appendix III.

2. Albert Henry Smyth, ed., *The Writings of Benjamin Franklin*, 10 vols. (New York: Macmillan Co., 1907), 8: 220.

3. *See* Zoltán Haraszti, *John Adams and the Prophets of Progress* (Cambridge: Harvard University Press, 1952), p. 302.

4. Charles Francis Adams, ed., *The Works of John Adams*, 10 vols. (Boston: Little, Brown & Co., 1856), 9: 351.

5. Ibid., pp. 558–59.

6. H. Trevor Colbourn, *The Lamp of Experience: Whig History and the Intellectual Origins of the American Revolution* (Chapel Hill: University of North Carolina Press, 1965), pp. 173, 186.

7. Andrew A. Lipscomb, ed., *The Writings of Thomas Jefferson*, 20 vols. (Washington, D.C.: The Thomas Jefferson Memorial Association, 1904), 8: 32.

8. Oscar Handlin and Mary Handlin, "James Burgh and American Revolutionary Theory," *Proceedings of the Massachusetts Historical Society*, 62 (1961): 57.

9. Ibid., p. 38.

10. Francis Dorothy Cartwright, ed., *The Life and Correspondence of Major Cartwright*, 2d ed., 2 vols. (New York: Augustus M. Kelley, 1969), 2: 135.

11. John Bigelow, ed., *The Works of Benjamin Franklin*, 12 vols. (New York: G. P. Putnam's Sons, 1904), 11: 77.

12. J. R. Pole, *Political Representation in England and the Origins of the American Republic* (Berkeley: University of California Press, 1966), p. 436.

13. Colbourn, *The Lamp of Experience*, pp. 200–203.

14. Smyth, ed., *Writings of Benjamin Franklin*, 4: 370.

15. Bernard Knollenburg, ed., "Thomas Hollis and Jonathan Mayhew: Their Correspondence, 1759–1766" *Proceedings of the Massachusetts Historical Society*, 15 (1949–50): 173.

16. Adams, ed., *Works of John Adams*, 9: 331–32.

17. H. Trevor Colbourn, "Thomas Jefferson's Use of the Past," *William and Mary Quarterly*, Series 3, 15 (1958): 64, 64n.

18. James Curtis Ballagh, ed., *The Letters of Richard Henry Lee*, 2

vols. (New York: Macmillan Co., 1911), 1: 160–64.

19. Julian Boyd, ed., *The Papers of Thomas Jefferson*, 18 vols. (Princeton: Princeton University Press, 1950–71), 1: 471, 477.

20. Ibid., p. 488.

21. Carl Van Doren, *Benjamin Franklin* (New York: Viking Press, 1958), pp. 319–22.

22. Charles E. Norton, "The Price Letters," *Proceedings of the Massachusetts Historical Society*, Series 2, 17 (1903): 287–88.

23. Page Smith, *John Adams*, 2 vols. (New York: Doubleday & Co., 1962), 2: 644.

24. Dumas Malone, *Jefferson and His Time: Jefferson and the Rights of Man*, 4 vols. (Boston: Little, Brown & Co., 1948–70), 2: 55–56.

25. Merrill D. Peterson, *Thomas Jefferson and the New Nation* (New York: Oxford University Press, 1970), pp. 59, 63.

26. Katharine Anthony, *First Lady of the Revolution* (Port Washington, N.Y.: Kennikat Press, 1972), p. 123.

27. Ibid., pp. 124–25.

28. Maud Macdonald Hutcheson, "Mercy Warren, 1728–1814," *William and Mary Quarterly*, Series 3, 10 (1953): 392–93.

29. Quoted from Lucy Martin Donnelly, "The Celebrated Mrs. Macaulay," *William and Mary Quarterly*, Series 3, 6 (1949): 194.

30. Jared Sparks, ed., *The Writings of George Washington*, 12 vols. (Boston: John B. Russell, 1837), 9: 111.

31. *See* Knollenburg, ed., "Thomas Hollis and Jonathan Mayhew: Their Correspondence, 1759–1766," pp. 102–93. These letters show how British and American radicals viewed the Stamp Act crisis and how the two groups' reliance upon information from each other often affected their evaluations, whether accurate or inaccurate, of imperial problems.

32. *See* Norton, ed., "The Price Letters," pp. 262–378. These letters between Price and numerous Americans range over the period from 1767 to 1790, including correspondence written during the Revolutionary War. The wartime letters are a telling account of the strong bonds between British and American radicals at a time when men like Dr. Price could have been prosecuted for communicating with rebels against the crown. Such actions were never taken against pro-American radicals, however. John Horne Tooke was the only Englishman jailed for his pro-American activities during the American war.

33. *See* Arthur M. Schlesinger, Sr., *Prelude to Independence: The Newspaper War on Britain, 1764–1776* (New York: Alfred A. Knopf, 1958).

34. Colbourn, *The Lamp of Experience*, p. 187. *Also see* Philip Davidson, *Propaganda and the American Revolution* (Chapel Hill: University of North Carolina Press, 1941).

35. Bernard Bailyn, *The Ideological Origins of the American Revolution* (Cambridge: Harvard University Press, 1973), p. 2.

36. Thomas R. Adams, "The British Pamphlets of the American Rev-

olution for 1774: A Progress Report," *Proceedings of the Massachusetts Historical Society*, 81 (1969): 31–84.

37. Ibid., p. 44.

38. Arthur M. Schlesinger, Sr., *The Birth of the Nation* (New York: Alfred A. Knopf, 1968), p. 231.

39. Ian R. Christie, *Crisis of Empire* (London: Edward Arnold, 1966), pp. 105–06.

40. Bernard Bailyn, ed., *Pamphlets of the American Revolution, 1750–1776*, 2 vols. (Cambridge: Harvard University Press, 1965), 1: 320.

41. Ibid., p. 454.

42. Ibid., p. 671.

43. Bernard Bailyn, "Political Experience and Enlightenment Ideas in Eighteenth Century America," *American Historical Review*, 62 (1961–62): 343–44.

44. Colbourn, *The Lamp of Experience*, p. 186.

45. Bailyn, *The Ideological Origins of the American Revolution*, p. 19.

46. William H. Nelson, "The Revolutionary Character of the American Revolution," *American Historical Review*, 80 (1965): 1011–14.

47. Benjamin Labaree, "The Idea of American Independence," *Proceedings of the Massachusetts Historical Society*, 82 (1969): 5.

48. Bailyn, *The Ideological Origins of the American Revolution*, p. 26.

49. Reginald Coupland, *The American Revolution and the British Empire* (London: Longmans, Green & Co., 1930), pp. 36–37.

Conclusion

1. Dean Tucker's views at the outset of the American war may be found in Josiah Tucker, *An Humble Address and Earnest Appeal*, 2d ed. (Printed by R. Raikes of Gloucester and sold by T. Cadell; London: 1775); Josiah Tucker, *The Respective Pleas and Arguments of the Mother Country* (Printed by R. Raikes of Gloucester and sold by T. Cadell; London: 1775); Josiah Tucker, *A Series of Answers to Certain Popular Objections against Separation from the Rebellious Colonies* (Printed by R. Raikes of Gloucester and sold by T. Cadell; London: 1776).

2. Josiah Tucker, *Cui Bono? or, An Inquiry, What Benefits Can Arise Either to the English or the Americans, the French, Spaniards, or Dutch, from the Greatest Successes, in the Present War?*, 2d ed. (Printed by R. Raikes of Gloucester for T. Cadell of London and sold by Evans and Hazel; Gloucester: 1782).

3. Ibid., p. 46.

4. Ibid., p. 87.

5. Thomas Pownall, governor in Massachusetts Bay and South Carolina during the Seven Years' War, urged administrative and economic reforms of such a scope in his *The Administration of the Colonies*, first published in 1763. He supported a plan that would transform the old imperial system of mother country and dependencies into an imperial

commonwealth governed in a more efficient, prosperous order. He urged a utilitarian approach to the American problem which, along with Tucker's proposals in 1782, anticipated Lord Durham's conclusions two generations later. Thomas Pownall, *The Administration of the Colonies*, 2d ed. (Printed for J. Dodsley and J. Walter; London: 1765); *also consult* John A. Schutz, *Thomas Pownall, British Defender of American Liberty* (Glendale, Calif.: Arthur H. Clark Co., 1951).

6. Quoted in R. L. Schuyler, ed., *Josiah Tucker: A Selection from His Economic and Political Writings* (New York: Columbia University Press, 1931), p. 38.

7. Ibid., p. 39.

8. Ibid., p. 461.

9. E. G. Bourne, "The Authorship of the Federalist," *American Historical Review*, 2 (1897): 454.

10. Francis Dorothy Cartwright, ed., *The Life and Correspondence of Major Cartwright*, 2d ed., 2 vols. (New York: Augustus M. Kelley, 1969), 1: 75.

11. Ibid., p. 77.

12. Ibid., pp. 55–59.

13. R. G. Adams, *Political Ideas of the American Revolution*, 2d ed. (New York: Facsimile Library, 1939), p. 58.

14. L. H. Gipson, *The Coming of the Revolution* (New York: Harper Torchbooks, 1962), pp. 232–33.

15. E. C. P. Lascelles, *Granville Sharp and the Freedom of Slaves in England*, 2d ed. (New York: Negro Universities Press, 1969), p. 40.

16. Ibid., pp. 41–42.

17. M. Dorothy George, *London Life in the Eighteenth Century* (New York: Capricorn Books, 1965), p. 137.

18. Cartwright, ed., *Life and Correspondence*, 1: 100.

19. J. R. Pole, *Political Representation in England and the Origins of the American Republic* (Berkeley: University of California Press, 1966), p. 463.

20. *See* Catharine Macaulay, *Observations on the Reflections of the Right Hon. Edmund Burke* (Printed by I. Thomas and E. T. Andrews; Boston: 1791).

21. John Emory, ed., *The Works of the Rev. John Wesley*, 4th ed., 14 vols. (London: John Mason, 1841), 11: 112.

22. Carl B. Cone, *Torchbearer of Freedom, the Influence of Richard Price on Eighteenth Century Thought* (Lexington: University of Kentucky Press, 1952), pp. 88–93.

23. Richard Price, *Additional Observations on the Nature and Value of Civil Liberty, and the War with America* (Reprinted by Hall and Sellers; Philadelphia: 1778).

24. Richard Price, *The General Introduction to the Two Tracts on Civil Liberty, the War with America, and the Finances of the Kingdom* (Reprinted by Hall and Sellers; Philadelphia: 1778).

25. Price's description of the British "Account of Customs" from 1772 to 1776 was as follows: from 1772 to 1776 gross receipts declined from £5,134,503 to £3,726,970; debentures, from £2,214,508 to £1,541,300; net receipts, from £2,441,038 to £1,633,380; payments into the Exchequer, from £2,525,515 to £2,460,402. *See General Introduction to the Two Tracts*, p. 14.

26. Cone, *Torchbearer of Freedom*, pp. 104–08.

27. Price's words quoted by Cone, *Torchbearer of Freedom*, p. 107.

28. Richard Price, *Observations on the Importance of the American Revolution, and the Means of Making It a Benefit to the World* (Printed for L. White, W. Whitestone, P. Byrne, P. Wogan, J. Cash, and R. Marchbank; Dublin: 1785).

29. Ibid., pp. 1–2.

30. Ibid., p. 85.

31. *See* Carl B. Cone, "Richard Price and the Constitution of the United States," *American Historical Review*, 63 (1947–48): 726–47.

32. Richard Price, *A Discourse on the Love of Our Country* (Reprinted by Edward E. Powers; Boston: 1790), p. 12.

33. J. H. Plumb, *England in the Eighteenth Century, 1714–1815*, 12th ed. (Baltimore: Penguin Books, 1966), p. 124.

34. Quoted in John Brooke, *King George III* (New York: McGraw-Hill Co., 1972), pp. 174–75.

35. Ibid., p. 175.

BIBLIOGRAPHY

GENERAL WORKS

Burt, A. L. *The Evolution of the British Empire and Commonwealth from the American Revolution*. Boston: Heath & Co., 1956.

Gipson, L. H. *The British Empire before the American Revolution*. 15 vols. New York: Alfred A. Knopf, 1936–70.

Halévy, Élie. *A History of the English People in the Nineteenth Century*. 6 vols. Translated by E. E. Watkin and D. A. Barker. New York: Barnes & Noble, 1961.

Keir, David L. *The Constitutional History of Modern Britain since 1485*. 9th ed. New York: W. W. Norton & Co., 1969.

Lecky, W. E. H. *A History of England in the Eighteenth Century*. 7 vols. Longmans, Green & Co., 1906.

Palmer, R. R. *The Age of the Democratic Revolution*. 2 vols. Princeton: Princeton University Press, 1959–64.

Plumb, J. H. *England in the Eighteenth Century, 1714–1815*. 12th ed. Baltimore: Penguin Books, 1966.

Rose, J. H.; Newton, A. P.; and Benians, E. H., eds. *The Cambridge History of the British Empire*. 8 vols. New York: Macmillan Co., 1929–40.

Watson, J. Steven. *The Reign of George III, 1760–1815*. Oxford: Clarendon Press, 1960.

BRITISH RADICALISM DURING THE AGE OF THE AMERICAN REVOLUTION

Contemporary Pamphlets and Books

Day, Thomas. *Reflections upon the Present State of England and the Independence of America*. Printed for John Stockdale; London: 1782.

Hollis, Thomas, ed. *The True Sentiments of America Contained in a collection of letters sent from the House of Representatives ... to several persons of high rank in this Kingdom*. Printed for John Almon; London: 1768.

Kippis, Andrew. *Considerations on the Provisional Treaty with America and the Preliminary Articles of Peace with France and Spain*. Printed for T. Cadell; London: 1783.

Paley, William. *The Principles of Moral and Political Philosophy*. Boston: Richardson and Lord, 1825.

Priestley, Joseph. *An Essay on the First Principles of Government and on the Nature of Political, Civil and Religious Liberty*. Printed for J. Johnson; London: 1771.

Shipley, Jonathan. *A Speech Intended to Have Been Spoken on the Bill for Altering the Charters of the Colony of Massachusetts Bay*. Reprinted by William and Thomas Bradford; London: 1774.

Society for Constitutional Information. *Pamphlets*. Written by a member of the Society for Constitutional Information; London: 1782. This volume of Society for Constitutional Information pamphlets is in the possession of the Department of Special Collections at the King Library, University of Kentucky.

Memoirs and Correspondence

Blackburne, Francis, ed. *Memoirs of Thomas Hollis*. London: 1780.

Cannon, Garland, ed. *The Letters of Sir William Jones*. 2 vols. Oxford: Clarendon Press, 1970.

Hazlitt, William Carew. *The Hazlitt Memoirs*. 2 vols. London: George Redway, 1897.

Knollenburg, Bernard, ed. "Thomas Hollis and Jonathan Mayhew: Their Correspondence, 1759–1766." *Proceedings of the Massachusetts Historical Society*, 15 (1949–50): 102–93.

Passmore, John A., ed. *Priestley's Writings on Philosophy, Science and Politics*. New York: Collier Books, 1965.

Teignmouth, Lord, ed. *Memoirs of the Life, Writings and Correspondence of Sir William Jones*. Philadelphia: William Foyntell & Co., 1805.

Biographies

George, Margaret. *One Woman's Situation: A Study of Mary Wollstonecraft*. Chicago: University of Illinois Press, 1970.

Keir, James. *An Account of the Life and Writings of Thomas Day*. London: John Stockdale, 1791.

Osborne, John W. *William Cobbett: His Thought and Times*. New Brunswick: Rutgers University Press, 1966.

Sherrard, O. A. *A Life of John Wilkes*. New York: Dodd, Mead & Co., 1930.

Stephen, Leslie and Lee, Sidney, eds. *The Dictionary of National Biography*. 23 vols. London: 1917.

Wallas, Graham. *The Life of Francis Place*. New York: Longmans, Green & Co., 1898.

Yarborough, Minnie Clare. *John Horne Tooke*. New York: Columbia University Press, 1926.

Other Works

Black, E. E. *The Association: British Extraparliamentary Political Organization, 1769–1793.* Cambridge: Harvard University Press, 1963.

Butterfield, Herbert. *George III, Lord North and the People, 1779–1780.* London: G. Bell & Sons, 1949.

Christie, Ian R. *Wilkes, Wyvill and Reform.* London: Macmillan & Co., 1962.

Clark, Dora Mae. *British Opinion and the American Revolution.* New Haven: Yale University Press, 1930.

Elsey, George M., ed. "John Wilkes and William Palfrey." *Publications of the Colonial Society of Massachusetts,* 34 (1943): 411–28.

Halévy, Élie. *The Growth of Philosophic Radicalism.* New York: Macmillan & Co., 1928.

Hinkhouse, Fred J. *The Preliminaries of the American Revolution as Seen in the English Press, 1763–1775.* New York: Columbia University Press, 1926.

LeMahieu, D. L. *The Mind of William Paley.* Lincoln: University of Nebraska Press, 1976.

Lincoln, Anthony. *Some Political and Social Ideas of English Dissent, 1763–1800.* Cambridge: Cambridge University Press, 1938.

Lovejoy, David S. "Henry Marchant and the Mistress of the World." *William and Mary Quarterly,* Series 3, 12 (1955): 375–98.

Maccoby, Simon. *The English Radical Tradition.* London: Charles and Adam Black, 1966.

Maier, Pauline. "John Wilkes and American Disillusionment with Britain." *William and Mary Quarterly,* Series 3, 20 (1963): 373–95.

Robbins, Caroline. *The Eighteenth Century Commonwealthman.* New York: Atheneum, 1968.

———. "The Strenuous Whig, Thomas Hollis of Lincoln's Inn." *William and Mary Quarterly,* Series 3, 7 (1950): 406–53.

Rudé, George F. E. *Wilkes and Liberty.* Oxford: Clarendon Press, 1962.

Schuyler, R. L. "The Britannic Question and the American Revolution." *Political Science Quarterly,* 38 (1923): 104–14.

———. "The Recall of the Legions." *American Historical Review,* 26 (1920): 18–36.

———. "The Rise of Anti-Imperialism in England." *Political Science Quarterly,* 37 (1922): 440–71.

Sutherland, Lucy. *The City of London and the Opposition to Government, 1768–1774: A Study in the Rise of Metropolitan Radicalism.* London: University of London, Athlone Press, 1959.

Veitch, George S. *The Genesis of Parliamentary Reform.* 2d ed. Hamden, Conn.: Archon Books, 1965.

BRITISH RADICAL SPOKESMEN ON IMPERIAL CRISIS, 1774–1776

Contemporary Pamphlets and Books

Anonymous [Richard Price and John Horne Tooke]. *Facts: Addressed to the Landholders, Merchants, Farmers, Manufacturers, Tradesmen, Proprietors of Every Description and Generally to All the Subjects of Great Britain and Ireland.* 3d ed. Printed by J. Johnson; London: 1780. A copy of this edition is in the Department of Special Collections, King Library, University of Kentucky

Burgh, James. *Britain's Remembrancer: Or, The Danger Not Over.* Reprinted by Benjamin Franklin; Philadelphia: 1747.

———. *Political Disquisitions.* 3 vols. Philadelphia: Robert Bell and William Woodhouse, 1775.

———. *The Dignity of Human Nature.* Reprinted by John W. Folsom; Boston: 1794.

———. *Thoughts on Education.* Reprinted by Rogers and Fowle; Boston: 1749.

Cartwright, John. *American Independence the Interest and Glory of Great Britain.* Printed by H. S. Woodfall and sold by J. Willkie; London: 1774.

Macaulay, Catharine. *An Address to the People of England, Scotland and Ireland on the Present Crisis of Affairs.* Reprinted by John Holt; New York: 1775.

———. *Observations on the Reflections of the Right Hon. Edmund Burke.* Printed by I. Thomas and E. T. Andrews; Boston: 1791.

Price, Richard. *A Discourse on the Love of Our Country.* Reprinted by Edward E. Powers; Boston: 1790.

———. *Additional Observations on the Nature and Value of Civil Liberty, and the War with America.* Reprinted by Hall and Sellers; Philadelphia: 1778.

———. *Observations on the Importance of the American Revolution, and the Means of Making It a Benefit to the World.* Printed for L. White, W. Whitestone, P. Byrne, P. Wogan, J. Cash, and R. Marchbank; Dublin: 1785.

———. *Observations on the Nature of Civil Liberty, the Principles of Government, and the Justice and Policy of the War with America.* Reprinted by John Dunlap; Philadelphia: 1776.

———. *The General Introduction to the Two Tracts on Civil Liberty, the War with America, and the Finances of the Kingdom.* Reprinted by Hall and Sellers; Philadelphia: 1778.

Schuyler, R. L., ed. *Josiah Tucker: A Selection from His Economic and Political Writings.* New York: Columbia University Press, 1931.

Sharp, Granville. *A Declaration of the People's Natural Right to a Share in the Legislature.* Printed for B. White; London: 1774.

Tucker, Josiah. *A Letter from a Merchant in London to His Nephew in North America.* Printed for J. Walter; London: 1766.

————. *A Letter to Edmund Burke.* Printed by R. Raikes of Gloucester and sold by T. Cadell of London; London: 1775.

————. *A Series of Answers to Certain Popular Objections against Separation from the Rebellious Colonies.* Printed by R. Raikes of Gloucester and sold by T. Cadell of London; London: 1775.

————. *An Humble Address and Earnest Appeal.* Printed by R. Raikes of Gloucester and sold by T. Cadell of London; London: 1775.

————. *Cui Bono? or, An Inquiry, What Benefits Can Arise Either to the English or the Americans, the French, Spaniards, or Dutch, from the Greatest Successes of the Present War?* 2d ed. Printed by R. Raikes of Gloucester for T. Cadell of London and sold by Evans and Hazel; Gloucester: 1782.

————. *The Respective Pleas and Arguments of the Mother Country.* Printed by R. Raikes of Gloucester and sold by T. Cadell of London; London: 1775.

————. *The True Interest of Britain.* Printed and sold by Robert Bell; Philadelphia: 1776.

Memoirs and Correspondence

Cartwright, Francis Dorothy, ed. *The Life and Correspondence of Major Cartwright.* 2 vols. 2d ed. New York: Augustus M. Kelley, 1969.

Hill, George Birkbeck, ed. *Boswell's Life of Johnson.* 6 vols. Oxford: Clarendon Press, 1934.

Johnson, R. Brimley, ed. *The Letters of Hannah More.* New York: Lincoln Macveagh, The Dial Press, 1926.

Norton, Charles E., ed. "The Price Letters." *Proceedings of the Massachusetts Historical Society,* 17 (1903): 262–378.

Biographies

Clark, Walter E. *Josiah Tucker, Economist.* New York: Columbia University Press, 1903.

Cone, Carl B. *Torchbearer of Freedom: The Influence of Richard Price on Eighteenth Century Thought.* Lexington: University of Kentucky Press, 1952.

Lascelles, E. C. P. *Granville Sharp and the Freedom of Slaves in England.* 2d ed. New York: Negro Universities Press, 1969.

Osborne, John W. *John Cartwright.* Cambridge: Harvard University Press, 1972.

Other Works

Adams, Thomas R. "The British Pamphlets of the American Revolution for 1774: A Progress Report." *Proceedings of the Massachusetts Historical Society,* 81 (1969): 31–103.

Baer, Harold M. "An Early Plan for the Development of the West." *American Historical Review*, 30 (1925): 537–43.

Barnes, W. H. F. "Richard Price—A Neglected Eighteenth Century Moralist." *Philosophy*, 17 (1942): 159–73.

Barrington, Daines. *Observations on the More Ancient Statutes*. London: J. Nichols, 1796.

Blackstone, William. *Commentaries on the Laws of England*. 2 vols. New York: W. E. Dean, 1850.

Bourne, E. G. "The Authorship of the Federalist." *American Historical Review*, 2 (1897): 443–60.

Coke, Sir Edward. *Institutes of the Laws of England*. 2 vols. Philadelphia: Robert H. Hall, 1853.

Cone, Carl B. "Richard Price and the Constitution of the United States." *American Historical Review*, 53 (1948): 726–47.

Copleston, Frederick. *A History of Philosophy*. 8 vols. New York: Image Books, 1964.

Donnelly, Lucy Martin. "The Celebrated Mrs. Macaulay." *William and Mary Quarterly*, Series 3, 6 (1949): 173–207.

Ford, Paul L. "Josiah Tucker and His Writings." *Journal of Political Economy*, 2 (1893–94): 330–47.

Handlin, Oscar and Handlin, Mary. "James Burgh and American Revolutionary Theory." *Proceedings of the Massachusetts Historical Society*, 73 (1961): 38–57.

Hay, Carla H. "Crusading Schoolmaster: James Burgh, 1714–1775." Ph.D. dissertation, University of Kentucky, 1972.

Hooker, Richard S. "The American Revolution Seen through a Wine Glass." *William and Mary Quarterly*, Series 3, 11 (1954): 52–77.

Hudson, William D. *Reason and Right: A Critical Examination of Richard Price's Moral Philosophy*. London: Macmillan Co., 1970.

Lutnick, Solomon. *The American Revolution and the British Press*. Columbia: University of Missouri Press, 1967.

The Statutes-at-Large. 29 vols.

The Gentleman's Magazine.

The Monthly Review.

THE WHIG OPPOSITION

Contemporary Pamphlets and Books

Burke, Edmund. *A Letter to the Sheriffs of Bristol*. Printed by William Pine; Bristol: 1777.

———. *Thoughts on the Cause of the Present Discontents*. Printed for J. Dodsley; London: 1770.

Pownall, Thomas. *The Administration of the Colonies*. 2d ed. Printed for J. Dodsley and J. Walter; London: 1765.

Memoirs and Correspondence

Barker, G. F. R., ed. *Horace Walpole: Memoirs of the Reign of George III.* 4 vols. New York: G. P. Putnam's Sons, 1894.

Copeland, Thomas W., ed. *The Correspondence of Edmund Burke.* 9 vols. Cambridge: Cambridge University Press, 1958–70.

Emory, John, ed. *The Works of the Rev. John Wesley.* 14 vols. London: John Mason, 1841.

Fortesque, Sir John, ed. *The Correspondence of King George III.* 6 vols. Macmillan Co., 1927.

Hoffman, Ross J. S. and Levack, Paul, eds. *Burke's Politics: Selected Writings and Speeches of Edmund Burke.* New York: Alfred Knopf, 1949.

Mahoney, Thomas H. D., ed. *Edmund Burke: Selected Writings and Speeches on America.* New York: Bobbs-Merrill Co., 1964.

Russell, Lord John, ed. *Memorials and Correspondence of Charles James Fox.* 2 vols. Philadelphia: Blanchard & Lea, 1853.

Steuart, A. Francis, ed. *The Last Journals of Horace Walpole during the Reign of George III from 1771 to 1783.* 2 vols. London: John Lane, 1910.

Thomas, George, Earl of Albemarle. *Memoirs of the Marquis of Rockingham.* 2 vols. London: Richard Bentley, 1852.

Biographies

Brooke, John. *King George III.* New York: McGraw-Hill Book Co., 1972.

Cone, Carl B. *Burke and the Nature of Politics.* 2 vols. Lexington: University of Kentucky Press, 1957, 1964.

Fitzmaurice, Lord Edmund George. *Life of William, Earl of Shelburne.* 3 vols. London: Macmillan Co., 1876.

Hoffman, Ross J. S. *The Marquis: A Study of Lord Rockingham, 1732–1782.* New York: Fordham University Press, 1973.

Magnus, Sir Philip. *Edmund Burke.* London: John Murray, 1939.

Schutz, John A. *Thomas Pownall, British Defender of American Liberty.* Glendale, Calif.: Arthur H. Clark Co., 1951.

Sherrard, O. A. *Life of Lord Chatham.* 3 vols. London: The Bodley Head, 1958.

Trevelyan, George Otto. *The Early History of Charles James Fox.* New York: Harper & Bros., 1904.

Williams, Basil. *The Life of William Pitt, Earl of Chatham.* 2 vols. New York: Octagon Books, 1966.

Other Works

Annual Register. London: J. Dodsley, 1758–80, 1781–92. 34 vols.

Bredvold, Louis I. and Ross, Ralph G. *The Philosophy of Edmund Burke.* Ann Arbor: University of Michigan Press, 1960.

Cobbett, William, ed. *The Parliamentary History of England*. 36 vols. London: T. C. Hansard, 1806–20.

Coupland, Reginald. *The American Revolution and the British Empire*. London: Longmans, Green & Co., 1930.

Donoughue, Bernard. *British Politics and the American Revolution: The Path to War, 1773–75*. London: Macmillan Co., 1964.

George, M. Dorothy. *London Life in the Eighteenth Century*. New York: Capricorn Books, 1965.

Guttridge, G. H. *English Whiggism and the American Revolution*. University of California Publications in History, vol. 28. 2d ed. Berkeley: University of California Press, 1966.

———. *David Hartley, M.P., An Advocate of Conciliation, 1774–1783*. University of California Publications in History, vol. 14. Berkeley: University of California Press, 1926.

Harlow, Vincent T. *The Founding of the Second British Empire*. 2 vols. London: Longmans, Green & Co., 1952, 1964.

Namier, Lewis B. *England in the Age of the American Revolution*. 2d ed. London: Macmillan Co., 1963.

Namier, Lewis B. and Brooke, John. *The History of Parliament: The House of Commons, 1754–1790*. 3 vols. New York: Oxford University Press, 1964.

Norris, John. *Shelburne and Reform*. London: Macmillan Co., 1963.

Olson, Alison G. *Anglo-American Politics, 1660–1775*. Oxford: Oxford University Press, 1973.

Philips, N. C. "Edmund Burke and the County Association Movement." *English Historical Review*, 76 (1961): 254–78.

Pole, J. R. *Political Representation in England and the Origins of the American Republic*. Berkeley: University of California Press, 1966.

Williams, Basil. "Chatham and the Representation of the Colonies in the Imperial Parliament." *English Historical Review*, 22 (1907): 756–58.

THE AMERICAN CONNECTION

Contemporary Pamphlets and Books

Bailyn, Bernard, ed. *Pamphlets of the American Revolution*. Vol. 1. Cambridge: Harvard University Press, 1965.

Memoirs and Correspondence

Adams, Charles Francis, ed. *The Works of John Adams*. 10 vols. Boston: Brown & Co., 1856.

Ballagh, James Curtis, ed. *The Letters of Richard Henry Lee*. 2 vols. Macmillan Co., 1911.

Bigelow, John, ed. *The Works of Benjamin Franklin*. 12 vols. New York: G. P. Putnam's Sons, 1904.

Boyd, Julian, ed. *The Papers of Thomas Jefferson.* 18 vols. Princeton: Princeton University Press, 1950–71.

Lipscomb, Andrew, ed. *The Writings of Thomas Jefferson.* 20 vols. Washington, D.C.: The Thomas Jefferson Memorial Association, 1904.

Smyth, Albert Henry, ed. *The Writings of Benjamin Franklin.* 10 vols. New York: Macmillan Co., 1907.

Sparks, Jared, ed. *The Writings of George Washington.* 12 vols. Boston: John B. Russell, 1837.

Biographies

Anthony, Katharine. *First Lady of the Revolution.* Port Washington, N.Y.: Kennikat Press, 1972.

Lee, Richard Henry. *Life of Arthur Lee.* 2 vols. Boston: Wells & Lilly, 1829.

Malone, Dumas. *Jefferson and His Time.* 4 vols. Boston: Little, Brown & Co., 1948–70.

Peterson, Merrill D. *Thomas Jefferson and the New Nation.* New York: Oxford University Press, 1970.

Smith, Page. *John Adams.* 2 vols. New York: Doubleday & Co., 1962.

Van Doren, Carl. *Benjamin Franklin.* New York: Viking Press, 1958.

Other Works

Adams, R. G. *Political Ideas of the American Revolution.* 2d ed. New York: Facsimile Library, 1939.

Bailyn, Bernard. "Political Experience and Enlightenment Ideas in Eighteenth Century America." *American Historical Review*, 62 (1961–62): 339–51.

———. *The Ideological Origins of the American Revolution.* Cambridge: Harvard University Press, 1973.

Bemis, Samuel Flagg. *The Diplomacy of the American Revolution.* 7th ed. Bloomington: Indiana University Press.

Colbourn, H. Trevor. *The Lamp of Experience: Whig History and the Intellectual Origins of the American Revolution.* Chapel Hill: University of North Carolina Press, 1965.

———. "Thomas Jefferson's Use of the Past." *William and Mary Quarterly*, Series 3, 15 (1958): 56–70.

Davidson, Philip. *Propaganda and the American Revolution.* Chapel Hill: University of North Carolina Press, 1941.

Gipson, L. H. *The Coming of the Revolution.* New York: Harper Torchbooks, 1962.

Hans, Nicholas. "Franklin, Jefferson, and the English Radicals at the End of the Eighteenth Century." *Proceedings of the American Philosophical Society*, 97 (1954): 406–26.

Haraszti, Zoltán. *John Adams and the Prophets of Progress.* Cambridge: Harvard University Press, 1952.

Heimert, Alan. *Religion and the American Mind*. Cambridge: Harvard University Press, 1968.

Hutcheson, Maud Macdonald. "Mercy Warren, 1728–1814." *William and Mary Quarterly*, Series 3, 10 (1953): 378–402.

Labaree, Benjamin. "The Idea of American Independence." *Proceedings of the Massachusetts Historical Society*, 82 (1970): 3–20.

Mullett, Charles F. *Fundamental Law and the American Revolution, 1760–1776*. New York: Columbia University Press, 1933.

Nelson, William H. "The Revolutionary Character of the American Revolution." *American Historical Review*, 70 (1965): 998–1014.

Ritcheson, Charles R. *Aftermath of Revolution: British Policy toward the United States, 1783–1795*. Dallas: Southern Methodist University Press, 1969.

Robson, Eric. *The American Revolution in Its Political and Military Aspects, 1763–1783*. Hamden, Conn.: Archon Books, 1965.

Savelle, Max. *Seeds of Liberty*. New York: Alfred A. Knopf, 1948.

———. *The Colonial Origins of American Thought*. Princeton: D. Van Nostrand Co., 1964.

Schlesinger, Arthur M., Sr. *Prelude to Independence: The Newspaper War on Britain, 1764–1776*. New York: Alfred A. Knopf, 1958.

———. *The Birth of the Nation*. New York: Alfred A. Knopf, 1968.

Sweet, William Warren. *The Story of Religion in America*. New York: Harper & Bros., 1950.

Trevelyan, George Otto. *The American Revolution*. 4 vols. 2d ed. London: Longmans, Green & Co., 1909.

Wood, Gordon S. *The Creation of the American Republic*. New York: W. W. Norton & Co., 1972.

INDEX